JOHN CLEARE'S
FIFTY BEST
HILL WALKS
OF BRITAIN

JOHN CLEARE'S
FIFTY BEST HILL WALKS OF BRITAIN

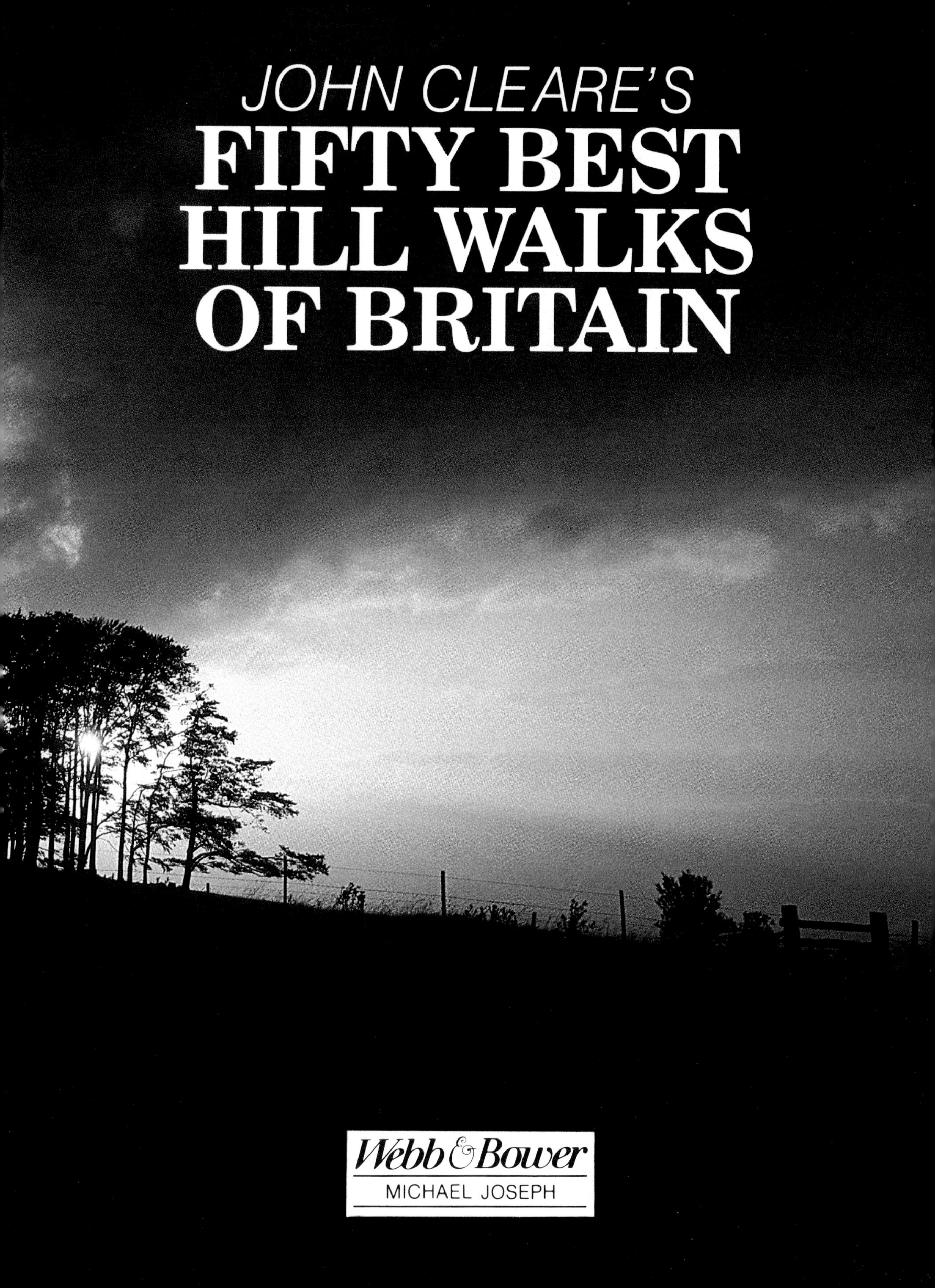

Webb & Bower

MICHAEL JOSEPH

For my ever-patient Joey
who always had the kettle on.

Half-title
Sunset over Llyn Fan Fawr, the lonely tarn that lies below the
steep east scarp of Bannau Brycheiniog. The Carmarthen
Fan is in the distance.

Frontispiece
Evening on Cherhill Down above the Vale of Calne, Wiltshire.

First published in Great Britain 1988 by
Webb & Bower (Publishers) Limited
9 Colleton Crescent, Exeter, Devon EX2 4BY
in association with Michael Joseph Limited
27 Wright's Lane, London W8 5TZ

Designed by Vic Giolitto

Production by Nick Facer/Rob Kendrew

Text and illustrations Copyright © 1988 John Cleare
Maps Copyright © 1988 Ordnance Survey

British Library Cataloguing in Publication Data
Cleare, John
John Cleare's fifty best hill walks of
Britain
1, Mountaineering—Great Britain—
Guide-books 2. Great Britain—Description
and travel—1971– —Guide-books
I. Title
796.5'22   DA632

ISBN 0–86350–142–7

Typeset in Great Britain by Keyspools Limited, Golborne,
Lancashire

Colour reproduction by J Film Process, Bangkok, Thailand

Printed and bound in Spain by Graficromo, Cordoba

Contents

Introduction

'The true mountaineer is a wanderer . . .'

Albert Mummery 1893

Hill-walking – or fell-walking as it is often known in Britain – is the quintessential craft from which all other mountain sports are born. Without the basic ability to move safely over upland country there would be little rock-climbing, no fell-running or ski-touring and certainly no mountaineering. Climbing the snow and ice of a Himalayan giant is only an extreme extension of basic hill-walking techniques, an extreme to which relatively few aspire, while for thousands of folk hill-walking is a meaningful and enjoyable end in itself.

I was fortunate enough to become involved with mountains at a tender age and luckily the schoolmaster who led our climbing holidays – a real mountain man – ensured that though our days might start on steep rock, they would continue upwards to a summit and conclude with a circuit over the tops whatever the weather. Although rock was my early interest, I soon learnt to appreciate and then to cherish the walking. It was all part of the overall mountain game, and long days on the British hills have stood me in good stead among the mountains of six continents. For me too, hill-walking has become an end in itself.

Thus I make no apology that I, as an alpine and expeditionary mountaineer, should write a book on British hills, a book which includes such global trivia as the Wiltshire Downs between the same cover as Ben Nevis. Frank Smythe, the famous thirties mountaineer, considered the moody Surrey eminence of Holmbury Hill almost as much a mountain as many of his Himalayan summits. He knew that sheer height is no arbiter of what is a mountain.

In the British uplands the dividing line between hills and mountains may well depend on the weather or even the walker. Personally I enjoy my Wiltshire Downs even as I enjoy my Himalayan peaks, but I believe that reward is commensurate with effort, accomplishment with challenge. The walker who puts his all into an ascent of Bidean has achieved no less – in context – than the experienced climber on

Everest's summit. We play the same game, which is surely about delight rather than glory.

What then are the parameters of a *best* hill-walk? I have my own ideas, but the coverage of this book demanded routes to intrigue the experienced northern fell-walker with a week's holiday besides the aspiring chap from suburbia with a single day. I'm grateful to thirty friends – from Aberdeen to Kent – who gave me their opinions: a surprising concensus with some interesting gems. My initial list of one hundred walks included several *musts* if it was to be credible, the common denominator was ambience – the mood of the high places whatever the scale – while I ignored obviously 'coastal' walks. In eighteen months I walked, or repeated, them all. Practical considerations finally limited the present volume to just fifty routes, spread evenly over the British uplands.

Perhaps some words of explanation are pertinent. Each itinerary is a circuit from a reasonable parking place. The effort should go into the walking, not planning an expedition and it seemed pointless to recommend one-way routes requiring complex car shuttles or a non-walking partner. Every route in this book is a shorter or longer 'day's walk' save one – my own favourite in South Uist to which I was first introduced by the late great Tom Patey – and that actually requires a sleeping bag.

The main text, I hope, will enthuse, inform and inspire while the route itineraries are designed to be copied, as necessary, for use on the hill in conjunction with a compass and the relevant OS 1:50,000 or 1:25,000 map. For each route I have given only distances and height gained but never times. Time is subjective, folk walk at different speeds and I, for one, dawdle to take photographs, but all hill-walkers should be familiar with Naismith's Rule and should know how their own performance compares: they can thus estimate **their own** time. WW Naismith was a prominent Scottish mountaineer of the 1880s and 90s whose habit it was to walk, in a fairly direct line, from his home near Glasgow to the various Highland meets of the SMC, from this experience he concluded that his average speed was 3 mph with an extra half hour for every thousand feet he ascended, a formula that works surprisingly well. In modern metric terms read the Rule as: **5 kms/hour on the map plus 300 metres/$\frac{1}{2}$ hour on the ascent**. Allow a little longer for halts, bad weather, strong winds or really rugged ground.

Itinerary distances are from the map and are given to the nearest convenient half kilometre or quarter mile. For yards, of course, read metres. The meaning of the many abbreviations should be obvious: L for left, N for north – for instance – YDNP for Yorkshire Dales National Park, NCC for Nature Conservancy Council, RoW for Right of Way, and so on. The *true* bank of a stream is always that when facing downstream. Main routes on the maps are marked with a continuous line while a broken line indicates useful variations.

Summits, tops and significant eminences are named in capitals; an asterisk ⋆ against a Scottish height denotes a separate mountain in Munro's Tables. For those unfamiliar with the term, a Munro is a Scottish summit about 3,000 feet, first classified and listed by Sir Hugh Munro in 1891. The latest revision includes no less than 281 separate mountains plus a further 287 tops or significant lesser summits, the difference between the two being quite a complex matter! Today Munro bagging is almost a sport in itself

and I would direct interested readers to both *The High Mountains* and *Munro's Tables* listed in the bibliography on page 206. *Bridge's Tables* is a similar summit catalogue for England and Wales listing also the County Tops.

Which leaves me only to thank, firstly those patient companions with whom I have shared these walks, who appear in my pictures and whose company I have greatly enjoyed: Caroline Aisher, Irvine Butterfield, John Chapman, Joss Cleare, Barry Cliff, Ronnie Faux, John and James Fowler, Carl Gilham, Emma van Gruisen, Ian Howell, Hywel and Caerwyn Lloyd, Joe Mitchell, Johnny Noble, Bill O'Connor, Alastair Stevenson and various folk from Glenmore Lodge. Secondly, for their understanding help with maps, Jim Page and his team at Ordnance Survey. And last but not least the colleagues whose advice, input and enthusiasm have kept the words flowing: Delian Bower, by publisher, Vic Giolitto, my designer, and my editor Alyson Gregory.

'Of Paradise can I not speak properly, for I have not been there,' wrote John Mandeville in 1360. But our British hills *are* accessible and the best of them are as beautiful as any in this world. I wish you as much delight walking among them as I have had.

Mid Craig Hill looks down on Loch Skeen, source of the Grey Mare's Tail.

The West Dartmoor Tors Devon

1″ Tourist Map, No. 1 'Dartmoor' (OS 1 : 50,000 Sheet 191)

Dartmoor is known for its ponies, its prison, the Hound of the Baskervilles and Widecombe Fair. Admittedly it is a moody place but as the largest and wildest tract of open country in southern Britain it allows a freedom to the walker unknown south of the Pennines. In 1951 the whole of Dartmoor, some 190 square miles of moorland, 128 square miles of farmland and 33 square miles of forest, was designated a National Park and the Dartmoor Commons Act of 1985 legalized free public access to almost all the wild country.

The moor itself is a great boss of granite from which time has stripped the overlying crust of softer Carboniferous rock. It has been eroded by rivers and frost – but was never glaciated. Today it forms two high, rolling plateaux mostly covered with a thick layer of peat, carpeted with heather, purple moor grass, bilberry and bent, studded with characteristic craggy tors and cut by fast-flowing streams in typically deep and narrow valleys.

Much of the larger northern plateau lies above 500 metres (1,500 feet) with the most dramatic heights rising in the north-west where two summits actually exceed 2,000 feet (620 metres) – High Willhays is the loftiest point in England south of Kinder Scout. Military use of Dartmoor dates back to 1870 and unfortunately the MOD still controls most of this area, although there is public access when training is not in progress (see the accompanying notes). Because of its height and the way the high ground drops abruptly to the rolling green chequer-board landscape of central Devon, this north-western sector of the moor is a favourite with many discerning walkers. This itinerary provides a good intro-

The River Tavy tumbles off the high moor through Tavy Cleave, an impressive defile originally carved by the torrential run-off of Ice Age thaws.

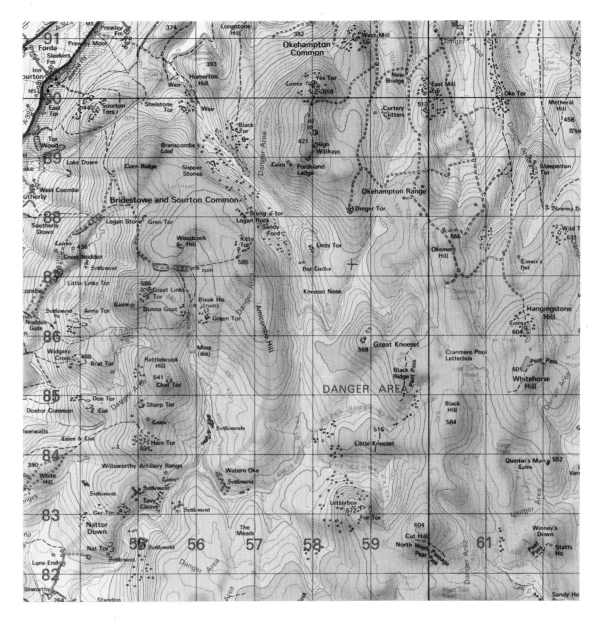

duction to the area while the longer variation visits its most interesting points.

Initially both routes ascend the picturesque defile of Tavy Cleave, where the rushing Tavy tumbles off the high moor in a series of rapids and small cascades between craggy granite outcrops. Such valleys – gorges almost – around the periphery of Dartmoor were originally carved by the torrential run-offs of Ice Age thaws and now contain rivers boisterous with an annual rainfall of around 260 centimetres (100 inches) on the high ground. Such rivers may not always be easy to cross. The path leads over green meads

and through scatters of lichen-covered boulders, so called 'clinter', prised from the jagged tors ranged along the skyline by the shattering action of Ice Age frost.

On a grassy terrace above the river lie the hut circles of Watern Oke. There are a couple of dozen of them – rings of rough stones mostly 3–5 metres across (10–15 feet) and rising about 1 metre from the ground. They date back some 3,500 years to a warmer and dryer climate than today and may mark the site of a summer pasture or sheiling. The huts would have been conical with a central post supporting a thatched

roof rising from the low granite walls. It is a thought-provoking place.

Northward a vague ridge of tussocky grass and stunted heather leads towards Kitty Tor. Alternatively, the river can be followed eastward and a careful route plotted across a boggy green desert to Cranmere Pool – reputed to be the middle of Dartmoor and its least accessible point. A century ago Cranmere Pool was a real pond but now it is merely a boggy hollow containing several puddles – and a Dartmoor letterbox. In 1854 James Perrot, a Chagford guide, started a custom whereby visitors to the Pool would leave postcards in a jar which the next visitors would recover and post. Over the years the tradition grew and now a series of usually inconspicuous letterboxes are situated at remote points all over Dartmoor; they contain a visitor's book and a rubber stamp and enthusiasts set out to locate and visit them all. The modern letterbox is sited on the west 'shore'.

In good weather a bee-line can be made to High Willhays closeby the distinctive and sharper silhouette of Yes Tor; once the strange, pinnacled cairn is reached the most difficult navigation and worst going is over. Yes Tor, the

This is the most impressive of the several granite towers that comprise Great Links Tor.

Two Circuits on West Dartmoor

Length: short circuit 15.5 kms/9¾ miles
            long circuit 24 kms/15 miles
Height gained: short circuit 430 m/1,410 ft
                  long circuit 722 m/2,370 ft
Difficulty: this is wild, rough and boggy moorland susceptible to quite fierce conditions. Competence with map and compass necessary even in clear weather. **Grid** bearings are given.
Warning: although usually accessible, this entire corner of moor is a military training area where live ammunition sometimes used. Red flags fly when training in progress – there is one near start. Check times with local post office, police, or phone Okehampton (0837) 2939

Start: Willsworthy Lane End, muddy parking area off farm track at 537823. (300 m/985 ft).

Short Circuit
(1) Track, then good path, leads E past barn to follow leat contouring into narrowing Tavy Cleave gorge. From weir rough path follows true R bank of river and gradually disappears. At major confluence cross L fork 100 m to N, continue 700 m along R fork to bend, then strike up steep bank to area of hut circles at 565834. (580 m/1,900 ft).
4 kms/2½ miles

(2) Follow high ground NW then N to flag post at summit of KITTY TORR (585 m/1,919 ft) and descend W to old workings before easy but boggy ascent WSW leads to summit and trig point GREAT LINKS TOR (586 m/1,923 ft).
6 kms/3¾ miles

(3) Descend S along high ground, crossing CHAT TOR (541 m/1,775 ft) to flag post among rocks HARE TOR (531 m/1,742 ft). Faint pony track leads SSW to flag post and rocks on GER TOR (448 m/1,470 ft). Descend SW, bridge crosses wide leat on direct line to car-park.
5.5 kms/3½ miles

Long Circuit
(1) As (1) above to river bank below hut circles, continue E along Amicombe Brook and Black Ridge Brook to final confluence at 593845. Strike NW via stream source over featureless ground to boggy hollow Cranmere Pool or follow compass bg 36° **grid** to reach Pool more surely. Letterbox on W bank. (560 m/1,837 ft).
9.5 kms/6 miles

(2) Cross undulating, featureless, often boggy moorland NW aiming at High Willhays visible just left of conspicuous Yes Tor. Or follow compass bg 326° **grid** to scattered rocks and tall narrow cairn on HIGH WILLHAYS summit. (621 m/2,039 ft).
4.5 kms/3 miles

(3) Descend SW into narrow steep-sided valley of West Okement river and ascend, steep at first, to summit flag pole KITTY TOR (585 m/1,919 ft). Continue as (2) above to rocky summit GREAT LINKS TOR (586 m/1,923 ft). Return to car-park as (3) above.
9.5 kms/6 miles

second 2,000-foot summit, is worth a short detour for its craggy top and wide views. The West Okement river must be crossed at Sandy Ford to reach Kitty Tor with its conspicuous flag post, while old tin workings are passed *en route* to Great Links Tor, the next summit. Great Links is actually several separate tors, each exhibiting interesting weathering patterns: another letterbox is located under the north-east corner. Onwards the wide ridge is easier ground though there are three more tors to ascend before the final rocks of Ger Tor above the mouth of Tavy Cleave are reached and the circuit completed.

Cheddar Gorge and the Mendip Somerset

OS 1:50,000 Sheet 182

'. . . a stupendous chasm, quite through the body of the adjacent mountains. It appears as if the hill has been split asunder by some dreadful convulsion of nature.'

Thus was Cheddar Gorge described in 1784 by the New British Traveller, and indeed 200 years later it is still considered the most spectacular physical feature in southern Britain. This route makes a circuit of the gorge itself and continues over the Mendip Hills to the summit of Beacon Batch, their highest point.

An anticlinal outcroping of Mountain – or Carboniferous – limestone, the Mendip is a rather bleak and featureless plateau of drystone-walled pastures pitted with swallow-holes, scattered with farms and criss-crossed by narrow lanes and few roads. In several places the fold has eroded away to expose the more resistant old red sandstone beneath, forming several hills, such as

Blackdown, which rise above the general elevation of around 250 metres (800 feet). This is karst country where the water flows underground and where caves and pot-holes proliferate, attracting the 'spelunkers' who explore them. Along the plateau edge are several deep and narrow defiles originally cut by running water but left dry when the land rose and the water found a course underground: though less spectacular than the Cheddar Gorge, Burrington Coombe and Ebbor Gorge are such formations worth visiting.

Our route, shaped like a figure of eight, starts in the middle – the confluence of the several dry valleys which converge to form Cheddar Gorge

The route passes above these crags on the southern rim of the gorge known as 'the Pinnacles' which fall some 400 feet (over 120 metres) to the road at the Horseshoe Bend. Cheddar village and Brent Knoll on the Somerset Levels are seen in the distance.

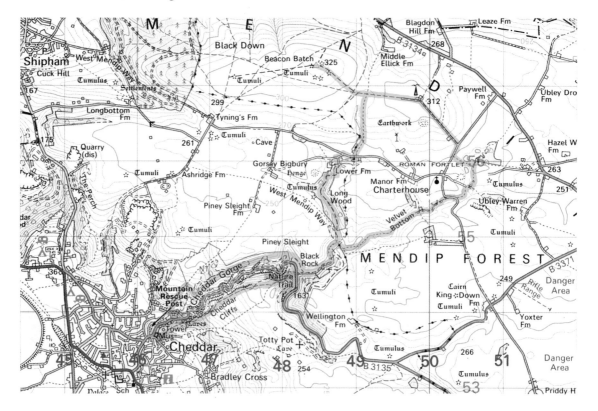

itself – allowing the walker to complete either circuit or both, depending on one's energy. The initial section climbs to open windswept downland on the southern side of the gorge where grey rocks protrude through the long grass and from where there are superb views southward over the broad Somerset Levels to Glastonbury Tor – the legendary Isle of Avalon – and the Quantock Hills beyond. The path runs close to the cliff edge, sometimes abrupt but often the highest of several tiers, the ledges bushy with ash and dogwood and the dark green of stunted yews. Several great gullies cut back into the cliff top and there are glimpses of the twisting road far beneath, but due to the strike of the limestone beds this is the steeper side of the Gorge, the northern side is less spectacular and little can be seen of the great cliffs below.

After descending into Cheddar village, in season a thriving tourist trap, the route ascends to National Trust territory on the northern side of the gorge from where the full majesty of the southern cliffs can be appreciated. The great wall of High Rock – a slightly overhanging 430 feet – is the tallest limestone cliff in Britain; Coronation Street, the now classic rock-climb pioneered by Chris Bonington, Tony Greenbank and the present author in 1965, runs straight up the middle. There are now many harder and more intimidating climbs hereabouts but most rise sheer above the road or various car-parks and climbing is banned between Easter and October. There are few easy routes however, the rock is loose and friable, and all Cheddar climbs are serious undertakings.

Apparently the ivy which today mantles much of the cliffs first arrived around the turn of the century when first the road was built. Where today cars and coaches grind round the tight bends and pedestrians take their lives in their hands, a narrow footpath once picked its way between the boulders beneath pristine pinnacles of gleaming limestone. A special feature of the limestone is its prolific and characteristic flora, best seen in early summer on this south-facing flank. This is the home not only of the rare Cheddar Pink but also of numerous adders – summer walkers should tread with care. The wild flowers are of course protected by law.

Returning to the start at Black Rock Gate, the route now follows the ancient drove road up the

winding and attractive Black Rock valley. This is a Nature Reserve and interesting descriptive leaflets are available at a map board 200 metres up the track where a donation should be made. Access is permitted through the adjoining Long Wood Reserve where the entrances are passed to the important Longwood Swallet/August Hole cave system and the Rhino Rift pot-hole, and then a field path leads up onto the swelling heathland of Blackdown and through heather, gorse and, in summer, clumps of rippling pink willow-herb, to Beacon Batch. The wide panorama from the summit stretches from the Cotswolds to Exmoor and across the Bristol Channel to Flat Holm and Cardiff.

The return leg to Black Rock Gate follows the interesting Velvet Bottom dry valley, another Nature Reserve notable not only for its unusual ecology but also for the remains of the lead mines which were worked here from pre-Roman times until 1885 and are now scheduled as an Ancient Monument. This certainly is a fascinating and very varied walk.

This overgrown path on the slopes of Beacon Batch or Blackdown Hill – the highest point of the Mendip – leads over from Charterhouse to Burrington Coombe.

A Mendip Circuit

Length and height gained: Gorge circuit: 6 kms/3¾ miles, 300 m/1,000 ft
Blackdown circuit: +10.5 kms/6½ miles, +200 m/650 ft
Difficulty: easy walking but complete circuit involves considerable ascent
Warning: route often passes close to cliff tops where rock is loose and grass is slippery. On paths stones too can be very slippery when damp

Start: limited parking at Black Rock Gate layby 482545. (160 m/525 ft). Alternatively park in Gorge below High Rock or elsewhere.

(1) Good path waymarked 'Draycott W Mendip Way' ascends through woods from W side of road opposite layby. At junction above woods leave W Mendip Way taking RH fork to open grassland plateau (253 m/830 ft) whence path descends gradually close above cliff top to Jacob's Ladder tower. RoW now bears left through undergrowth to reach cottages, follow steep lane down into Cheddar village (15 m/50 ft).
2.25 kms/1¼ miles

(2) Go 500 m up main road to top end of small lake and take RH of two lanes leading off left. After 200 m just before first cottage on RHS a marked RoW leads up to larger path ascending through wood, cross stile and take RH path to more open ground and wall near bush-lined cliff edge at 468543. Various paths now lead eastward along gorge lip and converge to become narrow main trail signed 'Black Rock' which is followed along lip, via several stiles and a steep re-entrant, eventually to Black Rock Drove (lane) 200 m E of car-park.
3.75 kms/2¼ miles

(3) Follow drove road E through Black Rock Nature Reserve up dry valley past old quarry to stile and waymark 'W Mendip Way', 200 m onward stile by white gate is signed 'Longwood Nature Reserve', enter and continue through thick woods up narrow valley. Plank over stream just past August Hole cave entrance, then wooden steps lead up right to field edge and lane, tarmac drive leads R to road. Cross stile 100 m E opposite white bungalow onto RoW leading up little valley. At green lane on crest go W through gate onto open heathland of Blackdown. Ascend broad track to summit trig point of BEACON BATCH (325 m/1,067 ft).
4.25 kms/2½ miles

(4) Retrace route to green lane and continue past radio masts down metalled drive to road. 150 m S iron stile on LHS leads into Blackmoor-Charterhouse Nature Reserve. Cross 'dam' and follow track S to car-park before turning off left to reach road and crossing into Velvet Bottom Nature Reserve. Good track, then path, leads down dry valley which after 2 kms rejoins Black Rock Drove.
6.25 kms/4 miles

Wiltshire Downs – Cherhill and Oliver's Castle

OS 1:50,000 Sheet 173

'Wiltshire is a pleasant county, and of great variety. I have heard a wise man say that an ox left to himself would, of all England, choose to live in the north, a sheep in the south part hereoff, and a man in the middle betwixt both . . .'

Thomas Fuller,
History of the Worthies of England – 1675

Wiltshire has changed much in 300 years. Though still a pleasant and varied county, the oxen have gone and the great open chalk downs where once roamed myriad sheep have mostly surrendered to the plough – or the army. Fragments of these fragrant grasslands remain however, typically prolific with flowers in spring and summer, often where the scarp is too steep to cultivate. The questing walker can usually guarantee an interesting route by searching on maps for paths along the steepest scarps and among the most convoluted contours.

One will not have to look far for what the OS label as 'Antiquities', for Wiltshire has the greatest concentration in Britain. In prehistoric times these downs were the main inhabited region of our island and the scarp edges are scattered with the mounds and ditches of ancient hill forts, usually occupying – by no accident – the most spectacular sites. This particular route leads along the final westerly bastion of the chalklands of southern England, a scarp as convoluted as any and – though passing no famous monument or celebrated ruin – spanning some 5,000 years of Wiltshire history. It is perhaps epitomized by the delicate hang-gliders which on a summer's day soar out from the Iron

The great scarp of Oliver's Castle is seen to the south-east from the path that runs round below the hill from Heddington.

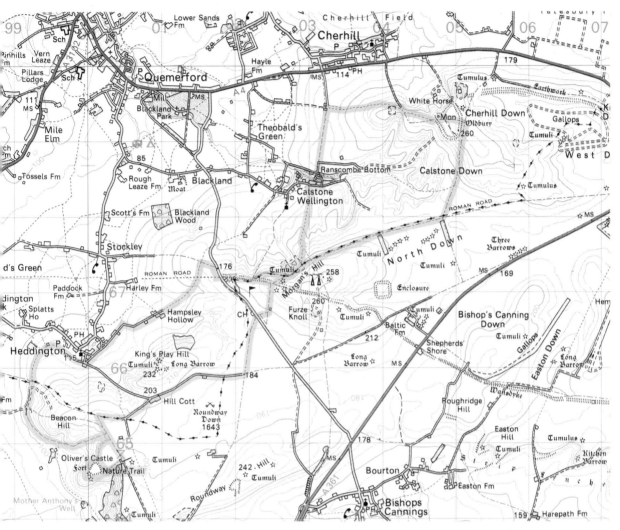

Age ramparts of Oliver's Castle, high over the 'Bloody Ditch' where the Parliamentary troopers perished, to float across the spreading cornfields of the Avon vale.

The Roman highway from Silchester to Bath and Wansdyke, the sixth century defensive ditch which stretches from Marlborough to the Bristol Channel, converge on a modern minor road on the slopes of Morgan's Hill where a convenient county council picnic site gives the start. The route can be broken if necessary into two circuits, one northward, one to the south. The objective of the former, Cherhill Down, is conspicuous right from the start for close to its summit rises the 37-metre (120-feet) obelisk of the Lansdown Column erected in 1845 and now in a somewhat dangerous state. The hilltop itself is crowned by Oldbury Castle, an impressive

Iron Age fort over a kilometre in circumference from where there are extensive views westward towards Calne and the Bristol conurbation: in mid-distance a distinctive beech clump caps the crest of the ascent ridge.

Cherhill is best known, however, for the White Horse which prances across its north-west-facing coombe and is best seen from the main A4 Bath road beneath. Alas, it is no ancient symbol for it was cut in 1780 on the instigation of a local Dr Alsop who directed his workmen by megaphone from over a mile away! The whole hilltop belongs to the National Trust. To the north-east the hill overlooks Yatesbury Field, until the early Sixties the site of a huge RAF training camp, no doubt remembered by many National Servicemen. Two kilometres of Roman Road lead back to Morgan's Hill.

Cherhill Down is best known for the white horse carved on its northern flank and which is familiar to motorists using the A4 road.

Below
Seen to the north-east from Morgan's Hill, Cherhill Down is crowned by the conspicuous obelisk of the Lansdown Column.

The circuit southward follows old and muddy rights of way under the hill, via the ancient village of Heddington with its strange dormer-windowed church, into the steep downland coombe between the swelling flank of Beacon Hill and the jutting prow of Oliver's Castle – a superb defensive site if ever there was one. Initially the return route lies along the scarp top before meeting the line of the Old Bath Road on Beacon Hill and following it eastwards between hedges of hawthorn, crab-apple and sloe onto Roundway Down. On old maps this shallow valley is named King's Play Down, possibly because of the bloody happenings here on 13th July 1643 when the King's army achieved its most decisive victory of the Civil War. Briefly, a small Royalist cavalry force, hoping to lift the siege of Devizes, tired after their hurried march from Oxford and outnumbered three to one, attacked a Parliamentary army of 2,000 horse and 2,800 foot who were drawn up across the valley. Avoiding the powerless infantry, they routed the cavalry and drove them from the field. Apparently the hapless Parliamentary horsemen fled south-west, only to find themselves plunging down very steep slopes into the coombe immediately south of Oliver's Castle where many perished. Meanwhile the Parliamentary infantry were rounded up by the Royalists aided by fresh troops who had sallied forth from Devizes.

Past Hill Cott the old road is metalled, a legacy of the Second World War when it became the artery of a large military camp of which little else now remains. A wide green lane leads to the North Wilts Golf Club beside an incongruous pig farm and so once more onto Morgan's Hill.

Cherhill Down and Oliver's Castle

Length: 21 kms/13 miles
Height gained: 300 m/1,000 ft
Difficulty: easy walking but paths may be very muddy or overgrown in places

Start: good parking at Smallgrain Plantation picnic site 020671. (190 m/623 ft).
Alternative start from Oliver's Castle picnic site 005648. (200 m/656 ft).

(1) Muddy lane at N side picnic site leads E to gate into Morgan's Hill Nature Reserve, take LH track 700 m to E corner of coppice where field path descends N to Calstone Wellington hamlet. At lane go 200 m R then fork L past farm to cross brook in Ranscombe Bottom. Narrow footpath leads uphill avoiding cottages to rejoin lane for 200 m before bridle-path strikes N across fields towards Cherhill. At path junction by barn 032694 footpath strikes E up hillside to reach lonely clump of beech trees. Several paths lead across National Trust property to conspicuous obelisk and Oldbury Castle hill fort (260 m/853 ft). From E ramparts path leads S down fields to join good track returning WSW to Morgan's Hill and road beyond car-park.
10 kms/6¼ miles

(2) Footpath immediately opposite leads between road and golf course 150 m NW to bridle-way signed 'Stockley', follow this 200 m to track junction and turn S down footpath descending to Hapsley Hollow stables – muddy. Metalled lane leads onwards under hill to Heddington village. At final muddy lane junction S of church go R through gate onto greenlane which becomes narrow track between high hedges behind village houses. At cottage 994663 high-hedged path contours S under hill to cross chalk lane leading steeply uphill. Path beyond completely overgrown but a few metres uphill a parallel tractor track continues its line, contouring below steep hillside into coombe between Beacon Hill and Oliver's Castle and climbs to hilltop. Turn R to Oliver's Castle and car-park at head of rough chalk lane. (200 m/656 ft).
6.5 kms/4 miles

(3) From Oliver's Castle, bridle-way leads NW to join chalk lane on Beacon Hill, follow it E to metalled lane bearing NE to Hill Cott. Continue to barn and 500 m beyond turn N onto wide green lane leading to golf clubhouse on road. Signpost on road indicates RoW N across golfcourse to Morgan's Hill, whence retrace route to Smallgrain Plantation car-park.
4.5 kms/2¾ miles

The Malvern Hills   Hereford and Worcester

OS 1:50,000 Sheet 150

'Mauborn hills or as some term
them the English Alps'

Celia Fiennes,
'Journeys' c 1690

They rise sheer from the flat Severn vale and to the unsuspecting visitor hurrying down the M5 at Worcester or breasting the Cotswold edge at Birdlip their long mountainous silhouette will seem improbable, a spectacular anomaly in this wide and gentle landscape. The Malvern Hills are certainly unusual, a narrow 12-kilometre (8-mile) crest of Precambrian volcanic rocks — mostly gneiss — found elsewhere only in the far north-west Highlands and as old as anything in Britain.

The Malvern ridge, steep-flanked and at its widest just over 1 kilometre ($\frac{3}{4}$ mile), holds fifteen named summits — ten of them rising above a thousand feet, and forms a natural boundary between the ancient shires of Worcester and Hereford — and Gloucester at its far southern point. Major gaps divide the crest into four distinct sections. Grassy and almost rugged, the higher more elegant northern tops are scattered with small rocky outcrops and in season with patches of rosebay willow-herb, gorse and broom, while the more intriguing southern hills rise above a woodland cloak of ash and oak and here especially exemplify the best of rural England. Certainly the poet William Langland thought so when he wrote the *Vision of Piers Plowman* towards the end of the fourteenth century: 'Ac on a may morwening/on Malverne hulles Me byfel for to slepe/for weyrynesse of wandryng.' and with the wide-spreading Severn plain below, the Cotswold edge lining the distance and hills and woods tumbling westward towards the dark shapes of the Black Mountains, he dreamt his famous dream of rustic England. Over the centuries many others have found inspiration here, most notably Sir Edward Elgar who was born nearby and was always closely associated with the hills. Malvern itself is a charming spa town with a strong cultural tradition.

The greater part of the hills and surrounding commons is under the jurisdiction of the Malvern Hills Conservators, a Body Corporate dedicated to protecting the land for the public benefit: they prevent encroachment, provide car-parks, check erosion and ensure free public access to some 3,000 acres. Obviously the traverse of the entire Malvern ridge is a classic walk but at first sight a one-way trip necessitating the use of two cars or barely existing public transport. The ridge crest itself involves considerable ascent but an almost level return route is suggested here which visits flanks of the hills usually unseen by the one-way walker while still being within the bounds of a fair day's hike.

Midsummer Hill, its bare summit crowned by a complicated Iron Age fort, rises above Holybush; careful navigation is required to find the best descent through steep woods directly to the Gullet, a deep defile where an imposing aban-

Herefordshire Beacon is crowned by the extensive ramparts of 'British Camp': in the distance beyond the shoulder of Broad Down stretches the Vale of Gloucester.

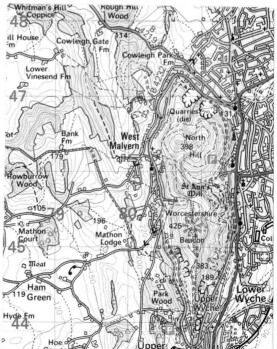

doned quarry holds a neat lake. A viewing ledge above its western lip displays the junction of the primeval Malvernian rocks with younger Silurian strata. From Swinyard Hill the route onwards becomes straightforward, following the prominent 'Shire Ditch' or 'Red Earl's Dyke' virtually the whole way. Constructed around 1290, the dyke was a boundary between the hunting preserves of the red-haired Earl of Gloucester and those of the Bishop of Hereford – it is said that the fence along its crest was so constructed that the Bishop's deer could leap eastward but the Earl's could not escape west! Herefordshire Beacon is the first 'thousand footer' and is crowned by British Camp, a very impressive thirty-two-acre hill fort built during the third century BC. 'One of the goodliest vistas in England', wrote the diarist John Evelyn of the summit panorama, and who would disagree?

North of the Wynds Point pass with its car-parks and café, the Pinnacle Hill massif is a particularly narrow switchback crest above almost precipitous eastern slopes. The Wyche pass beyond is the route of an ancient saltway from the Severn – only 7 kilometres (4½ miles) distant – into Wales: the actual cutting dates to 1840. The ascent to Worcestershire Beacon leads past the site of a long abandoned gold mine (at 769441), avoids with difficulty a metalled drive-way leading to an ugly café, and arrives at a sharp summit with a view that on a clear day extends over fifteen counties and must be one of the best in Britain. Now the crest curls round Green Valley to the final summit – North Hill – from where there are views down 800 feet (260 metres) into the town itself; with luck strains of a brass band will waft up on the wind.

The return to Hollybush is a long but gentle walk, often through woods and passing several points of interest including Clutter's Cave below Broad Down said to have been a hiding place of Owain Glyndwr. If energy permits, a short diversion to the conspicuous Eastnor obelisk is worth making. The circuit of the two southern-most hills, Ragged Stone and Chase End, is conveniently made from Hollybush. Certainly the most characterful of the Malverns, Ragged Stone Hill is surely the most shapely – though be careful! An old legend claims that they are cursed on whom its shadow falls!

The Malvern Circuit

Length and height gained:

Hollybush to North Hill	11.5 kms/7¼ miles
	850 m/2,790 ft
North Hill to Hollybush	13 kms/8 miles
	175 m/575 ft
Ragged Stone Hill circuit	3.5 kms/2¼ miles
	255 m/840 ft

Difficulty: easy walking on good paths

Start: parking beside track off N side A438 at Hollybush 759369. (160 m/525 ft) 'Pay + display' parking facilities at numerous points N.

(1) Ascend N up hillside to wood where well-defined path climbs diagonally L to gain crest and shelter MIDSUMMER HILL (286 m/938 ft). At rampart 200 m N take bridle-path descending back R. After 130 m turn L at second group of 3 ash trees onto narrow track through bracken following Shire Ditch then dropping steeply L into re-entrant descending to Gullet Quarry (150 m/490 ft). At E corner of lake ascend through fir copse onto brackeny hillside, climb steeply to rejoin Shire Ditch by fence on ridge. Follow crest over SWINYARD HILL (272 m/892 ft) and subsidiary summits of HANGMAN'S HILL and BROAD DOWN to British Camp earthworks and summit HEREFORDSHIRE BEACON (340 m/1,115 ft). Descend to road at Wynds Point pass. (236 m/774 ft).
4.5 kms/3 miles

(2) Go N 100 m up B4232 road, path leads up R behind hotel to ridge and Shire Ditch, follow crest N over BLACK HILL (308 m/1,010 ft), PINNACLE HILL (357 m/1,171 ft) and PERSEVERANCE HILL (325 m/1,066 ft) to road at Wyche Cutting (258 m/846 ft).
3.5 kms/2¼ miles

(3) Take R fork ahead, Beacon Road, for 150 m then strike R to ridge crest and continue N over minor top SUMMER HILL to summit WORCESTERSHIRE BEACON (425 m/1,394 ft). Descend N over SUGARLOAF HILL (368 m/1,210 ft) and TABLE HILL to NORTH HILL (398 m/1305 ft).
3.5 kms/2¼ miles
Short easy descents to Malvern (c 175 m/575 ft) if necessary.

(4) Return to Hollybush: Good paths contour E flank Worcestershire Beacon rejoining crest at Summer Hill. From road 50 m E of Wyche Cutting by cottage, path leads S contouring E flank Pinnacle Hill massif to road 300 m E of Wynds Point pass. From car-park path contours E flank British Camp to Broad Down, then contours W flank past Clutter's Cave and Hangman's Hill. At col beyond ('Pink Cottage') drop R to join wide track through News Wood to junction at 757380 and continuing S below W flank Midsummer Hill to Hollybush.
13 kms/8 miles

(5) Ragged Stone Hill and Chase End Hill: Track climbs S from A438 road just W of phone box. After 150 m path leads off R uphill behind cottage to summit RAGGED STONE HILL (254 m/833 ft). Descend narrow ridge S to track junction, continue SE over stile to lane. 70 m track leads onto CHASE END HILL, climb R to summit (191 m/627 ft). Path descends NW to lane and Whiteleaved Oak hamlet. Just N of Ragged Stone Cottage good contour track through gate on R returns to Hollybush.
3.5 kms/2¼ miles

Below the slopes of Pinnacle Hill the chequer-board fields stretch towards the Severn.

Stiperstones – the Devil's Doing Shropshire

OS 1: 50,000 Sheets 126, 137

Once upon a time the Devil's apron strings broke and he was forced to drop the load of rocks he was carrying. Falling to earth they scattered along the crest of a high ridge of heathland that runs close to the Welsh border some ten miles from Shrewsbury. The rocks remain there to this day, a line of jagged quartzite outcrops standing along the spine of Stiperstones hill.

More akin to the wilder hills of North Wales than to the other more gentle hills of Shropshire, the Stiperstones is actually the second highest summit in the county and has a unique atmosphere engendered largely by its geology and resultant history. The hill is said to be the traditional meeting place of Shropshire witches; certainly the Devil's proximity will come as no

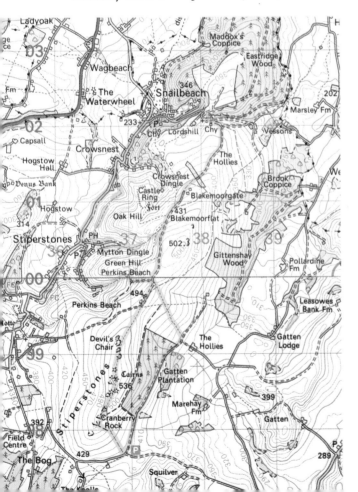

In this view from the Long Mynd the Stiperstones ridge is seen across the East Onny valley. Along the crest rise the outcrops of Cranberry Rocks (left), Manstone Rock and the Devil's Chair (right).

surprise to those who have traversed the Stiperstones on a misty winter's day! Geologically speaking however, the seven-mile-long Stiperstones ridge is the eroded crest of an anticline of Ordovician strata some 480 million years old, later folded by the 'Caledonian' earth movements responsible also for the Snowdonian mountains. A narrow band of light grey quartzite running almost vertically forms the hill crest and is flanked on the west by a steep band of standstones known as the Mytton and Tankerville Flags which contains veins of lead and barytes. From Roman times these minerals supported a mining industry which reached its zenith in the 1850s when no less than ten percent of Britain's lead originated in this small area, and which has so influenced the detail of the surrounding landscape.

Besides its quartzite spine, the other notable feature of the Stiperstones is the striking 'dingles', the narrow steep-sided valleys that cut deeply into its western flank and cradle long-abandoned mine shafts and adits. On the heathery western hillsides, linked by overgrown tracks and surrounded by crumbling walls and derelict hedges, stand relics of the smallholdings where the miners supplemented their livelihood. The main centres of mining activity were at The Bog, Pennerley and Snailbeach – where work ceased only in 1916: chimneys, the remains of engine houses, and tips of shiny calcite waste mark the old mine workings. Because of its geological and biological significance, the latter as an important acid moorland habitat, the Stiperstones has been protected as a National Nature Reserve since 1982 and the Nature Conservancy Council is intent on preserving its special wilderness quality.

The figure-of-eight circuit described here traverses the entire crest of the hill and visits its four contrasting flanks and thus gives much scope for individual route variations. The first section links the four main rock outcrops which were carved from the ridge by frost erosion during the last Ice Age when the Stiperstones stood as a nunatak above the surrounding glaciers: today they rise from blocky scree on a whaleback moor of heather and bilberry. Frost polygons and stripes – stone patterns characteristic of a permafrost landscape – are still discernable, particularly south-west of the second out-

crop, Manstone Rock, which is the highest point. The remarkable panorama from its summit extends from Snowdon – some 93 kilometres (58 miles) distant – to the Brecon Beacons; from the Malverns to the Peak District. The famous Devil's Chair, a pinnacled knife-edge arete, is the third and steepest outcrop. Beyond the saddle north of Scattered Rock the character of the hill starts to change as the path, less frequented now and grassier, crosses the shoulder of the final rounded hilltop and gives an impressive glimpse down into the depths of Mytton Dingle. An ancient wind-blasted hedge appears as angles ease and the Shropshire Plain spreads out ahead, sweeping wide from Earl's Hill to the Wrekin. Green lanes, a copse, and sheep pastures lead to a pretty wooded valley with cottages and a chapel and the first hints of bygone mining activity, and past the derelict smelting mill itself to Snailbeach village. South of the village the road runs for a while beside the course of the abandoned narrow gauge Snailbeach Railway but after passing Crowsnest Dingle it can be avoided by a narrow right of way which contours the flanks of Oak Hill. Be prepared here for rough going between high hedges of bracken. The Stiperstones Inn may offer convenient refreshment before the ridge is regained by very steep slopes at the head of either of the two dingles, Mytton or Perkins Beach: both are interesting, the former containing traces of a wartime aircrash and the latter of an abandoned village. Once over the crest on the eastern flanks the character of the Stiperstones changes yet again as the final section of the route contours the edge of a gentler landscape of little tumbling hills that fall to the Onney Valley and rise beyond to the great bank of the Long Mynd.

If transport can be organized, an excellent traverse can be made along the Stiperstones crest to GR 383020 and then striking north-east to Habberley before climbing steep and imposing Earl's Hill with its Iron Age hill fort and descending to Pontsford: the route, of about 12 kilometres ($7\frac{1}{2}$ miles), follows rights of way except on Earl's Hill which is a nature reserve with permitted public access.

Manstone rock, the highest point on the Stiperstones crest, is seen here from the south.

A Traverse of the Stiperstones

Length of circuit: 13 kms/8 miles
Height gained: 415 m/1,360 ft
Difficulty: easy walking on good but sometimes rough and rocky tracks: one steep ascent
Note: this is a National Nature Reserve, please observe byelaws posted on car-park noticeboard which include strict control of dogs and prohibition of fires. Grouse shooting may take place between 12th August and 10th December
Warning: beware of old mine shafts

Start: Nature Reserve car-park at 369977. (420 m/1,380 ft).

(1) Take wide track to NW diagonally up hillside to first rocky tor, CRANBERRY ROCK, then follow ridge crest path past MANSTONE ROCK (trig pt 536 m/1,759 ft), DEVIL'S CHAIR and SCATTERED ROCK (pt 494 m) to track junction and cairn on broad saddle at 373999.
3 kms/1¾ miles

(2) Main track continues NE along ridge passing W of SHEPHERD'S ROCK (pt 502 m) gradually descending W flank of final rounded hill through several gates to track junction below power lines. Fork left to join metalled lane at gate by chapel at 380021 and descend into Snailbeach. Cut corner by lead smelter ruins, join road and continue SW to Stiperstones village.
6 kms/3¾ miles

(3) By Stiperstones Inn turn E into righthand of two lanes, leading first SE then S into deep valley of Perkin's Beach. Climb steeply from head of cwm to rejoin saddle at 373999.
1.5 kms/1 mile

(4) Descend path down E flank of ridge towards The Hollies until reaching jeep track 200 yards above farm, follow track S through forestry back to car-park.
2.5 kms/1½ miles

Variation

(2.A + 3.A) Follow (2) past Snailbeach and Crowsnest to 368014 opposite tower of old mine works. Ascend drive through gate to cottages, RoW passes in front of upper cottage and as a narrow path contours Oak Hill along intake fence into Mytton Dingle. Path ascends very steeply to ridge crest track below Shepherd's Rock. Continue S to saddle at 373999.
7.5 kms/4¾ miles

Pride of the Peak District – Kinder Scout

OS 1 : 50,000 Sheet 110

'A country beyond comparison uglier than any other I have seen in England, bleak, tedius, barren, & not mountainous enough to please one with its horrors.'

Thomas Gray: letter 1762

'Kinder Scout offers solitude and established stillness, older than the world'

E A Baker: *Moors, Crags and Caves of the High Peak* 1903

Time changes, and with it man's perception of the wilderness. And Kinder Scout, hardly a mountain, more a great mesa that holds the highest point in the Peak, is today a much loved wilderness. Together with Bleaklow, its slightly lower but even wilder neighbour, Kinder is the quintessence of the Dark Peak, that high and brooding gritstone moorland that sits astride the spine of England, the final link of the Pennine Chain. But Peak it is not: in Saxon times the region was known as Peaclond – literally 'Hill Country' – later travellers described the whole area as 'The Peak'; the Ordnance Survey in its first map of the region in 1864 misleadingly appended the name to the five-square-mile plateau surrounding its highest point while carefully lettering in the name 'Kinder Scout' along its western lip where the plunging stream of Kinder Downfall is the major feature. Cyn

Beyond the Kinder reservoir the moors sweep up to the western edge of the Kinder plateau: on the right is the dark gorge of Kinder Downfall and on the far left rises the shoulder of the so-called Upper Western Buttress.

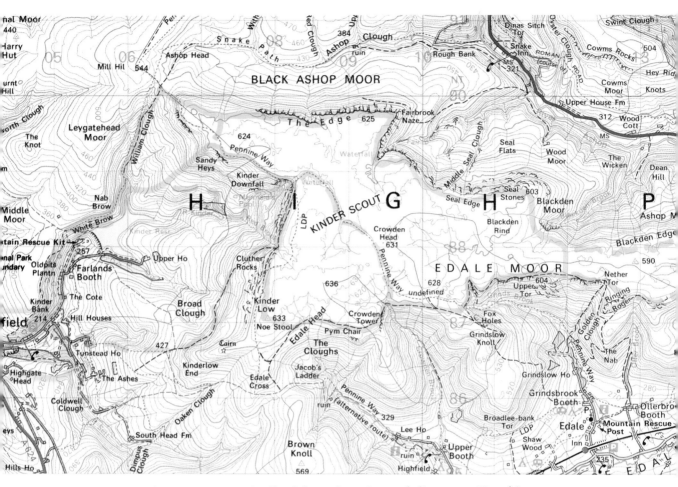

dwr Scwd in Anglo-Saxon means 'Hill of the Waterfall', so this at least seems an apt and proper title. Geologically, Kinder and Bleaklow are gritstone islands perched on the crest of the so-called Derbyshire dome, all that remains of the upper rock layer in the centre of this great anticline, the rest having been worn away to expose the layers beneath – notably the Limestone of the White Peak – but leaving gritstone verges to east and west. Practically, the Kinder Scout plateau is a desolation of shallow dunes of peat, sometimes heathery, often boggy, crisscrossed by 'groughs' – deep runnels – that make bee-line travel tedious and exhausting. Once clothed in broad-leaved forest after the permafrost melted, poorly drained, burned by man, grazed by animals, eroded and soured by atmospheric pollution, this is the landscape John Hillaby described in his *Journey through Britain* as '. . . land at the end of its tether . . .' likening the maze of chocolate-brown peat-hags to the

droppings of dinosaurs. Yet this monotonous plateau is fringed by steep edges, often rocky, sculpted and spectacular and if Kinder's heart is stern and uncompromising, its beauty lies round its perimeter.

Historically Kinder Scout played an important part in the development of both fell-walking and National Parks in Britain. Set midway between the great cities of Lancashire and Yorkshire and close to the industrial Midlands, the empty moors and challenging landscape had attracted hardy walkers as early as 1880 when the first rambling club was formed in Manchester, despite the fact that virtually the entire upland was jealously preserved grouse moor. An early test piece of the 'bog-trotters' – as they were soon known – was the now-classic Marsden to Edale walk across Black Hill, Bleaklow and Kinder in 1902. In the depression years of the Thirties rambling exploded as a natural escape from the frustrations of the cities and pressure for

Kinder Downfall and the Perimeter Circuit

Length: 22.5 kms/14 miles
Total ascent: 560 m/1,850 ft
Difficulty: a stout walk, rough often muddy paths along edges, short trackless sections across plateau rugged, strenuous. (1A) involves short stiff scramble
Note: this is serious country subject to fierce changeable weather. Typically featureless, navigational skills essential. Specific areas occasionally closed for shooting 12th August – 10th December, enquire PNP phone 062–981–4321

Start: PNP car-park at 048869, Bowden Bridge above Hayfield (215 m/705 ft).

(1) Ascend road 800 m, cross bridge continuing on path above river, crossing again to Pump House. Ascend L to contour path above reservoir, continuing E to N arm of lake whence descend to footbridge crossing outflow William Clough, ascend N of E to shoulder, hints of path, then up narrowing ridge – Upper Western Buttress – to bouldery promontory plateau lip. Follow well-defined path SE to head of cliffs Kinder Downfall (600 m/1,970 ft).
5 kms/3 miles

(2) Edge path continues S to OS pillar KINDER LOW (633 m/2,077 ft) whence strike 300 m SE, rough ground, to meet edge path near anvil-like Noe Stool rock, follow path E along southern edge past Pagoda Rocks, Woolpacks boulder field, above crag Crowden Tower to cross muddy swarth Pennine Way, swing N to craggy head Grindsbrook Clough (590 m/1,936 ft).
5.5 kms/3½ miles

(3) Following edge path to crags Upper Tor, continue 400 m E then strike N 400 m, rough ground, to join northern edge path above Blackden Brook. Follow path L, bearing first N to Seal Stones then W along Seal Edge, round craggy Fairbrook Naze and along Ashop Edge to conspicuous Boxing Glove stones (590 m/1,936 ft).
6 kms/3¾ miles

(4) Path continues along fading edge, descends to boggy saddle Ashop Head (500 m/1,640 ft), junction, whence descend path L down William Clough, rejoining ascent route above reservoir.
5.5 kms/3½ miles

Alternatives
(1.A) For experienced scramblers only: from William Clough bridge ascend to shoulder then contour rough hillsides due E 500 m, descending to W end small wood and Kinder River (direct route below wall crosses private non-access land). Ascend rugged valley beside river to scrambly boulders below waterfall/cliffs Kinder Downfall. Go 100 m L to corner whence stiff scramble up short vertical blocky wall into alcove leads to plateau above.

(2.A) Shorten route by using well-marked muddy Pennine Way linking Downfall to Grinsbrook Clough direct, or visa versa.
3 kms/2 miles

(4.A) If (1A) used in ascent, 700 m W of Boxing Glove stones strike S 300 m to join western edge path near summit Upper Western Buttress, descend (1) to reservoir.

access to the moors became intense for even by the mid-Thirties there was still not one public right of way on the upper fifteen square miles of Kinder Scout. Land that two centuries before had been criss-crossed by packhorse tracks and free for all was now barred by cordons of zealous gamekeepers, many of them not averse to strong-arm tactics, and walkers often developed commando methods to reach the tops. One unpleasant incident in 1932 was a Mass Trespass by some 600 ramblers up William Clough – a right of way above Hayfield since 1898 – and on towards the forbidden Kinder plateau: there was violence and five ramblers went to prison. Nevertheless, wheels were in motion and in 1939 Parliament examined the whole question of rights of way, finally passing an Access to Mountains bill which led eventually to the designation of Britain's first National Park – the Peak District – in 1951.

Today, with almost unrestricted access, there are many excellent walking routes on the Kinder massif but the finest is the lengthy perimeter circuit taking in the steep plateau edges where lies the best scenery. The approach suggested here allows competent scramblers to approach the Downfall, the most famous single feature on Kinder, up the wild gulch of the Kinder river from below where the 30-metre (100-foot) waterfall is seen at its most spectacular – especially in spate or when frozen. Non-scramblers can approach with caution but they cannot reach the plateau and must descend and detour via the Mermaid's Pool – where immortality is threatened for those who glimpse her on an Easter morning – to regain the recommended route up the pleasant ridge of the Upper Western Buttress. Going south the path approaches the marked 'summit' of Kinder Low, the unmarked highest place – point is hardly accurate – is some 800 metres distant towards the middle of the plateau and just three metres higher. Along the southern edges stands a sequence of grotesque boulders and outcrops such as the strange throne of Pym Chair, the tapering tor of the Pagoda, the scattered blocks of the weird Woolpacks – often known as 'Whipsnade' – and the imposing crags of Crowden and Grindsbrook Towers above the popular ascent routes from Edale.

Above Grindsbrook Clough energetic purists may consider extending the circuit a further 5½ kilometres (3½ miles) eastward to the spur-end of the plateau at Crookston Knoll before striking back westward to Blackden Edge. Here the northern edges are less frequented and more atmospheric and the path passes above the steep Chinese Wall on Seal Edge before striking north round the head of Fairbrook Naze and its sharp prow and west again over Black Ashop Edge –

where stand the famous Boxing Glove Stones – to complete the circuit. A lasting impression of Kinder Scout in perfect weather is one of 'Big Sky Country' – as they say in Montana.

Kinder Downfall: this is a winter view of the famous falls which gave Kinder Scout its name.

White Peak and Dark Peak – A Hope Valley Horseshoe   Derbyshire Peak District

OS 1: 50,000 Sheet 110

'The Peak of Derby being extraordinarily noted, I could not in my travels omit to visit it, especially upon the account of the dreadful cave called the Devil's Arse . . .'

William Lithgow,
Rare Adventures and Painful Peregrinations – 1614–32

Celebrated especially for its subterranean sights, the Hope Valley lies along the junction of the gentle limestone plateau of the White Peak and the frowning gritstone moorlands of the Dark Peak. Peak Cavern – as William Lithgow's cave is now more genteelly known – is just one of a

number of impressive caves that open into the valley close to the village of Castleton. The surrounding surface landscape is as dramatic and interesting as any in the Peak and the walk suggested here samples something of the contrasting countryside on both sides of the valley.

Castleton, a charming village and something of a tourist venue in season, is both a convenient place to start and a refreshing place to finish the walk. Once a medieval model town, it is dominated by the imposing ruins of Peveril Castle perched on a great crag rearing between

the twin clefts of Peak Cavern and Cave Dale, a stronghold built by William Peveril, bastard son of the Conquerer, when Steward of the surrounding royal hunting preserve of Peak Forest.

After crossing farmland and fields the ascent of the graceful cone of Lose Hill is straightforward and the excellent summit panorama stretches from the gritstone edges beyond the Derwent to the moody folds of the Kinder Scout massif at the head of the Edale sanctuary below. Across the portal of Edale and crowned with a rocky 'Pike' stands shapely Win Hill which can be added to the walk for the penalty of a few more miles. Apparently a bloody Dark Ages battle took place hereabouts – possibly on the Roman Road that runs along the western flanks of Win Hill – between Edwin of Northumbria and Cuicholm of Wessex. On the eve of battle the former king camped on Win Hill and won the day, the latter king on Lose Hill and lost it!

Of a mountainous style almost unique in the Peak District, the crest westward from Lose Hill is comparatively narrow, runs over two intermediate tops and is generally known as the Great Ridge. From Back Tor, the first top, the path picks its way down the edge of shattered cliffs, a manifestation of the shales – neither gritstone nor limestone – of which the ridge is composed, and which appear again on the culminating point of the ridge, Mam Tor. Its east face scooped out to form a huge striated cliff, Mam Tor – the so-called 'Shivering Mountain' – is a dramatic landmark. The triangular cliff, falling around 100 metres (300 feet) from near the summit but not particularly steep, is the result of incessant landslips which have exposed layer upon layer of crumbling shales and siltstones. Solidified under snow and ice the face provides an esoteric winter climb though first ascended as long ago as 1898 in summer by the redoubtable J W Puttrell! The hilltop is circled by the ramparts and ditches of a large and important Bronze Age hill fort which obviously predates the cliff over which a sizable section has fallen away: as recently as 1977 landslides permanently cut the main A625 road below the face.

The ruins of eleventh-century Pevril Castle guard the mouth of the dry limestone valley of Cavedale.

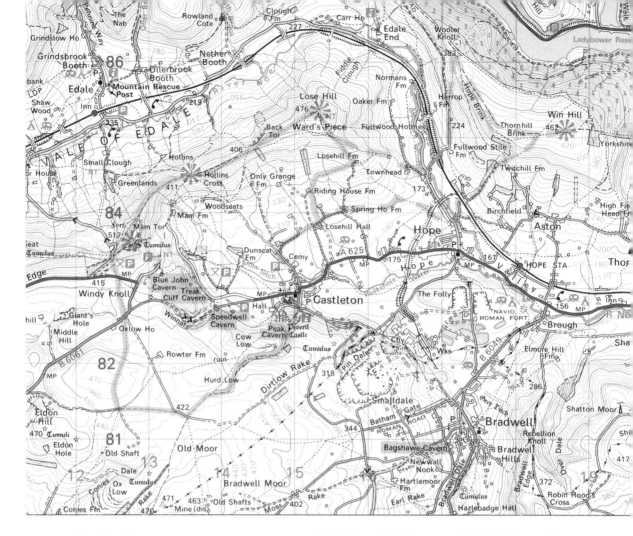

A Hope Valley Horseshoe

Length: 13 kms/8 miles
Total ascent: 435 m/1,425 ft
Difficulty: mostly good paths but a trifle rough in places
Note: try not to exacerbate footpath erosion on Great Ridge Section (2)

Start: most aesthetic start is Castleton car-park 149830. (290 m/950 ft) but other convenient car-parks are marked on map below Mam Tor and Hope, fees usually payable.

(1) From village centre take Hollowford Rd N 500 m to lane junction, follow farm track R, then field path to lane junction at Losehill Hall PNP Centre. Continue 100 m E where concessionary field path over stile leads N to pass R of Riding House Farm whence RoW ascends E across hillside almost to Lose Hill Farm, go up L to signpost from where path climbs to grassy spur and summit topograph LOSE HILL (476 m/1,562 ft).
3.5 kms/2 miles

(2) Follow well-worn path SW along ridge crest crossing BACK TOR (435 m/1,427 ft) with steep rocky descent and BARKER BANK (426 ft/1,398 ft) to track junction at Hollins Cross saddle (390 m/1,280 ft) then long gradual climb to summit trig pt MAM TOR (517 m/1,696 ft). Descend path and steps SW to lane at Mam Nick then footpath S to road.
4 kms/2½ miles

(3) RoW opposite leads 500 m over Windy Knoll to another road, go R to track junction whence path strikes S across pasture to wall continuing over low hill to track junction 126814. Go E beside wall to join stony lane at gate, continue E 200 m to gate by sheep pens where path strikes L across fields 400 m to fork in shallow depression, go R, through iron gates, deepening depression becomes narrow Cave Dale leading directly to Castleton.
5.5 kms/3½ miles

Variation to include Win Hill Pike

(1.A) From Losehill Hall continue track E to Hope Village, cross Edale Rd and river at Killhill Br, lane ascends under rly, go R then NE up track to Twitchill Farm whence RoW climbs to crest and trig pt, rocky outcrop WHIN HILL PIKE (462 m/1,516 ft). Descend ridge 2 kms W then NW to track junction almost at edge woods, descend L track across steep hillside S to lane crossing rly, then Edale Rd crossing river. After 50 m turn R up Townhead lane for 300 m, fork L, track then path climbs to grassy spur and Losehill Pike summit.
Extra 8 kms/5 miles, plus 325 m/1,0670 ft

The imposing east face cliffs of Mam Tor fall towards the head of the Hope Valley, the remains of the main road, finally obliterated in 1977, are seen below. In the distance, eastward, the Great Ridge stretches towards Lose Hill.

Mam Tor and a large surrounding area belong to the National Trust and the popular summit is usually reached from the lane on the narrow col of Mam Nick. A steep, rough and badly eroded (and currently closed) but infinitely more scenic route descends south-west down the cliff edge to the abandoned road which can be followed round to the entrance to Winnats or 'Wind Gates' Pass, now the only road, steep, narrow and twisting, down to Castleton: it is sobering to learn that in 1938 there were serious government proposals to blast a modern highway through this delightful limestone gorge! However, our route now gently ascends onto the limestone plateau, and dark gritstone dykes give way to walls of white rocks. Near its lowest point the path passes over Windy Knoll where excavations in Bone Cave below the old quarry have revealed bones of bison, wolf and bear. Further on the route crosses pastures riddled with the shafts and workings of lead mines abandoned some 200 years ago. Eventually the path drops into the interesting dry valley of Cave Dale, a narrow, twisting and rocky defile probably carved by glacial melt water after the Ice Age and the scene of mass rallies in the 1920s of ramblers protesting at the then forbidden access to 'Old Kinder Scout and the Moors roundabout' as the well known song puts it. Peveril Castle rises sheer above the craggy lower end of the Dale and the centre of Castleton is only a couple of hundred metres further on.

Along the Derwent Crest   Peak District

OS 1 : 50,000 Sheet 110

'... where Derwent rolls his dusky floods
Through vaulted mountains, and a night of
woods.'

Erasmus Darwin: The Botanic Garden 1789

The Peak District, remarkable for its dearth of natural lakes, is scattered liberally with over fifty made by man of which the largest and least incongruous are the three that impound the headwaters of the River Derwent – the Howden, Derwent and Ladybower reservoirs. Rising on the desolate Bleaklow plateau with its annual rainfall of some 150 centimetres (60 inches) the Derwent had little chance of escaping the East Midlands water engineers: the first two dams were completed in 1916 and the Ladybower, ten years in construction, in 1945. Derwent derives from the Celtic *derwen* meaning oak, and Derwent Dale must once have been a peaceful and attractive wooded valley, the surrounding moors were always sheep country and Ladybower alone drowned no less than ten farms besides the pretty villages of Ashopton and Derwent Chapel. Tragic though it was, the flooding of the dale and the subsequent reafforestation of its slopes – albeit with pine and larch – has created a comely lakeland landscape in harmony with the surrounding hills and high moors, an extremely popular 'lung' for the nearby Sheffield conurbation and a walking venue unique in the Pennines.

For serious walkers the area holds several excellent itineraries of which the most interesting is probably the circuit of the tops and edges – noted for their extraordinary rocky outcrops – that rise above the eastern shores. At Fairholme the National Park facilities provide a good starting point close to the awesome 35 metres (115 feet) castellated wall of the Derwent Dam. During the war the hills hereabouts echoed to the roar of 617 Squadron's Lancasters as they swept down the narrow valley to perfect their dangerous 'dambusting' techniques, but the lakeside is now tranquil and a good foresty track leads along it towards the Howden Dam that blocks the northern end of the valley. But before the dam is reached the route turns eastward to follow an ancient packhorse track up the narrow clough of the Abbey Brook: with its lively stream, slopes scattered with oaks and leading deep into the heart of the moors this is one of the most charming small glens in the Peak District. Walkers striding happily up this grassy track, secure in the midst of National Trust territory, should know that it was not always so peaceful. Although well used from times immemorial, by an Enclosure Act of 1816 this track was closed from the Derwent up to the watershed while the descent eastward to the Don valley remained a right of way, a ridiculous situation which rankled the militant hikers of the Twenties and Thirties when the surrounding moors were closely patrolled by gamekeepers: many a fracas occurred. In 1932 a mass trespass down the valley was confronted by a waiting band of keepers and police and a battle and several arrests ensued.

Lost Lad is the first summit and all routes up to it are rough and more or less boggy, it commands a wide view and is crowned with a useful topograph but it tells a sad tale. One springtime many years ago a shepherd noticed the words 'lost lad' scratched on a boulder here and found nearby the body of a young boy lost in bad weather the previous autumn. On the skyline rises the spectacular silhouette of a ruined castle which on closer aquaintance proves to be Back Tor – the highest point of the walk. 'The Spirit of the Moors has his home on Back Tor ...' wrote John Derry in his classic book *Across the Derbyshire Moors* in 1926, and surely this spiky gritstone palisade standing atop the wide and gently swelling moorland and guarded by grouse, curlew and mountain hares, is an imposing – and particularly in mist – an eerie place. In clear conditions however it is one of the best viewpoints in the Peak, not only towards the

At the southern end of the Derwent Edge, Whinstone Lee Tor looks down on the long ribbon of the Ladybower Reservoir: in the distance rears the Kinder Scout Plateau.

looming plateaux of Bleaklow and Kinder, but into Edale and to distant Axe Edge, while eastwards can be seen the towers and chimneys of Sheffield, Barnsley and the cities beyond the Peak.

The terrain ahead is almost flat but the path is often boggy and badly eroded. Near the Cakes of Bread a rocky scarp materializes along the eastern lip of the moor and a diversion here provides better going with glimpses of the lakes and the green vale below. To locate anything resembling a dove among the boulders littering the craggy edge of Dovestones Tor requires a powerful imagination but the weird Salt Cellar beyond is a conspicuous landmark. Now a great henge rears on the moorland horizon, the Wheel Stones, a clutch of bizarre towers which could well have been designed by Michelin men though from other angles the alternative name of Coach and Horses seems apposite: the scramble to the summit is easier than it looks. The Hurkling Stones, said to resemble crouching warriors, are the final strange outcrops before the path passes above the cliffs of Whinstone Lee Tor and starts descending towards Grindle Clough and moody Ladybower. There, as the lake-shore lane passes little Mill Brook Bay, it seems appropriate to give a poignant salute to Derwent village beneath the dark waters.

Right
Standing high on the Derwent Edge, the celebrated gritstone pillar of the Salt Cellar looks eastwards over the Ladybower Reservoir towards the distant plateau of Kinder Scout.

Like the ruins of a great castle, the rocky battlements of Back Tor rise from the moorland skyline: view from the north near Lost Lad.

A Circuit of the Derwent Crest

Length: 16 kms/10 miles
Total ascent: 380 m/1,250 ft
Difficulty: mostly easy, though sometimes boggy, paths but one section rough, damp and trackless
Note: almost entire route to Salt Cellar on National Trust land, many variations, short cuts, possible

Start: Fairholme PNP car-park/picnic site 173893 between Ladybower and Derwent reservoirs.

(1) Minor road leads E below Derwent Dam whence path ascends L to E end Dam, joining wide track leading N up shore Derwent Reservoir. At bend 200 m before bridge first major tributary, gated track leads R above plantation wall into Abbey Brook valley, grassy track continues ascending gradually across S slopes deep glen. Cross second stream to follow grassy path more steeply over shoulder, leave path at highest point striking R up steep grassy nose, continue over rough tussocky plateau ascending slightly R to join poor path leading S along wide ridge crest. Join bigger boggy path, ascend to junction, small cairn, go L, ascend to skyline cairn, topograph, LOST LAD (518 m/1,699 ft), boggy path continues SE to skyline rocks, OS cairn BACK TOR (538 m/1,765 ft).
6.5 kms/4 miles

(2) Follow wide path S, cross signposted junction, then near Cakes of Bread bear R along plateau edge, passing over rocky Dovestone edge to obvious Salt Cellar pillar. Path continues past conspicuous towers Wheelstones, across shallow col, signpost, to follow ridge curving R to rocky edge Whinstone Lee Tor (c 410 m/1,345 ft).
4.5 kms/2¾ miles

(3) Continue 100 m to gully on RHS shoulder, path cuts steeply back R under hill to join boggy contour track along wall, continue N to signpost 'Derwent/Moscar', continue 50 m then strike L on good path, pass plantation edge, ford stream to Grindle Clough barns. Go L through yard, gate, descend steep pasture to join lakeside lane, continuing N past Derwent cottages, etc, to Ladybower Reservoir head and Fairholme.
5.0 kms/3¼ miles

Variation

(1.A) Continue Abbey Brook track round shoulder to ascend valley third stream, Sheepfold Clough, towards Lost Lad. Path fades into bogs, reappears higher. This variation 1.2 kms longer, wetter, more gentle.

Stanage and the Hathersage Heights

Peak District

OS 1: 50,000 Sheets 110, 119

Probably the best known and certainly the most extensive of the gritstone edges that fringe the Peak District is Stanage, a stark battlement of coarse brown rock that lines the escarpment of the Hallam Moors high above the village of Hathersage in the verdant Derwent valley. Eastward from the bouldery edge-top a flat peaty plane of heather, crowberry and moor-grass wide to the wind ripples towards the Sheffield suburbs while westward, beyond steep bracken and green depths, the swelling uplands of the White Peak smile towards the brooding plateaux of the Dark Peak that line the horizon. Stanage Edge is an atmospheric place and its crest

Long-abandoned millstones litter the slopes beneath the gritstone crags of Stanage High Neb.

a popular walk while its 4 kilometres ($2\frac{1}{2}$ miles) of almost continuous cliffs between 12 and 25 metres (40–80 feet) high make it the busiest rock-climbing venue in the Peak with well over 500 guide-booked climbs dating back to 1890 and of every kind and standard.

But there is more on the heights above Hathersage than merely Stanage Edge and this route links interesting local features into an infinitely variable circuit. Completing the major ascents early on, the walk starts at the cwm-like head of the Burbage Brook, and descends over the prow of Higger Tor to the strange kopje of Carl Wark rising in the middle of the heathery expanse of Hathersage Moor. Higger Tor is variously claimed to mean 'Hill of God' or 'Higher Tor' and is celebrated among climbers for its imposing Leaning Block. Carl Wark however is an ancient hill fort where steep rocky edges on three sides and a stone-revetted rampart still 3 metres high (10 feet) enclose a small plateau: it has been described as 'a natural fortress improved by art' and is probably of Dark Ages origin. Leaving the wild moorland the route follows the pretty alder-lined Burbage Brook down a shallow green valley, part of the National Trust's 1,000-acre Longshaw Park estate, formerly home of the Duke of Rutland. Suddenly woods close in as the stream pours over a series of foaming cataracts and into a steep and narrow defile. This is Padley Gorge, deep and rocky but never precipitous, hung with stunted oaks, floored with mossy boulders and the habitat of uncommon birds, it is a beautiful place and a Nature Reserve.

Below the gorge the route climbs to the long-abandoned Lawrencefield Quarry hidden in a jungle of whispering birches, its slabby faces rising from a silent pool while rows of completed millstones nearby await transport that will never come. The famous Surprise Pass on the A625, noted for its sudden view across the Derwent valley towards Kinder, lies just above the cliff top and beyond rear the dark walls of Millstone Edge, its conspicuous quarried escarpment dominating the Hathersage dale. Here the most interesting of several tracks follows the base of the formidable cliffs, in places 40 metres

(140 feet) high, which were an important training ground for aid climbers in the '50s – though the old piton cracks and the blank walls between are today climbed free. A good path, initially steep and rough, leads through the cliffs, round the lip of Hathersage Moor and down into the hollow below Callow Bank which is a favourite launch site for radio-controlled gliders.

The steep Dale Bottom road climbs to Hook's Car where it joins the line of the old turnpike which runs below Stanage Edge and once linked the Woodlands Valley to Sheffield, continuing to a weathered plantation where the narrow road forks. Round the corner a right of way leads down through the trees towards North Lees Hall and although our route bears off almost immediately, the Hall is worth a short diversion: a battlemented tower-house originally built around 1410, it is the original of Thornfield House in Charlotte Brontë's novel *Jane Eyre*. At Dennis Knoll above lonely Greens House the ancient packhorse track over Stanage Edge meets the old turnpike while a short way north stands High Neb, almost the end of the Edge and the loftiest point in the area. Flaunting a series of impressive buttresses and the distinctive overhanging beak (or 'neb') of 'Qietus', for long one of the boldest climbing leads on gritstone, High Neb was, like all these moors, closely keepered and theoretically inaccessible until comparatively recently, and is still subject to access agreements between the National Park and the landowners.

Over a hundred millstones lie scattered beneath the edge hereabout, until the advent of synthetic carborundum killed the industry they would have been carved on site, fitted to wooden axles and rolled, two by two, to waiting transport. Now an easy path stretches along the edge-top, past the packhorse track, across the line of the 'Long Causeway' Roman road, above the sandy ledge of Robin Hood's cave – a favoured bivouac of early climbing pioneers – and past the tops of famous rock climbs busy every weekend. Then as the cliffs fade away the path rises easily to the final rocky tor above the Cowper Stone and the finish is in sight.

Stanage Edge and the Padley Gorge

Length: 20.5 kms/12½ miles
Total ascent: 570 m/1,870 ft
Difficulty: easy walking on good though sometimes stony paths
Note: route described may be changed at will with wide choice of obvious variations

Start: route described from car-park at 263829, Burbage Rocks, on Ringinglow – Hathersage road (410 m/1,345 ft). Other convenient parking places include: Hook's Car (244830) or PNP car-park Hollin Bank, toilets closeby, (237837).

(1) From Burbage Rocks follow road 300 m W, strike S on moorland path above edge to rocky nose Higger Tor, path descends over Carl Wark hill fort to Burbage Brook near A625 bridge (Toad's Mouth). Beyond road follow good path R bank Brook S to edge woods/Nature Reserve continuing on rocky main path down through forested Padley Gorge to grassy clearing. Strike up R past water-works building 50 m to gate whence narrow path climbs into woods, zigzags up through overgrown spoil tips to level birch woods below old Lawrencefield Quarry, good track continues to A625 road at 248801 (280 m/920 ft).
6 kms/3¾ miles

(2) Cross road, go R to take higher of two stony tracks leading N below cliffs Millstone Edge to good path contouring moor beyond to RoW sign on minor road 253817. Go R 100 m to RoW sign, path drops L across slope to valley bottom track, go L to join minor road, ascend R to Hook's Car junction, take road L below Stanage Edge, descending gradually to fork at small wood (305 m/1,000 ft).
5 kms/3 miles

(3) Follow R fork 100 m to track leading L through pines, grassy path soon breaks R across bouldery pastures below oak wood to stream, stepping stones, mill-pond. Path beyond continues, gates, stiles, to Greens House whence track ascends R to rejoin road at Dennis Knoll plantation. From corner 200 m L take good moorland track R until obvious path leads L below craggy Edge to High Neb. Continue N 500 m (or sooner) to ascend easily to cliff-top, whence good path leads R to OS pillar HIGH NEB (458 m/1,502 ft).
5 kms/3 miles

(4) Follow path SE above cliffs Stanage Edge to OS pillar near Cowper Stone (457 m/1,500 ft). Path continues E across moor to road at Burbage Rocks.
4.5 kms/2¾ miles

Stanage Edge, seen here above the Plantation, stretches away northward towards the distant prow of High Neb.

The Roaches Crest Staffordshire Peak District

'Here are also vast Rocks which surprise with Admiration, called the Henclouds and Leek Roches. They are of so great a Height and afford such stupendous Prospects that one could hardly believe they were anywhere to be found but in Picture'

Compleat History of Staffordshire: 1730

Stand on the gritstone battlements of the Roaches and look down upon the wide spreading Cheshire Plain fading away towards the distant soft Midland shires. Turn behind and gaze at rolling moors and serried hills – the sterner stonier upland landscape of the North. There can be few places in Britain where the frontier between lowland and highland is so manifest as this long gritstone ridge that dominates the Staffordshire border country north of Leek.

Ideally the traverse of the Roaches ridge should start from its far north-western end where Danebridge nestles in a smiling landscape of rounded hills, but it is only a small village and one should park with discretion in the narrow lane by the bridge. Field paths lead past a four-square farmhouse to the strange beak of Hanging Stone jutting from the grassy hillside. A plaque set into the rock commemorates *Burke, a noble mastiff . . . a gun and a ramble his heart's desire with the friend of his life the Swythamley Squire. 1874.* Here the corner can be cut by a narrow path – not actually a right of way – past a small tarn directly to the ridge crest. The first landmark beyond the bare whaleback ridge of Back Forest is the pass at Roach End with a remote keeper's cottage closeby. Now the moorland is more rugged with boulders scattered over the carpet of heather and bilberry, and rocks sometimes eroded into weird shapes such as the conspicuous Bearstone. Although the Roaches summit hardly justifies its name – obviously derived from the Norman-French *roche* – rock becomes very much in evidence thereafter as the path approaches the scarp-like lip of the almost unbroken line of crags that edge the ridge for two kilometres: an ancient larch plantation below the cliffs and the sharp shape of Hen Cloud now visible ahead add a real mountain ambience to the wide view. Doxey Pool is passed, a peculiar grass-fringed tarn on the ridge crest and mentioned in Domesday Book, and then the path drops into the straggly trees below the rearing crags. And what crags! This is one of the most celebrated climbing areas in the Peak and the gritstone walls and buttresses are laced with dozens of routes up to 30 metres (100 feet) high. Most famous is surely Sloth, a fierce and uncompromising line out over a huge overhanging neb, a truly spectacular lead pioneered by the great Don Whillans in 1952. 'Was it 'ard?' Asked an onlooker who watched the first ascent. 'Not if yer use yer loaf,' replied Whillans dryly.

At the edge of the wood stands Rockhall, a bizarre cottage built into the cliff, its rooms hewn from the living rock. Not surprisingly it has been the abode of a succession of eccentric characters, from highly aggressive gamekeepers to the recent Doug – self-proclaimed 'Lord of the Roaches' – but none stranger than Bowyer of the Rocks, a notorious moss trooper and local terror, and his daughter Bess who sheltered thieves, smugglers and deserters here. Her own lovely daughter had a beautiful voice and would sing among the rocks in a unknown tongue: but she was abducted and old Bess was left to die of a broken heart. If you are alone and unlucky you may see the spectre of a singing woman who haunts the Roaches. If you are lucky you may see a wallaby. Several escaped from a local menagerie years ago – together they say with a few musk oxen – and after travelling as far as Macclesfield (!) the wallabies settled in hereabouts: many unsuspecting visitors have been astonished to see these outlandish marsupials hopping around among the boulders.

From near Doxey Pool on a misty day, the Roaches escarpment takes on a strangely alpine character as it stretches away towards the distant prow of Hen Cloud.

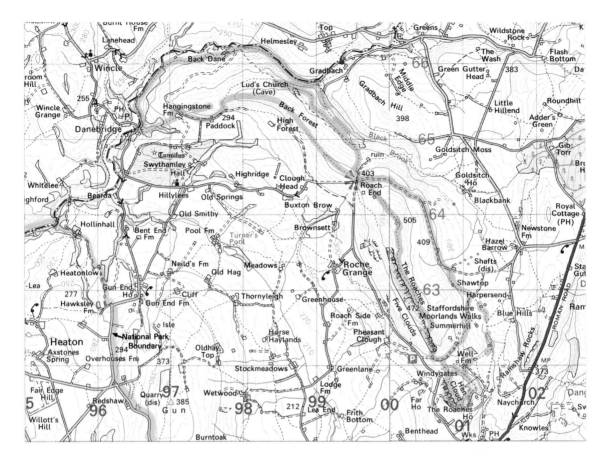

The Roaches Crest

Length: 18.5 kms/11½ miles
Total ascent: 580 m/1,900 ft
Difficulty: easy walk on good paths
Note: most aesthetic start to route is Danebridge, but parking problems may dictate alternative starts

Start: limited roadside parking at Danebridge 965652 (190 m/623 ft), better but still limited at Roach End 996645 (407 m/1,335 ft) or PNP car-park below Roaches at 004621 (340 m/1,115 ft).

(1) From road 100 m S of bridge waymarked path leads up L past cottages, continues NE through wood, up fields, through farmyard and L of Hangingstone Farmhouse to join contouring track below prominent 'Hanging Stone'. Go E past Paddock house and gate to track junction, turn N up to moorland, at ridge crest waymarked concessionary path strikes E along broad Back Forest Ridge, gradually bending SE to join rough track leading eventually to lane crossing ridge at Roach End.
4 kms/2½ miles

(2) Path continues along ridge crest, climbing past eroded Bearstone Rocks to summit trig point THE ROACHES (505 m/1,657 ft). Gradual descent onwards leads along edge of craggy scarp to Doxey Pool. 350 m beyond Pool by fence at shallow saddle easy gully drops R through gap in crags to path descending through woods, down steps, to Rockhall cottage and moorland track leading L to wide col (350 m/1,150 ft). Now concessionary path through stile leads across field to well-defined ridge, ascend to rocky summit HEN CLOUD (410 m/1,345 ft).
4 kms/2½ miles

(3) Path drops steeply SE to plantation, then R to wide track, go 50 m R to narrow trail branching up R to contour steep slopes below W face cliffs and rejoin ascent path. At col follow track NE for 1 km to gate, now strike NW to stile, pass Shawtop ruins to lane at Shaw House, follow lane L climbing gradually round hillside to Roach End.
4.5 kms/2¾ miles

(4) Descend N down track 100 m, cross stile L, follow path descending to edge of woods where lesser path branches L contouring through woods. Lud's Church lies on L some 250 m after slight ascent/descent. Path continues 200 m to junction where fork cuts back R descending to river and footbridge below Gradbach. Now take path L through woods along S bank river, then through fields above river and finally woods again to Danebridge.
6 kms/3¾ miles

The entire 1,000-acre Roaches Estate was acquired by the Peak National Park in 1979, so perhaps the wallabies are safe now.

Hen Cloud is one of the more imposing 'peaks' in the Peak District, a real mini-mountain standing aloof beyond the end of the Roaches ridge. The odd name comes from the Celtic *clud* meaning a rock. Our route now traverses Hen Cloud before turning back below the north-eastern slopes of the Roaches towards Danebridge. Do not miss Lud's Church as you descend into the secluded Dane valley on the return journey. Here, hidden in the depths of Back Forest, is a deep dark chasm in the gritstone, the result of an ancient landslip. A mossy and mysterious place, it has been identified as the Green Chapel of the classic medieval poem *Sir Gawain and the Green Knight* (the atmosphere is certainly appropriate) and also with the Lollards, precursors of the Reformation, who held illicit religious services here in the fourteenth century, indeed it is probably named from one of their number, Walter de Ludank. It was later a popular 'sight' for energetic Victorian pedestrians.

The final stretch leads through pretty woods and meadows along the banks of the tumbling Dane, here the border between Staffordshire and Cheshire.

The mysterious cleft of Lud's Church high above the upper reaches of the River Dane, was a meeting place of the fourteenth-century Lollards and has associations, it is said, with Sir Gawain and the Green Knight.

Ingleborough and the Karst Country

Yorkshire Dales

OS 1:50,000 Sheet 98

Ingleborough has been described as the most interesting mountain in England and though a comparison with, say, Scafell would be invidious, the mountain does have a unique appeal and is justly famed. Its massif dominates the countryside of west Craven and although the distinctive ramp-shaped summit is often invisible from the surrounding dales, Ingleborough projects its singular personality over a large area of the Pennines. It is the third highest summit in Yorkshire – though at one time held to be the highest in England. While unspectacular in mountain terms, the Ingleborough massif is scenically remarkable, a geological treasure trove besides having considerable botanic and archaeological significance.

Much of the mountain's special character results from the unique limestone landscape of its lower slopes, a major reason for the designation of the Yorkshire Dales National Park in 1954. Basically the massif is a huge moorland plinth of Great Scar or mountain limestone some 250 metres (800 feet) thick, on top of which repeated layers of shales, sandstones and limestones – the Yoredale Beds – form the final stepped 300-metre (1,000 foot) summit structure capped with a thin layer of millstone grit. Hillside streams flow downwards only to disappear underground on reaching the limestone. Gaping Gill is the most celebrated of more than a hundred such sinks or potholes which surround the mountain, the water often reappearing at resurgences along the base of the limestone above a lower impervious strata. Twenty thousand years ago deep glacier ice covered Ingleborough and many of its features are due to glacial action, not only did the ice grind out the scars and the vast areas of limestone pavement so characteristic of the Ingleborough moors but the powerful melt-water torrents carved valleys and gorges in the limestone when the ground was still frozen and the cave systems blocked, valleys long since abandoned by the water. It is textbook karst country and the finest cave region in Britain.

Our route leaves the pretty village of Clapham by the private Clapdale valley, its beautiful lake and delightful woods created in the early 1800s by members of the Farrer family of Ingleborough Hall at the top of the village. Various exotic shrubs and plants in the wood were planted by Reginald Farrer, the famous plant collector who died in 1920. Clapdale narrows beyond the woods and the path, now a right of way, passes the craggy portal of Ingleborough Cave, a fine show cave, and the closeby Beck Head resurgence where the Clapham Beck emerges from the inner recesses of the Ingleborough/Gaping Gill system beyond. Thereafter Clapdale becomes a classic dry valley, the path passing the Foxholes neolithic rock shelter on the left before turning ninety degrees into Trow Gill.

Probably cut by a retreating melt-water waterfall, Trow Gill is a small but imposing limestone gorge, its walls over 25 metres (80 feet) high and its head narrowing to a mere slot through which the path climbs over a steep boulder slope. Beyond the slot the Ice Age torrent once roared through a narrow green valley which twists through the limestone onto the plateau near the rocky hollow of Bar Pot where a black hole beneath a gnarled ash tree is the caver's regular entrance to the Gaping Gill system. Gaping Gill itself lies a little further on, where the Fell Beck, chattering down over the moor, suddenly plunges into a dark fern-hung abyss. It is the head of Britain's highest unbroken waterfall, albeit in darkness, and all of 104 metres (340 feet) high. It is given to few to visit the awesome base of the falls in a huge cathedral-like chamber over 150 metres (500 feet) long and 30 metres wide where the water – glinting with hints of daylight – pours through a shaft in the vaulted roof. Reaching this sanctum demands several hours strenuous caving or a descent

On the south-eastern slopes of Ingleborough the Fell Beck plunges into the vertical shaft of Gaping Gill – though underground, the highest unbroken waterfall in Britain.

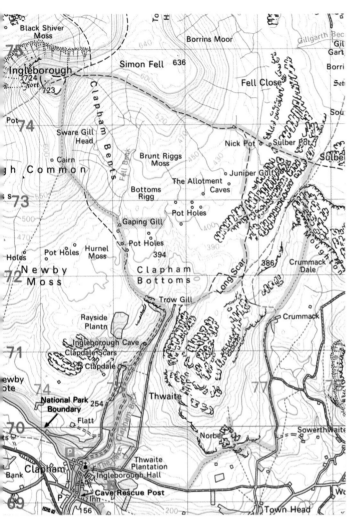

A Circuit over Ingleborough

Length: 17.5 kms/11 miles
Total ascent: 670 m/2,200 ft
Difficulty: easy walking on paths, often boggy, sometimes faint. Mountain is high and exposed, navigation awkward, especially stage (3), compass advisable and 1:25,000 map, showing walls, useful
Note: RoW to Clapdale Farm avoids Clapdale Wood toll. Ingleborough Cave open daily summer, weekends winter. YDNP visitor centre in Clapham car-park

Start: large YDNP car-park at 745692 near Clapham village centre, charge payable. Toilets, etc (160 m/525 ft).

(1) Go N to church, L across bridge, R to corner then L whence sign indicates route to Ingleborough Cave leading R through wood-yard past cottage, 10p payable. Follow good path N along lake shore, through woods into narrow valley. Pass Ingleborough Cave, continue through gate, sharp bend, into Trow Gill. Path emerges into shallow valley leading to stile and rocky depression Bar Pot. Muddy path bears N over flat moorland 400 m to fenced pothole Gaping Gill. (405 m/1,330 ft).
4.5 kms/2¾ miles

(2) Ascend steepening path over boggy moorland then gritstone scree NW to flat shoulder of Little Ingleborough. Muddy path continues N along plateau to second flat shoulder then ascends across rocky slopes on RHS to summit plateau, go 300 m W to

pation rather than to enjoy the wide view which in good conditions stretches from Pendle Hill and the Isle of Man to Scafell.

Initially the descent follows the badly eroded route of the famous 'Three Peaks Race' across the flanks of Simon Fell to an area of weird limestone landscape known as Sulber Scars. Here a desert of white pavement fretted by clints and grikes – blocks and fissures – stretches in every direction, though close examination will reveal a wealth of plant life flourishing in the protective grikes. Several routes now lead back to Clapham but navigation hereabouts can be confusing: the suggested route descends via mysteriously named Thieves Moss and Beggar's Stile, over two strange craggy amphitheatres and past a deserted Iron Age settlement into the head of charming little Crummack Dale. Down the dale lie the famous Norber Erratics, scores of slaty boulders plucked by the ice from an outcrop up the valley and deposited here on a limestone bench. The final stretch, Thwaite Lane, is a continuation of celebrated Mastiles Lane above Kilnsey, a section of that medieval monastic highway that crossed the southern Dales to link the lands of Fountains Abbey.

down the main shaft by the bosun's chair set up during summer bank holidays by local cave clubs. The intrepid French speleologist, Edouard Martel, was the first man to enter Gaping Gill, lowered down this main shaft in 1895, while in 1983, after more than a decade of concerted attempts, cave divers finally entered Gaping Gill to emerge in Ingleborough Cave.

The route up Ingleborough is now straightforward, crossing the shoulder of Little Ingleborough before climbing to the extensive summit plateau graced with its topograph and shelter-wall built to commemorate the '53 Coronation. Traces of ramparts encircle the plateau and nineteen hut circles have been located here, for this is Britain's highest Iron Age hill fort. It seems to have been built by the local Brigantes tribe in reaction to the Roman occu-

topograph, shelter wall, OS cairn INGLEBOROUGH
(724 m/2,374 ft).
2.5 kms/1½ miles

(3) From NE corner plateau, path descends R of ridge crest then
across S flank Simon Fell, eroded, boggy, to ruined shooting hut
767740. (425 m/1,395 ft). Level path continues over stile to
signpost whence follow single pointer 'Footpath' W through
expanse limestone pavement to lonely signpost at 778735 (Sulber)
whence go R signed 'Clapham'. At stile 400 m drop L through
wicket gate to Thieves Moss below rocky amphitheatre, follow
faint path through rocky pavement, cairns, to Beggar's Stile
notch in Moughton Scars escarpment. Cross stile, descend to
grassy terrace traversing W side Crummack Dale to stile above
farm. (300 m/985 ft).

The 'grikes' – or fissures – between the limestone 'clints' are
often sanctuaries for small plants. Our route crosses this area

(4) Join track W of Crummack farm, continue c 1.5 kms S to
tarmac, at bend strike R through stile to Nappa Scars craglet, stile
and signpost beyond at 766697 amid Norber Erratics, best just up
slope above. Follow sign 'Clapham' W below crags (Robin
Proctor's Scar), then SW to stile, lane leads W (Thwaite Lane)
eventually through tunnels to Clapham church.
5 kms/3 miles

Alternative

(3.A + 4.A) At first signpost past shooting hut faint path strikes S,
over area limestone pavement, to join ancient drove road at Long
Scar. Continue SW over hillside to gate and walled lane (Long
Lane) leading S to Thwaite Lane and Clapham.
Saves 2 kms/1¼ miles

of characteristic limestone pavement at Sulber below the
slopes of Simon Fell, Ingleborough's eastern satellite.

The Wharfedale Heights – Great Whernside Yorkshire Dales

OS 1 : 50,000 Sheet 98

> 'Our maps are candid charts of desolation
> And wear the Pennine weather on their
> sleeve'
>
> Ivor Brown: 'The Moorland Map' from *Landmarks*: 1943

Great Whernside is the monarch of the Eastern Dales. Not to be confused with Whernside, one of the famous 'Three Peaks' of Craven, Great Whernside rears its massive whale-back above upper Wharfedale, the fifth highest summit in Yorkshire, the most easterly two-thousand-footer in Britain north of the Peak. A typically unspectacular Yorkshire mountain, its gritstone summit sits on layers of shales, sandstones and limestones – the Yoredale beds – which rise from a plinth of Great Scar limestone. Accordingly, from high desolate moorland of peaty grass and dark boulders, its terrain changes to smiling hillsides slashed with white limestone scars and seamed with caves, while myriad shafts riddle the middle slopes, dotted with the abandoned workings of old lead mines to lend the mountain a hint of times-past, of melancholy even. Nevertheless its summit is windblown, aloof and atmospheric, far higher it seems than a mere 2,310 feet. Great Whernside is a worthy mountain.

One of the gems of Wharfedale, the picturesque small village of Kettlewell is mentioned in Domesday Book, it has a long history of marketing, mining and farming and still boasts no less than three inns, a reflection of one-time importance as a stage on the old coaching route

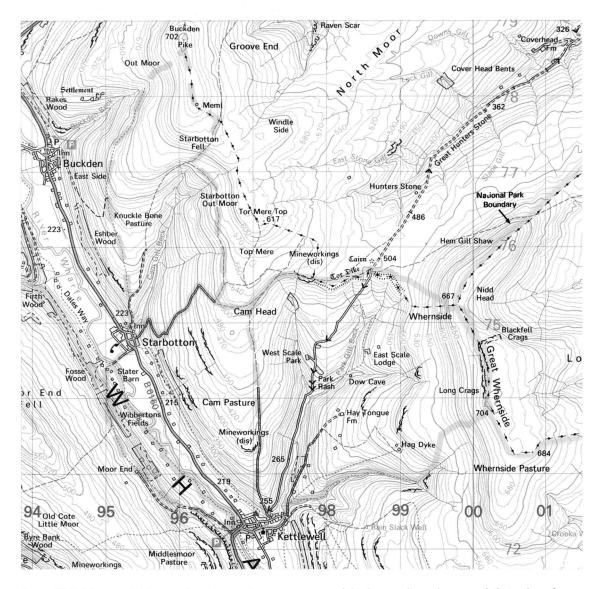

The route from Kettlewell onto Great Whernside follows
Dowber Gill, carved deeply into the limestone on the western
flanks of the hill.

from Keighley to Richmond. Our walk starts
through the village and enters the deep rugged
Dowber Gill, V-shaped and not quite a gorge
but set with limestone outcrops and initially
scattered with gnarled hawthorns and ash trees.
The tumbling beck pours over impressive little
cascades and waterslides but in summer its
waters often disappear and resurge in its rocky
bed. Then the limestone ends, the rocks darken
and the valley forks. High up on the right stand
the ruins of the old Providence lead mine, once

one of the largest hereabouts, while in the often-
dry stream bed below a metal manhole covers
Providence Pot. Here starts one of the classic
Pennine caving expeditions, following the water
through the extraordinary Dowbergill Passage
for over 1,500 metres – nearly a mile – to its
resurgence in the depths of Dow Cave in
Caseker Gill, the next valley northwards on the
flanks of Great Whernside.

Climbing out of Dowber Gill the route
crosses tussocky moorland and a terrace littered
with aircraft wreckage to a low edge of strange
gritstone boulders, crinkly surfaced and almost
rectangular, crowned by the huge cairn of Great
Whernside. Almost ringed by a horizon of

rolling Pennine tops, the best views are eastwards towards the distant Cleveland Hills. Continuing almost level over the bouldery outcrop of Blackfell Top and alternating between boggy patches and a shallow rocky edge, the crest drops towards Black Dike End and a view down to the twin Nidderdale reservoirs – a lake view unusual in the Yorkshire Dales. Then the path plunges down the massive rounded shoulder of Great Whernside to meet the lonely Coverdale road, once the Richmond stage coach route and unmetalled until 1953,. The rumpled flanks of Park Gill and Cam Gill frame a green glimpse of Wharfedale far below.

From the road a boggy route strikes across featureless moorland towards Tor Mere Top and Buckden Pike, but our 'edge' route – and a more interesting approach to the Pike – follows an old green lane along the line of the enigmatic Tor Dike. Nearly a mile of still-discernible Iron Age ramparts, the Dike follows the lip of the moorland plateau encompassing the natural limestone scars: it appears to defend the pass over to Coverdale and may have been built around 70 AD by the local Brigantes tribe, possibly against the Roman invader. The lane is the ancient trackway from Wharfedale, Arncliffe and Settle to Nidderdale; the Cam Head fork was once a busy junction and from it a direct descent can be made down the medieval 'Top Mere' track to Kettlewell. Meanwhile the walled lane, wide enough for a sheep or cattle drove, drops steeply to the dale floor at Starbotton, a now quiet hamlet but once an important crossroads which, all but destroyed by the catastrophic flash flood of June 1686, later became a flourishing mining village until the industry declined in the 1840s: the name means 'Stony Valley'. A modern footbridge takes the ancient route over the Wharfe, a noted trout stream, and the gentle riverside path now followed by the modern 'Dales Way' leads back southwards to Kettlewell while along the western flank of the valley a slightly longer alternative path shows the glacial trough of the dale to good advantage – although it existed before the ice – while one of Britain's finest lynchet or 'Celtic field' systems should be visible across the dale if the light is low.

On the wide saddle between Great Whernside and Tor Mere Top the route follows the line of the ancient Tor Dike. The Cam Gill valley beyond leads down towards Kettlewell.

A Great Whernside Circuit

Length: 15.5 kms/9½ miles
Total ascent: 550 m/1,800 ft
Difficulty: easy walking mostly on good paths/tracks, Great Whernside summit high and exposed, compass useful in poor conditions
Note: route lies within YDNP car-park, nearest Visitor Centre at Grassington

Start: large YDNP car-park at 968723 near Kettlewell bridge, charge payable (210 m/690 ft).

(1) From car-park go L, first R, pass toilets, church, continuing beside stream to rough track, Dowber Gill Bridge. Turn R into camp-site field, keep R, stile, on beckside path into narrow Dowber Gill following good path N bank of beck. At Providence Pot cave entrance beck forks, climb steeply N out of L fork, hints

of path, to open hillside above Hag Dike Scout centre, join well-defined path ascending easily NE to crest, OS and summit cairns GREAT WHERNSIDE (704 m/2,310 ft).
5 kms/3 miles

(2) Strike N 600 m along shallow ridge crest, poor path, boggy and rocky, past shelter ring to bouldery outcrop Blackfell Top. Path descends gradually NW to wall, stile, dropping steeply beyond to boggy plateau and unfenced road at hill lip. Across road green lane contours W round hill lip to Cam Head track junction, signpost, continue R round hillside, stiles, lane becomes walled, wide, stony, zigzagging steeply down to Starbotton village.
7 kms/4½ miles

(3) At S end village turn R off road through gate, lane leads to River Wharfe footbridge. Cross, go L joining Dales Way along W bank to Kettlewell.
3.5 kms/2¼ miles

Continuation to Buckden Pike

(2.A) At gate in walled lane 600 m beyond Cam Head junction strike up R, follow track 300 m, gate, then contour hillside above wall, past old mine workings, to junction above steep valley head, cairn. RH track climbs to boggy plateau meeting hillcrest path by wall. Follow path N onto wide ridge, past memorial cross, to OS cairn BUCKDEN PIKE (702 m/2,032 ft) extra ascent 230 m/760 ft).
8.5 kms/5¼ miles from Great Whernside

(3.A) Descend SW from cairn into hollow above Buckden Beck, traces of path, aiming at abandoned mine workings whence footpath contours S round hillside, gradually descending to join drove road above Starbotton. Continue to Kettlewell as for (3).
8 kms/5 miles

The Cleveland Crest North York Moors

Cleveland, they say, was originally 'cliff-land' – a region of steep and craggy scarps looking down on the flatlands of the twisting Tees and the green vale of its tributary the little River Leven. But the modern county of Cleveland comprises the industrial cities of Teesside and little more, leaving the closeby Cleveland Hills, as the north-western extremity of the North York Moors, to remain as they should be – part of North Yorkshire.

The North York Moors contain England's largest expanse of heather-covered upland – some 500 square kilometres (196 square miles) – one reason for their designation as a National Park in 1952, and although some areas are conserved as grouse shoots there is a tradition of

de facto access to the open moors and several long distance moorland walks have become renowned in recent years. Longest is the Cleveland Way which follows the western and northern scarps from Helmsley before taking the precipitous east coast southward to Filey – a distance of 150 kilometres (93 miles). Most classic is the Lyke Wake Walk from Osmotherly to the sea at Ravenscar, a test piece of 64 kilometres (40 miles) to be completed in under twenty-four hours. Originally a gruelling expedition, more than thirty years of use have worn a muddy trail

The sandstone crags of the Wainstones rise beside the Cleveland Way on the edge of Hasty Bank and overlook the Vale of Cleveland: across Garfitts Gap rise the slopes of Cold Moor.

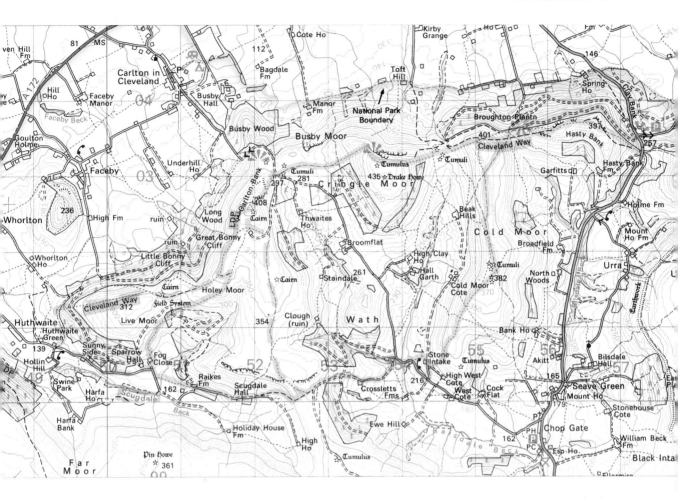

across expanses of once trackless moorland and erosion has now become a frequent problem.

Coincident with one of the best sections of both walks, the circuit suggested here savours all three intrinsic aspects of the moors: the imposing edge, the heather plateaux and the charming dales. Hasty Bank, the first summit, is easily reached and its long crest, supported by the dark crags of Raven's Scar, provides a magnificent view out over the Vale of Cleveland. Eastward the forest-hung scarp extends from Urra Moor to the strange pinnacle of Rosebury Topping above Captain Cook's boyhood home, the village of Great Ayton, with a distant glimpse of the ocean beyond. A thousand feet below the patchwork of fields sweeps northward to a horizon of towers, spires and chimneys, of steam, clamour and smoke – the Teesside conurbation.

Dropping off Hasty Bank the route passes the Wainstones, an inviting area of shattered sand-

stone boulders and grotesque towers which catches the sun and is the most important climbing crag in the area: the name is said to derive from a Danish chieftain who was slain here. Cold Moor rises beyond Garfitts Gap and its wide heathery crest is followed south to Point 382 m where the right of way leading directly down into Raisdale becomes lost in knee-deep heather – not overly strenuous if taken in **descent**. Some walkers may prefer to continue the traverse of the northern edges from Garfitts Gap in one continuous section, although that necessitates a strenuous **ascent** of these slopes on the return. Other indirect paths do exist on this grouse moor.

Raisdale is a smiling and pretty valley with moors swelling high on either side but its narrow lane is a through route and the dale is not as secluded as Scugdale which is reached by a long but gentle ascent over Barker's Ridge. A deserted cottage stands in a blind coombe below craggy bracken-cloaked hillsides at the head of Scugdale and rough pastures dotted with stunted oaks and hawthorns fall to a burbling beck. A line of grey spoil heaps scattered across the hillside are among the few signs of the jet mining industry that once flourished in this charming and venerable-seeming dale.

The secret oak-forested hollow above Fog Close is known as Snotterdale. The long climb above it on to heathery Holey Moor is never steep and the Cleveland Way is soon joined. One can continue down Scugdale to join the Way – indicated by acorn symbol waymarks – at Huthwaite, but the price is an extra two kilometres. The upper section of Holey Moor where it narrows towards the summit of Carlton Bank is the home of the Newcastle and Teesside Gliding Club and while the soaring gliders are graceful creatures of the wind, the discordant paraphernalia of hangers and huts, winches and wires, adds nothing to the ambience of this fine hill.

Cringle Moor, the next top, is the second highest point on the North York Moors but the path avoids the actual summit and follows the scarp edge. According to the memorial topograph agreeably sited at the head of the northern spur the superb vista extends as far as Cross Fell and Ingleborough. Signs of long-abandoned alum and jet workings are common among the hollows as the edge continues over the northern end of Cold Moor and drops once more to Garfitts Gap from where a forestry track – once an old jet miner's trail – leads back to Clay Bank avoiding Hasty Bank. If it is evening however, connoisseurs will return along the high edge to savour the Teesside lights glinting beyond the wide vale.

From Barker's Ridge our route drops into the secluded head of Scugdale. In the distance the nose of Lime Kiln Bank rises above Swainby village.

The Cleveland Crest

Length: 19.5 kms/12 miles
Total ascent: 940 m/3,080 ft
Difficulty: mostly good paths, RoW through trackless heather on Cold Moor
Note: high moors subject to changeable weather. Route sometimes badly eroded on N scarps, follow NP erosion control signs. Grouse shooting may take place Cold Moor 12th Aug to 10th Dec, enquire locally

Start: good FC car-park Clay Bank 572035. (240 m/787 ft).

(1) Cross road to woods, steps lead to wide forestry track, ascend L 200 m to corner, cross stile on to open moor, join well-used path climbing steeply W to flat top and edge HASTY BANK

(397 m/1,302 ft). Continue along edge, descend past Wainstones crags to wide saddle Garfitts Gap (300 m/984 ft) now poor path ascends steeply SW across hillside to wide sandy track on crest Cold Moor, continue 1.3 kms S to tumuli (382 m/1,253 ft then strike SW down wide shoulder, RoW overgrown, to gate, wall, Stone Intake Cottage. Descend lane W to Raisdale bridge 540005 (185 m/607 ft).

(2) 100 m W track forks L past Raisdale Mill up to Crossletts Farm and Barker's Ridge saddle beyond (330 m/1,083 ft) where path forks R descending across hillside by power lines to narrow lane at Scugdale Hall. Descend lane to Raikes Farm, RoW cuts corner, take drive to Fog Close farm where sunken trackway above intake wall leads up around hillside, through wood to stile at N corner, now join sandy track ascending NE across Holey Moor, after 800 m strike L to join Cleveland Way along W lip of moor, continue N – beware gliders, winch cables – to OS trig pt and finger stone CARLTON BANK (408 m/1,338 ft).
7 kms/4½ miles

(3) Descend NE round old quarry edge then down through old alum workings to road 523030 (290 m/951 ft), go R 30 m to Cleveland Way path and climb to stone seat, topograph on spur CRINGLE MOOR (c 410 m/1,345 ft), continue round N edge, descend steeply to Raisdale saddle (310 m/1,017 ft) and ascend over COLD MOOR (401 m/1,316 ft) to meet outward route Garfitts Gap. Cross stile N to wide forestry track contouring round E below Hasty Bank scarp to start.
6 kms/3½ miles

Variation avoiding Scugdale
(2.A) From Barker's Ridge saddle (527001) path strikes NW between craglets 800 m to track junction by small Brian's Pond. Continue N to gliding access track and summit Carlton Bank.
Saves 2.5 kms/1½ miles and 165 m/550 ft ascent

High Cup Nick and the Northern Pennines

OS 1 : 50,000 Sheet 91

Nowhere is that backbone of England, the Pennine Chain, more impressive that at its northern end where for nearly 50 kilometres (30 miles) between the Stainmore and Tyne Gaps a great west-facing escarpment falls steeply from the barren moors into the green and fertile Vale of Eden. Rising to almost 3,000 feet (900 metres) on Cross Fell, the Pennine's loftiest summit, this mountain wall echoes – though more forcefully – the jumbled hills of the Lake District of similar height but so very different in style, that face it across the Vale. Indeed, a clear view of this formidable rampart from one of the higher Lakeland fells, especially in winter, is possibly the most remarkable upland vista in England. This northern section of the Pennines – the 'Alston Block' – is formed by a thick platform of mountain limestone, capped by gritstone and uptilted westward to where the scarp edge lies along a great fault and in the aeons since the slippage occurred the Vale beyond has been covered with a layer of new red sandstone.

Craggy outcrops of igneous Whin Sill dolerite intruded into the rocks of the scarp form High Cup Nick, the unique feature of our route.

Dufton is one of several picturesque villages that lie beneath the scarp, owing much of their prettiness to the colourful sandstone so characteristic of the older buildings. The Pennine Way drops to the village on its journey from upper Teesdale to Cross Fell and our walk initially follows its route from Dufton back up to the Pennine crest. Set on gently rising pastures, Bow Hall farm is the last habitation and offers teas and accommodation to weary hikers before the walled green lane beyond climbs high onto the hillside and views open up across the smiling Vale. Wild Boar Fell and the Howgills appear on the horizon, the lane becomes a path and the dark, shapely pyramid of Murton Pike looms

This weird pinnacle stands among the dolerite cliffs that line the slopes of High Cup Nick close below the Pennine Way path.

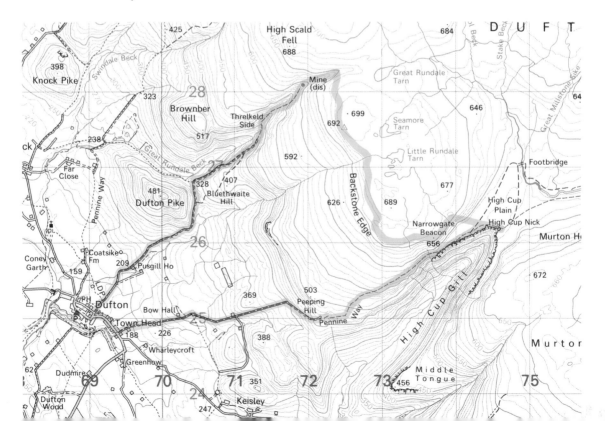

across the glinting river twisting below in the deep mouth of High Cup Gill: the dull crump of artillery is often heard from behind the Pike. As the Gill narrows lines of cliffs appear around its lip and the path crosses a couple of cascading becks – awkward when frozen – to follow a gentle terrace of greensward round the crag-hung hollow to the wide saddle of the Pennine watershed ahead. Precipitous grass slopes fall beneath the crags into the blind and secluded head of this curious valley where there is only the odd sheep to hint that the scale is less than it looks. One should traverse the cliff top below the path to admire the shattered columnar structure of the dolerite and several spectacular pinnacles. This is High Cup Nick, cutting right back into the spine of the great escarpment, a place to pause before climbing northwards to the conspicuous rocky cairn of Narrowgate Beacon that has already overlooked so much of the route.

Beyond the Beacon a shallow and intermittent gritstone edge lines the lip of the empty windswept moors of what is loosely known as Dufton Fell and the stern and almost featureless foreground presents a remarkable contrast to the green chequer-board of Edenside far below. A trickling beck issues from a miniature canyon in the peat, gushing over the edge on its journey to the Solway and flowing from lonely Little Rundale Tarn nearby where just 200 metres distant another shallow pool empties to the North Sea. Ahead the white radar dome on Great Dun Fell points the way to the Backstone Edge OS pillar while the cairn of the true summit, invisible from afar, stands a short way into the moor. Hidden until the last moment, the deep re-entrant of Great Rundale has recently been scarred with a rocky jeep track; a ramshackle bothy lies at its head beside Great Rundale Tarn but our route follows the track down, past the long abandoned workings where lead and barytes were won in the mid nineteenth century, to the ugly devastation of the modern mine. Rugged and crag-ringed, Great Rundale is not open like High Cup Gill but strangely enclosed, its mouth choked by the rearing cone of Dufton Pike, a delectable valley until recently when, at its most imposing level, its bottom was ripped out in the quest for barytes, a mineral used in paint and by the oil industry. Ironically, at the time of writing, the bottom has dropped out of the barytes market and the valley is again silent. The track leads easily down through the attractive lower valley and round Dufton Pike back to the village.

High Cup Nick and Backstone Edge

Length: 15.5 kms/9¾ miles
Total ascent: 550 m/1,800 ft
Difficulty: easy walking on good paths or tracks, fairly rough but flat on high exposed moorland where compass essential
Note: empty moorland section (2) is regularly walked but is not RoW. Live firing at military training area centred Hilton 5 kms S. This route and Pennine Way do not pass through Danger Area

Start: no formal car-park Dufton village (690250), limited parking possible with discretion by village green, at gravel dump 688253 or in Bow Hall Lane 695249. Do not inconvenience residents.

(1) From village green follow Appleby road SW 400 m to hollow, Bow Hall lane strikes L waymarked 'High Cup Nick'. Ascend metalled lane past Bow Hall farm, green lane beyond, gated, to open fell. Beyond last gate good path continues, climbing easily to horizontal terrace above steep flanks High Cup Gill leading eventually to wide saddle above Gill head. High Cup Nick (580 m/1,900 ft).
6 kms/3¾ miles

(2) Return 300 m to signpost inscribed 'footbridge', strike W, no path, to ascend easy grass slopes R of screes joining narrow path on plateau lip above. Follow path L to prominent cairn NARROWGATE BEACON (656 m/2,152 ft) continuing round edge W then N, poor path, to cairn/shelter walls. Path fades, edge soon disappears, strike R 200 m, boggy, to higher less pronounced edge followed by faint path to Little Rundale beck, and on to OS cairn 692 m, summit cairn BACKSTONE EDGE 200 m NE (699 m/2,292 ft). Continue N, descend boggy trackless slopes to join jeep track in deep re-entrant 725283.
4 kms/2½ miles

(3) Descend track W, through mine workings, down S side Gt Rundale valley, L round Dufton Pike, crossing fords, to reach centre Dufton village.
5.5 kms/3½ miles

A little brook trickles over the steep lip at the very head of High Cup Nick, a peculiar valley that cuts deeply into the great western scarp of the Pennines.

The Roman Wall

Northumberland

OS 1 : 50,000 Sheet 86

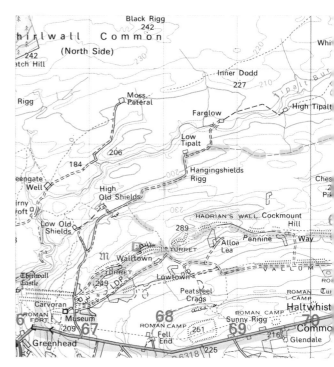

> 'Old men who have followed the Eagles since boyhood say nothing in the Empire is more wonderful than first sight of the Wall!'
>
> *Puck of Pook's Hill*: Rudyard Kipling

This walk along the Wall will set you thinking. Thinking of the Roman legionnaires who built it over 1,800 years ago; of the Imperial auxiliaries who guarded it for two and a half centuries and the Pictish barbarians who finally overran it as the Dark Ages began. This was the stormy North-West Frontier of the Roman Empire, it marked the edge of civilization. What do we share with those soldiers of Rome as we pace their Wall? There are still larks in the summer sky and curlew on the hill, the autumn bracken was as golden then as now and the winter wind as sharp as it sweeps in from Scotland with snow in its teeth. Their Wall may be shrunk and broken and its garrison long gone but it is still the most impressive boundary on the map of Britain.

The Wall – Hadrian's Wall – spans England at its narrowest point and the best section of its seventy-three-miles length is where it crosses the backbone of England as the Pennines blur towards the Cheviots. Not only is this the most scenic countryside, but up here the Wall and its supporting roads, ditches and forts have been best preserved from centuries of stone-stealing vandals and the march of progress and lie within the Northumberland National Park. Walls do not naturally lend themselves to meaningful circuits but the one suggested here covers much of the best of the Wall itself besides sampling a little of the surrounding countryside it so dominates. The route described gives a reasonable day's hike but is easily broken into shorter outings or extended to provide a 20-mile (32-kilometre) marathon, as desired.

Canny military engineers, when they built the Wall between AD 120 and 130, took advantage of a remarkable geological feature, a rippling ridge of igneous rock – a quartz-dolerite called Whin Sill – intruding into the surrounding

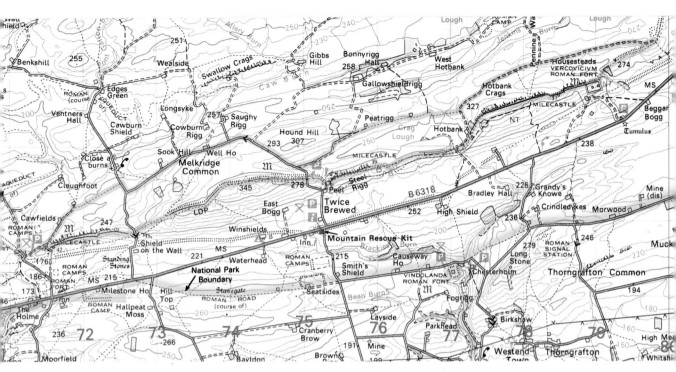

The most photogenic section of Hadrian's Wall is this stretch over Cuddy's Crags looking eastward towards Housesteads Crags. The Wall continues over the distant prow of Sewingshields Crags.

sedimentary strata and characteristically form-ing a craggy scarp frowning steeply to the north. The Wall follows the scarp crest to form a superb defence line. The Steel Rigg to House-steads section is typical, running above a se-quence of steep cliffs of which one – Highshield Crags rising over 35 metres (80 feet)) vertically above the dark waters of Crag Lough (pronoun-ced 'loff') – is the most famous rock-climbing venue in Northumberland.

At the time of writing National Trust arch-aeologists are working on the Steel Rigg section and it is fascinating to watch them at work, both excavating and renovating, carefully replacing each stone in its original position with new mortar. The Wall hereabouts was originally some 5 metres (15 feet) high of which the top third – the breast-work – has fallen while the lower third is buried in the detritus of centuries. The turf has been cut back in places on the northern side to expose as many as eight previ-ously hidden courses of stonework and here the Wall rears an imposing ten feet and more, though throughout most of our route it rises only half that height and has sometimes even been entirely dismantled and replaced at some juncture by a dry stone shepherd's wall. Three Milecastles – 39, 38 and 37 – stand between Steel Rigg and Housesteads, there was one every Roman mile (1,481 metres/1,620 yards) with two 'turret' guard posts between them. Just west of impressive Milecastle 37 is Cuddy's Crags – so named from St Cuthbert whose body was supposed to have been laid here *en route* from Lindisfarne to Durham – the most popular and photographed section of the entire Wall, leading shortly to the major fort of Vercovicium at Housesteads where the 1,000-man garrison has been replaced by a car-park, a visitor centre and a small museum under the care of English Heritage. The site is well worth a diversion and if one descends from the Wall to enter it the usual fee should be paid. However, the Knag Burn Gateway closeby, a unique fourth-century customs post virtually in the centre of England, is on the Wall itself and can be visited for free.

The return route westward along old tracks and footpaths running below the northern scarps is not without interest for this is the viewpoint of the Wall that would have discouraged would-be attackers, though rough pasture and grassy fields have largely replaced the moorland of heather, bracken, birch and alder scrub that lay below the Wall in times past. Look to the walls of field and farmhouse for army-issue quarried stones, obvi-ously filched long ago from the Wall itself. At reclaimed Cawfields Quarry our route rejoins the Wall and returns eastward over fairly rugged country to Steel Rigg. Beyond the deep Shield Gap the Wall, unfortunately not here at its structural best, climbs towards its highest point on Winshields summit. From here the view is extensive, the dark conifers of Wark Forest roll northward towards the Cheviot outliers and the Scottish Liddesdale Hills, southward the Pen-nines rise towards Cross Fell while the giant cooling towers of Annan power station stand westward above the Solway flats: no, it is no longer quite as the Romans saw it!

It is worth diverting a few yards from the Wall at Housesteads to explore the ruins of the Roman fort of Vercovicium: this is the remains of the headquarters or administration block.

A Circuit of Hadrian's Wall

Length of circuit: 21 kms/13 miles
Total ascent: 570 m/1,870 ft
Difficulty: easy going on the Wall, some muddy fieldpaths elsewhere
Note: background knowledge is essential to appreciate fully any walk along Hadrian's Wall. Several guides and handbooks are available, OS special 2 inch: mile map 'Hadrian's Wall' is useful. Especially interesting are nearby musems at Vindolanda Fort (771664) with full-size replica of Wall section, and Museum of the Roman Army (667658) near Greenhead. County Council plan Theme Park at reclaimed Walltown Quarry (668659)

Start: good car-park at Steel Rigg 751676 (280 m/920 ft) – toilets.

(1) At SE corner car-park gate leads onto Wall, follow it up and down E above Peel Crags, over Steel Rigg, past Milecastle 39, over Highshield Crags (330 m/1,085 ft) above Crag Lough, then through woods to Hotbank lane. Climb now past Milecastle 38 to crest Hotbank Crags (320 m/1,050 ft) and Cuddy's Crags, past Milecastle 37, through wood to ruins large Housesteads Fort. Wall crosses Knag Burn at wide saddle and ascends again above Broomlee Lough, continue to stile/gate through wall 100 m past 2nd top (King's Wicket 798694).
5.5 kms/3½ miles

(2) Pass N through Wall, yellow waymarks lead W over boggy ground to stile – poor path – and through new plantation to poorly defined green lane. After crossing Pennine Way near ruined kiln, lane becomes muddy tractor track. As track turns S to Hotbank, yellow waymark indicates poor path through gate leading W across fields, past two barns to farm track and lane N of Steel Rigg. Follow lane NW then SW past Melkridge Common to junction 726674. 100 m N faint RoW leads through gate over fields to farm track and Cawfields Farm, continue 500 m to Cawfields car-park/picnic site (713666: 180 m/590 ft).
11.5 kms/7 miles

(3) Take path (Pennine Way) leading W along N shore lake to Wall and Milecastle 42, continue along crest Cawfield Crags, pass Thorney Doors step, Turret 41A, descend to lane at Shield Gap. Climb steeply to ridge crest where Wall continues, up and down, to rocky summit and trig point WINDSHIELDS CRAGS (345 m/1,132 ft) descends to lane at Steel Rigg.
4 kms/2½ miles

Variation
(3.A) From Cawfields car-park continue W along line of Wall (Pennine Way) past inconspicuous ruins Great Chesters fort, over Cockmount Hill to impressive section of Wall along Walltown Crags to Point 249 m. (**5 kms/3 miles** thus far). To return Cawfields either descend S to small car-park at 675663 and follow farm lane E (not RoW) past Lowtown and along line Roman vallum, or descend N from Turret 44B (680666) and follow lanes and RoW N of Wall E via Low Tipalt. From Cawfields follow (3) as above.
Total extra 11 kms/6¾ miles

High Street and the Kentmere Horseshoe Lake District

OS 1 : 50,000 Sheet 90

High Street, a strange name for a mountain! Were it more shapely it might well have been dubbed 'pride of the eastern fells' for it is the principal eminence in that rather formless area of Lakeland where the high tops start to fade away eastward. Its main claim to fame, of course, is the Roman Road which traverses its whaleback plateau, but it is also the apex of the longest high ridge in the Lake District, over 13 kilometres (8 miles) between Yoke and Loadpot Hill continuously above 600 metres (2,000 feet), and the hub of a complex valley system. Formed from

the erosion-resistant rocks of the Borrowdale Volcanic series – the same rocks that shape the rugged mountains of central Lakeland – High Street's dull crest belies the spectacular scenery of its boney flanks and its several handsome satellites. A horseshoe ridge-walk that samples much of the best encircles Kentmere, central of the three parallel valleys that probe towards High Street from the south. Kentmere once held two natural lakes and the relict mere in the lower valley, drained a century past and now unobtrusively excavated for diatomite, is all that

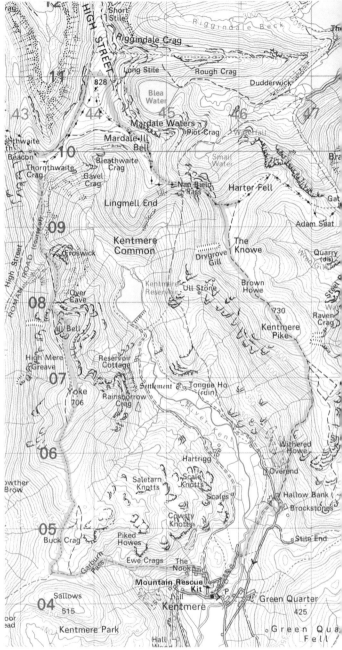

There is a fine view from Star Crag on the north ridge of Yoke into the head of the Kentmere valley: Ill Bell rises on the left and the route follows the skyline over distant High Street, Mardale Ill Bell, the Nan Bield Pass – above Kentmere Reservoir – and Harter Fell on the right.

remains. A second lake, silted up in ancient times, lay in the secretive upper valley, hidden beyond the rocky knolls and wooded moraines beneath which stand the church, a scattering of cottages and Kentmere Hall, a farmhouse incorporating a fine Pele Tower built against fourteenth-century Scottish raiders. Though the farm is private, a nearby right of way makes an alternative start to the walk, rejoining the scenic Garburn Pass packhorse road near the huge boulder known as Badger Rock, laced with climbing problems. At the head of the pass a gentle ascent commences towards Yoke, avoiding a fierce bog and giving glimpses into the pretty Troutbeck valley: higher up as the summit approaches, impressive views open up down the length of Windermere and over to Coniston and Langdale. Now the ridge takes on a most distinctive form, rising and falling northwards over the splendid conical summits of Ill Bell and Froswick above the dark waters of Kentmere Reservoir and the wild hollow of Hall Cove. From this side the three peaks appear as green triplets, the lower pair echoing their bell-shaped brother.

On Thornthwaite Crag, its domed grassy summit graced with a peculiar dry-stone column 14 feet high (4.25 metres) and often avoided, the ridge takes a sharp bend, dissolving into the gently swelling moorland of High Street. Climbing from Troutbeck over the shoulder of Thornthwaite, the straight scar of the Roman Road stretches ahead. Built in the first century AD to link the Roman forts at Ambleside and Brougham beside Penrith, it was a ridge-way before the Romans came and has been trodden continuously since they left, though there is now little to show for it but a well-used path and the hint of ditches. The summit of High Street some little way off is disappointing though the name 'Racecourse Hill' marked on the 1:25,000 map recalls the time when this wide expanse was the scene of an annual shepherd's meet, a great occasion when strayed sheep were exchanged, horses were raced, wrestlers fought, and ale was swilled. Mardale was the nearest community, just three kilometres away below the formidable eastern flank of High Street at the head of a remote valley with a bonny lake. 'The Inn at Mardale is full a mile from the water' observed the guide-

book writer Harriet Martineau in 1855. But in 1936 this pretty village was engulfed by the rising waters of Haweswater Reservoir, raised by no less than 29 metres (95 feet) to slake the thirst of Manchester.

On High Street the route turns back southward to Mardale Ill Bell, the first shoulder on the ridge, preferably following the lip above the fine eastern coombes. Though hardly a summit, Mardale Ill Bell appears suitably impressive from the shores of Haweswater, rearing over two wild and craggy coombes, each cradling a perfect glacial tarn: Blea Water and Small Water are among the grandest in Lakeland. Crossing the narrow ridge above Small Water is the old packhorse pass of Nan Bield linking Kentmere to Mardale, rocky and with a shelter wall on its desolate crest it has the distinct flavour of a

Himalayan pass. Steep zigzags now climb to the green dome of Harter Fell, crowned with its bizarre iron cairn and an excellent vantage point over Haweswater – a majestic lake when the water is high, an ugly travesty when it is low – before broad grassland undulates onwards towards Kentmere Pike. From this angle Froswick, Ill Bell and Yoke appear especially shapely and the latter is now seen to hold a huge cliff, Rainsborrow Crag, some 150 metres high (500 feet), its base riddled with abandoned quarries. Though its summit is unprepossessing, Kentmere Pike has an unusual 'edge-of-the-world' atmosphere and its descent, if easy, is not always simple to follow, but the latter stages especially, through the comely Kentmere valley, make a satisfying conclusion to an airy itinerary.

The Kentmere Horseshoe

Length: 19 kms/12 miles
Total ascent: 1150 m/3,770 ft
Difficulty: easy walking mostly on grassy paths, sometimes boggy, rarely steep. These are high and exposed mountains, appropriate equipment essential

Start: limited parking, with care, at 456041 by Kentmere church, popular at weekends. LDNP plans (1987) public car-park nearby (175 m/575 ft).

(1) Follow lane NW from church, keeping L, to yard entrance. Cart track goes R, signed 'Garburn Pass', bends L to gate, continues W, steady stony ascent to gate, crest Garburn Pass (447 m/1,467 ft). Continue 250 m to bend whence path strikes R over moorland, initially faint, boggy, cairns, then dryer track ascends gradually N to wall, follow to stile. Now path ascends steeply R to grassy plateau, cairn YOKE (706 m/2,315 ft). Continue along ridge to small rocky summit, 4 cairns ILL BELL (757 m/2,482 ft).
6 kms/3¾ miles

(2) Descend ½L, steepish, follow ridge over summit FROSWICK (720 m/2,361 ft) to long saddle, 700 m beyond low point take path ½L to plateau, wall, tall summit pillar, THORNTHWAITE CRAG (784 m/2,571). Strike ESE to join major path gradually ascending wide moorland NE, continue 800 m till near LH plateau edge, strike E 100 m to broken wall, OS pillar HIGH STREET closeby on E side –828 m/2,718 ft).
4 kms/2½ miles

(3) Go SE across moorland to scarp lip, poor path follows edge R to join larger path, shallow descent to vague top, twin cairns, MARDALE ILL BELL (761 m/2,496 ft). Stony path descends to outcrops, narrow Nan Bield Pass (625 m/2,050 ft) then ascends steeper rocky ridge to plateau lip and 200 m E to iron-post-cairn HARTER FELL (778 m/2,552 ft). Path, often boggy, follows fence then wall S along broad moorland crest to summit, OS pillar E side wall, KENTMERE PIKE (730 m/2,396 ft).
4.5 kms/2¾ miles

(4) Path descends S, forks where fence bends L, go R to stile, descend across W flank hill. At green spring, cairns, path zigzags steeply down, indistinct, to lower grooved path descending easily L across rougher slopes to lane at Hallowbank cottages. Go L through white gate 200 m, turn R signed 'Mardale Bridle Path' to muddy lane, go L to gate, stone steps through wall R, near huge boulder, lead to footbridge and lane beyond, go L to Kentmere church.
4.5 kms/2¾ miles

Nordic skiers run the crest of Kentmere Pike northwards towards Harter Fell. On the left, across the Kentmere valley, rise Ill Bell (left), Froswick and Thornthwaite Crag.

The Narrow Crests of Blencathra

Lake District

OS 1 : 50,000 Sheet 90

'. . . moorish Skiddaw and far-sweeping Saddleback (are) the proper types of majestic form . . .' wrote John Ruskin in 1889. Indeed, the two major peaks of the Northern Fells both embody classic mountain shapes. But Skiddaw, its noble cone rising from a clutch of graceful satellites and one of the four Lakeland peaks topping 3,000 feet, on close aquaintance is a cragless hump, while Saddleback – or Blencathra as it is more generally known – an almost isolated and complex mountain, flaunts a succession of challenging features and despite its modest stature as only the thirteenth highest, is acknowledged to be one of the grandest peaks in the Lake District. Sculpted from the easily eroded Skiddaw slates, as are all the Northern Fells, the public face of Blencathra – its southern and eastern flanks – has somehow avoided the rounded outlines of its lumpy neighbours. Rearing above the broad pastoral Glenderamackin valley and the busy A66 trunk road, a trio of matching ridges bounded by a pair of boggy grassy buttresses and separated by four deep ravines form its symmetrical south face. These ridges are steep and narrow and rise to pointed tops on a scalloped crest, all three demand to be climbed but the central or Hall's Fell Ridge, its upper section known as Narrow Edge and finishing abruptly on the actual summit, provides the most entertaining route. Cradled on the eastern flank however, a secret and spectacular coombe holds moody Scales Tarn beneath a knife-edge rock arete, the finest such feature in England – Sharp Edge. Only to the north and west where the undulating moorland flanks are known as Mungrisdale Common, does Blencathra disappoint. When seen from the east the mountain assumes a distinctive saddle-shape, and the name Blaencathair, Celtic in origin, appears to reflect this.

Though comparatively short, this particular traverse of Blencathra is one of the best expeditions in the Lakes and can easily be varied to suit weather and inclination. It is described in an anticlockwise direction ascending over Sharp Edge and descending Hall's Fell, but should the prospect of scrambling along Sharp Edge sound too daunting, a clockwise circuit up Hall's Fell but descending through Foule Crag Cove to avoid Sharp Edge is an excellent alternative. Certainly the horizontal rock crest of Sharp Edge is the closest the Lake District comes to Snowdonia's Crib Goch arete, and although it is rather exposed and a steady head is useful, in good conditions the difficulties on the crest are minimal and hands are necessary in only a few places, the lower 'escape' paths seem only to complicate the route. The black tarn below adds atmosphere to the ascent. Surrounded by steep craggy slopes it seems rarely to catch the sun, indeed so dark are its waters that they were once believed to reflect the stars at midday! The famous Abraham brothers, pioneering rock

The path to Scales Tarn crosses the shoulder of Scales Fell into the upper Glenderamackin valley, ahead rears the imposing prow of Foule Crag with the black crest of Sharp Edge below it. The ascent is by no means as desperate as it looks here!

climbers and mountain photographers, first practiced their sport here in the 1890s but the rock is poor and it seems unlikely that anyone has climbed here since, except in winter when the broken crags are sealed tight in snow and ice.

Above the arete the east wing of Foule Crag rears up as a blunt headwall, appearing from a distance far steeper than it is: the easiest line is the direct one taking the obvious and well-scratched central weaknesses where the scrambling is slightly technical for a short way and the exposure as great but less apparent. On the close-cropped grass at the top you wonder what all the fuss was about, although descending in winter verglas is a very different proposition! A strange feature on the plateau-like northern ridge is a great cross of quartzite pebbles laid into the grass. Some five metres in length it was constructed in the late Forties by a local man as a memorial to a walker who had died nearby. Seen from here Blencathra's summit is a low-key affair but the southerly view across the deep green vale to the serried fells beyond, to High Street and Helvellyn, to Scafell Pike and the hills beyond Derwent Water, is superb. Especially imposing is the distant wall of the High Pennines lining the south-east horizon. A short diversion along the plateau lip to Gategill Fell Top, Blencathra's western summit, is rewarding and puts the topography of the south face into perspective. Narrow Edge drops straight below the small summit cairn, at first the path descends a steep grassy buttress and then, as the angle eases, the crest becomes narrow and rocky with the path winding between the outcrops and occasionally over short patches of glacis. In ascent, by selecting the rockiest sections of blunted crest, almost continual easy scrambling can be enjoyed for some 500 metres. But the path avoids all difficulties before again descending steeply through bracken and heather to the intake wall at the mouth of the deep Gategill ravine where remains of an old lead mine, worked from the seventeenth century until before the First World War, still stand beside the tumbling beck.

A Traverse of Blencathra

Length: 8 kms/5 miles
Total ascent: 685 m/2,250 ft
Difficulty: in good conditions Sharp Edge demands simple though rather more awkward, easier in ascent. Narrow Edge any difficulties avoidable, simple scrambling if desired. Elsewhere easy grassy paths. This is a high and exposed mountain, appropriate equipment essential
Note: route described anticlockwise, see text

Start: 340268 on A66 road 300 m W of Scales, park at layby 150 m W on N side road, or layby S side road at Scales (215 m/705 ft).

(1) Between two roadside cottages track leads up to wall, gate, signpost, diagonal path ascends R across hillside, up grassy spur, round corner above broken slopes to wide saddle. Follow good contour path L side narrow Glenderamackin valley, cross Scales Beck and ascend L, steep stony path, to Scales Tarn, Sharp Edge rises on RHS. Path leads up R to grassy shoulder, traverse narrow horizontal rock arete, 150 m easy scrambling, exposed – or narrow awkward paths RHS below crest – to little nick. Scramble directly up more difficult rocky headwall above – Foule Crag – to grassy plateau. Either follow path L round Tarn Crags edge or take broad ridge above, past cross, tiny tarn, to small cliff-edge cairn BLENCATHRA summit (868 m/2,847 ft).
4.5 kms/2¾ miles

(2) Immediately below cairn grassy Hall's Fell Ridge drops S, initially steep. Path descends easily, avoiding simple scrambly sections Narrow Edge as desired. Beyond flat shoulder path descends R to meet Gate Gill above intake wall. Good contour path leads L above wall, crossing two narrow valleys/streams, past scattered conifers to gate, signpost, at start.
3.5 kms/2¼ miles

Alternative

(1.A) Avoiding Sharp Edge: at Scales Beck continue on traverse path, after 150 m either taking L fork ascending into Foule Crag Cove to gain grassy ridge on far side, or R fork leading to col at head of Glenderamackin valley before striking L up same grassy ridge. Then ascend slaty Blue Screes to summit Foule Crag. Continue as for (1).
Extra 1 km/½ mile

On Blencathra's south face the narrow crest of Hall's Fell Ridge leads directly to the summit providing a fine route for ascent or descent.

The Newlands Fells – Grasmoor and the Coledale Ridges   Lake District

OS 1 : 50,000 Sheet 89

'I shall return to Cumberland & settle at Keswick . . . I shall have a tendency to become a God, so sublime and beautiful with be series of my visual existence.'

Samuel Taylor Coleridge: letter 1800

Walk down from Keswick to the shores of Derwent Water and gaze out across the tranquil lake, as Coleridge must have done, to the massed mountains ranked above the wooded western shore. One sharp peak stands out from the interlocking crests and domes of the Newlands Fells: obviously not the highest, it is certainly the most distinctive, and once identified Causey Pike will seem an omnipresent landmark hereabouts. Like Blencathra, carved from rocks of the Skiddaw Slate series, these north-western fells are typically rounded and genteel – in contrast to the scarred and rugged mountains like Scafell to the south, hewn from the harder

Borrowdale Volcanics. Here the slates have formed a central clump of higher tops throwing out characteristic narrow ridges above long deep valleys, the gabled crests, seen end-on, sometimes assuming handsome shapes. There are crags among the innermost recesses but they are shattered and shaly while the many abandoned workings bear witness to a rich history of mining – for lead, copper, silver, even gold – going back before the Tudors. Today these fells are justly famed for superlative ridge-walks.

This walk starts near old workings above Farm Uzzicar in the heart of the Newlands Vale. Here once lay Uzzicar lake, drained in the thirteenth century to expose cultivatable land – hence the name 'New Lands'. As the elegant ridge curves over the shoulder of Rowling End towards Causey Pike the view unfolds across lush Newlands to Derwent Water and the majestic shapes of Skiddaw and Blencathra,

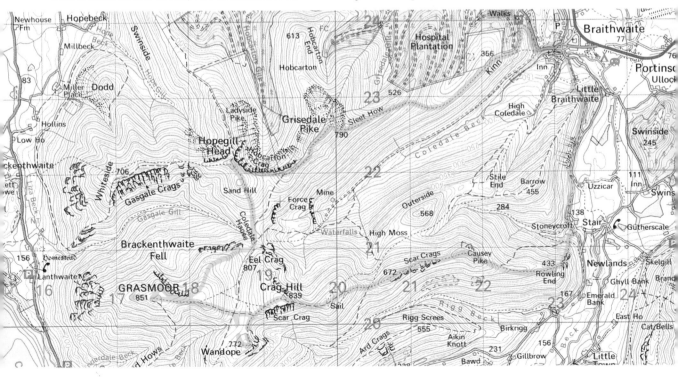

surely one of the most exquisite prospects in the Lakes. Most people will use their hands on the final rocky brow leading to Causey's popular summit which proves to be one of five knobs on an undulating ridge, disappointing perhaps but aloof enough to provide intriguing glimpses into the deep coombes of the neighbouring Derwent Fells. The pleasant ridge continues to Sail Hause, a useful pass with an abandoned cobalt mine below its northern flank, before a steep climb leads over Sail to Crag Hill, the highest 'Hill' in England, an unworthy appellation for such a massive crag-girt eminence which is the twenty-third highest point in the country! Perhaps this is why it is popularly known as Eel Crag, really the name of its rugged northern ridge-end above Coledale Hause. Tucked under the southern flank lies deep Addacomb Hole, the most perfect hanging valley in Lakeland, and a short diversion round

its lip to Wandope is recommended before pushing onwards to Grasmoor. Thrusting out its enormous bastion high above Crummock Water, isolated Grasmoor is the giant of the area and there are spectacular views from the outer lip of its turfy dome over the deep gulf of Buttermere to the knot of high mountains surrounding Scafell. Gras-moor derives from the Norse 'grise' – a wild-boar – and this is still tough hunting country where the fox is hunted on foot.

Coledale Hause, the wide green saddle between Crag Hill and Hopegill Head, is the focal point of the Newlands Fells. Below its east flank the little Pudding Beck tumbles over a rocky wall, High Force cascade, into a hanging amphitheatre from which it cascades again – as Low Force – over a taller crag into the head of long, narrow Coledale. It is a strange place but unfortunately a working barytes mine scars the

base of Force Crag. However, Hopegill Head is a pleasant surprise after the dull plod up from the Hause, its rocky peak – the meeting point of three narrow crests – jutting out above the imposing cirque of Hobcarton Crags, the prospect marred only by the angular geometry of the conifer plantation invading the lonely gill below. These dark cliffs, almost 150 metres (500 feet) high, are shaly and vegetatious and the only known English habitat of the red alpine catchfly, *Viscaria alpina*, a pretty herbaceous flower closely related to the famous Cheddar Pink. The crags continue below the cliff-edge path until it begins its stony climb to Grisedale Pike. Its sharp summit again the junction of sharp ridges and presenting a handsome end-on profile to the Derwent valley. The descent is long but pleasant and leads past the Royal Oak in attractive Braithwaite village – which may well ensure an easy return to Uzzicar.

Causey Pike, Grasmoor and the Coledale Horseshoe

Length: 18 kms/11 miles
Total ascent: 1450 m/4,750 ft
Difficulty: mostly easy going, grassy paths, occasional rocky sections: high and exposed mountains, appropriate equipment essential
Note: almost entire route National Trust property

Start: roadside parking at 233217 E side Stair-Braithwaite road. (125 m/410 ft).

(1) Go S 500 m, beyond Stonycroft bridge good path ascends directly up shoulder past wooden set, keeping L then following crest steeply to flatter ridge Rowling End whence path climbs steeply to 25 m (80 ft) semi-scramble and summit CAUSEY PIKE (637 m/2,090 ft). Path continues, grassy, hummocky, over flat summit SCAR CRAGS (672 m/2,205 ft) to shallow saddle Sail Hause, then more steeply, shaly, up rounded shoulder to dome, small cairn SAIL (773 m/2,536 ft). Narrow ridge, easy rocky steps, leads to broad slaty plateau, OS pillar, CRAG HILL (or Eel Crag, 839 m/2,753 ft).
5 kms/3 miles

(2) Descend easily WSW to wide grassy saddle, two tiny pools, climb W across broad shoulder, cairns, hints of path, to wide plateau, shelter cairn GRASMOOR (852 m/2,795 ft). Strike NE to cliff top, follow edge R then shoulder N to descend grassy slopes E, above waterfall, to broad saddle, Coledale Hause (600 m/1,970 ft). Ascend path N to round shoulder Sand Hill continuing to crag edge, go L to sharp rocky summit, slightly exposed, HOPEGILL HEAD (770 m/2,525 ft). Retrace path along crag lip continuing round cliff edge to follow broken wall to rocky minor top, now ascend steeper narrower stony crest to small summit GRISEDALE PIKE (791 m/2,594 ft).
7 kms/4½ miles

(3) Continue 70 m, drop R onto E ridge, stony path, initially steeper, then grassy. When ridge flattens path drops steeply R to long green spur, at stile by forest edge keep L till path cuts back R dropping to road. Go R to village, follow Stair road to bend 100 m past bridge whence take Braithwaite Lodge drive RHS, RoW passes through farmyard to contour L above wood rejoining road 600 m from start.
6 kms/3½ miles

Coleridge must have been familiar with this view across Derwent Water towards the sharp peak of Causey Pike and the Coledale summits beyond.

The Napes, Pillar and the Mosedale Crest

Lake District

OS 1:50,000 Sheet 89

'Mosedale . . . a noble amphitheatre of dark mountains . . .'

'. . . the famous Pillar Rock springs up vertically from the steep fellside, with a north face like a cathedral-front . . .'

Owen Glynne Jones: 1897

Wasdale, for its mountains and its mood, has no peer in all England. From its old and still-hospitable inn the great pioneers – men like O G Jones and the Abraham brothers, Haskett Smith, Cecil Slingsby and Norman Collie – would set off in their tweeds and hob-nailed boots at the turn of the century to explore the surrounding crags and fells. Indeed, rock-climbing was born here. Luckily Wasdale is a dead-end valley opening to the remote side of Lakeland, much of the dale and its enclosing mountains are protected by the National Trust so most of its visitors are mountain-orientated folk rather than mere tourists, and the atmosphere remains unspoilt. The sanctuary of Wasdale Head is a jigsaw of stone-walled pastures enclosed on one side by the Scafell massif, on the other by a chain of respectable peaks cradling the deep and deserted side valley of Mosedale. This itinerary almost traces the Mosedale crest – but not quite – for it extends the regular 'Mosedale Horseshoe' to include some of the most spectacular and adventurous walking in Lakeland.

The deep-walled lane leading past the tiny church of St Olaf – where victims of several early climbing accidents lie buried – provides intriguing glimpses into Mosedale before Burnthwaite, the last farm, where the sharp-angled pyramid of Great Gable seems to block the valley head. The fluted ribs jutting from Gable's flank are the 'glorious jumble of the Napes' and our route, climbing first across the bottom of the scree-covered hillside to the wide saddle of Sty Head, crosses back along a tenuous and rugged path known as the 'Climbers Traverse' to their base, before angling round the spur of Gavel Neese to the col of Beck Head visible on the left.

Named from the Norse 'stee' – a ladder – Sty Head was once a busy packhorse crossing and is still an important pedestrian pass, though as recently as 1934 there were moves to drive a road over it! Soon after the pass the little crag is Kern Knotts where the obvious crack was a celebrated test piece for many years, while at the base of the intricate Napes ridges, laced with

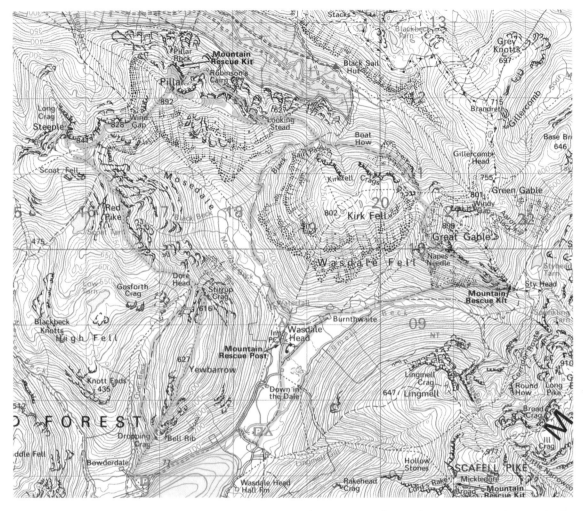

classic climbs, the famous Napes Needle is unmistakable. The first ascent of this remarkable 18-metre (60-foot) pinnacle by Walter Haskett Smith, solo, in 1886, is considered to mark the birth of rock-climbing as a distinct sport. Easier ground leads to Beck Head and pleasant walking continues round the desolate head of Ennerdale to join the usual Mosedale circuit at Black Sail Pass.

The ridge leads onwards to Pillar mountain via the fine vantage point of Looking Stead, but an ingenious traverse – the High Level Route – threads its way round the steep northern fellside to Pillar Rock, together with Scafell Crag and Dow Crag, one of the three greatest Lakeland

There is a fine view of Great Gable from the Styhead path just above Burnthwaite Farm: our route links Styhead Pass, seen on the right, to the saddle of Beck Head, seen on the left, across the south face of Gable below the Naples.

cliffs. At Robinson's Cairn, an impressively situated pile erected in 1906 to remember that notable early cragsman and principal discoverer of the High Level Route, Pillar Rock comes into sight, a dramatic view of this 'noblest of rock monuments' towering above moody Ennerdale. With its crenellated summit – High Man – rising nearly 230 metres (750 feet) above its lowest point, Pillar Rock is seamed with fine climbs ancient and modern, and though first ascended by an Ennerdale shepherd, John Atkinson, in 1826, and long considered an adventurous feat, its summit is still for climbers only. One character it attracted was the Reverend 'Steeple' Jackson, self-styled 'Patriach of the Pillarites', who climbed the Rock in 1875 at the age of 79. Unfortunately he was killed attempting his third ascent three years later. The narrow path winds sensationally up above Shamrock buttress ('sham–Rock', from some angles mistakable for the real thing) to the narrow neck linking the Rock to the main hillside before ascending the final 120 metres (400 feet) onto the rounded grassy plateau of Pillar mountain.

Wind Gap, a stony col, separates Pillar from Black Crag, a distinct and worthy summit until recently ignored on OS maps, whence the gentle sward of the northern edge provides spectacular views of shapely Steeple and Ennerdale Water as it is followed onwards to the old wall on which the summit cairn of Scoat Fell is actually perched. A short diversion will include Steeple's

tiny top before the route drops southwards to join the Red Pike ridge. Surprisingly the path avoids the sharp crest of this fine mountain, and with it the summit, its cairn seeming to overhang the broken precipices that plunge into the lonely head of Mosedale. On the long descent to Dore Head look out for a conspicuous outcrop where the Chair, a rudely constructed and ancient stone seat once famous but of unknown origin, sits among the boulders. Yewbarrow is the final summit and its northern bastion, Stirrup Crag, rears up imposingly above Dore Gap. Indeed a well-used path

descends the Over Beck valley to avoid the mountain, but the short scramble is far easier than it appears and the long aloof crest of Yewbarrow is the finest viewpoint in Wasdale, a fitting finale to a fascinating expedition. Now the path drops steeply towards Bowderdale farm, home of Joss Naylor the famous fell-runner, before cutting back to the Wastwater shore and the start.

Yewbarrow is the final summit of the Mosedale circuit: Stirrup Crag, the northern buttress of the mountain, rears above the saddle of Dore Head.

A Napes, Pillar Rock and Mosedale Circuit

Length: 21.5 kms/13¼ miles
Total ascent: 1460 m/4,800 ft
Difficulty: a strenuous expedition, high and exposed, much easy going but one short scramble pitch and several very rugged sections. Appropriate equipment essential

Start: NT car-park/camp site 182075, N end Wastwater (70 m/230 ft), limited parking out-of-season Wasdale Green 186085.

(1) Go NE through camp site, path fords river – or follow E bank to footbridge – continues to Wasdale Green. Walled lane passes church to Burnthwaite Farm whence main path ascends valley bottom before climbing diagonally across stony S face Gt Gable to Sty Head Pass, Rescue Box, path junction (480 m/1,575 ft).
5 kms/3 miles

(2) Avoid main Gt Gable (NW) path, cut back L (W) on tenuous traverse path below Kern Knotts cliff, huge boulders, then rising easily over rocky steps, across large scree shoot to broken ground below Napes crags where paths proliferate. Choose best traverse path passing well below conspicuous Napes Needle, across second scree shoot, descending slightly round SW corner of Mt to cross gentle scree flanks to grassy Beck Head saddle (620 m/2,040 ft). Good path descends NW from 2nd small tarn, traverses grassy N flanks Kirkfell, crosses rocky gully to ascend, indistinct, boggy, to cairn Black Sail Pass (550 m/1,800 ft).
4.5 kms/2½ miles

(3) Follow ancient fence posts NW over grassy summit LOOKING STEAD (627 m/2,058 ft) to saddle. Ascend rocky crest 150 m to platform, continue 20 m to low cairn whence narrow path drops R over edge, to traverse, undulating, round steep N flanks Pillar Fell to conspicuous Robinson's Cairn (1 km). Path continues towards unmistakable Pillar Rock, descending then climbing steeply L, scree, to slabby terrace leading R above crags to narrow neck behind Pillar Rock whence path zigzags steeply up rocky slopes to summit plateau, cairns, PILLAR (892 m/2,928 ft).
3 kms/2 miles

(4) Descend SW, grassy then shattered crest, to Wind Gap col (750 m/2,460 ft), ascend easily to stony crest, cairn BLACK CRAG (828 m/2,717 ft). Grassy slopes continue to wall, summit SCOAT FELL (841 m/2,760 ft). Path descends grassy slopes SE to wide saddle, ascend ridge crest to cliff-edge cairn RED PIKE (826 m/2,709 ft), descend long slopes, path, to Dore Head saddle (480 m/1,575 ft).
4 kms/2½ miles

(5) Ascend steep buttress ahead – Stirrup Crag – scramble, short, simple, to grassy top, cairns. Path along crest leads 900 m to cairn, summit YEWBARROW (628 m/2,058 ft), descend gradually onwards to narrow rocky neck – Great Door – drop R to shallow gully, easiest RHS, then descend steep grass L to good path crossing pasture to stile, descend far side wall until path strikes L to Wastwater shore, road returns to start.
5 kms/3 miles

Variation
(1.A + 2.A) Ascend direct to Black Sail Pass: behind Hotel take path E bank river 300 m to junction, fork L, good path leads into Mosedale then climbs R to Pass.
5 kms/3 miles

The Scafell Crest Lake District

OS 1: 50,000 Sheet 89

'The summit is bare of everything that grows … blocks and inclined planes of slate rock … compose the peak … the greatest mountain excursion in England.'

Harriet Martineau: 1855

'The Pikes of Scawfell are bold and picturesque but their precipices are slight …'

Owen Glynne Jones: 1897

Scafell Pike is indeed the highest point in England, a noble rocky mountain that is not unworthy of its crown. And the other descriptions, if not strictly accurate, do present a fair impression of a summit that despite demanding a long and rough walk to reach it, must be one of the most popular in the country. However, another summit standing one kilometre southward is only slightly lower, massive and moody it is girt with formidable defences and far less frequented: Scafell is unquestionably the finest mountain in England. Centuries ago the rugged high ground between the heads of Wasdale and Eskdale was known as Scaw Fell, possibly meaning 'Fell of the Rocky Tops', but as time went by the name became appended to the singular, most distinctive and seemingly highest summit of the massif while the less imposing tops became the Scawfell Pikes. To be strictly accurate there are three 'Pikes' – the others are Broad Crag and Ill Crag – before the undulating stony plateau from which all three rise rears up in the final bastion of Great End. In all the Lake District the Scafell massif has no peer.

Rising at the hub of a series of radiating valleys and accessible from many other starting points, Scafell and its great crags frown down upon Wasdale Head which has always been inexorably linked with these mountains in word and

From Styhead the route ascends the northern flanks of Great End by the shoulder known as The Band, seen here reflected in the moody waters of Styhead Tarn.

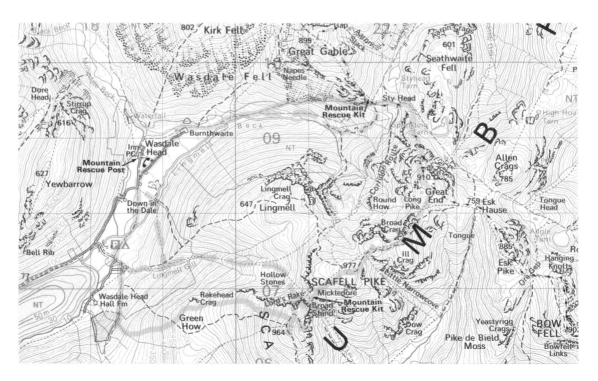

deed besides geography, and here our traverse starts, climbing first to the 'grand junction' of Sty Head. A more pleasant if slower alternative to the usual route previously described follows the old path up the valley bottom instead of mounting across the stony face of Great Gable. Then the northern ridge of Great End, its craggy butt dominating busy Sty Head and its dark tarn, is ascended by a less beaten path taking the easiest line, not always obvious, through fairly steep and rocky ground to the stony, mossy expanse of the summit plateau. From the lip one can peer down several impressive gullies, celebrated winter climbs, which slash deep into the large broken cliff that falls north-east above Sprinkling Tarn. The true summit, highest of three outcrops rising from the plateau, stands close to the cliff edge and provides impressive glimpses down Borrowdale to Derwent Water and unmistakable Skiddaw.

Now the tourist route from Esk Hause is joined, a highway almost, and followed to Scafell Pike, although connoisseurs will make short and obvious diversions to the bouldery summits of the other two Pikes, Ill Crag (927 m/3,040 ft) and Broad Crag (931 m/ 3,054 ft) both excellent vantage points – the latter summit is reputed to be the roughest in the Lakes. On a fine day folk will queue to ascend the monumental 3-metre (10-foot) cairn which crowns Scafell Pike: constructed in 1921, it dedicates the highest forty acres in England as a memorial to Lakeland men who died in the First World War. But the best views, especially down into Eskdale and Wasdale, are from the more lonely plateau edge while Scafell dominates the southern horizon as the path descends – or rather boulder-hops – to the narrow red crest of Mickledore and a nasty surprise. Formidable cliffs defend the entire northern flank of Scafell. Mickledore leads into the cliff and stops. Although a route does surmount the wall straight ahead, it is polished, exposed and often slimy if technically straightforward – a nasty place and scene of many accidents, Broad Stand is for climbers only. Two reasonable routes however outflank the precipice to left and right, the easier Fox's Tarn route involving a considerable descent. Classic and more interesting, the route via Lord's Rake contours down beneath the awesome cliffs of Scafell Crag, over 150

metres high (500 feet) and the greatest in England, passing the start of many famous climbs besides a discrete cross carved in the rock, a memorial to four climbers who died here in 1903 and are buried in the tiny Wasdale head churchyard. And so into the forbidding crag-walled gully of Lord's Rake itself. 'Reik' is old norse for a steep hillside path, and this one, floored with loose and now badly worn scree, is unwelcoming, but it is hardly scrambling and after a few minutes the gully is abandoned for the grassy shelf of the West Wall Traverse leading into the yawning portals of Deep Ghyll. The rocky scenery hereabouts is sensational, and the situation as atmospheric as any in Cumbria. A grassy plateau surrounds the wide gully mouth and the summit outcrops rises a short way southward from where the broad seaward prospect across

the shimmering sands of Morecombe Bay and the Duddon and Ravenglass estuaries is marred only by the incongruous towers of the Seascale nuclear facility rising against the distant shape of the Isle of Man. Nevertheless Scafell is a summit on which to linger. Despite its strong northern defences there are easy descents to south and west, the latter – the once popular Green How route dropping to the head of Wastwater – is swift and easy although the path fades low down and the final steep slopes should not be descended too soon.

The best views of the Scafell massif are from the summit crest of Yewbarrow. Here the entire route is visible from the green fields of Wasdale Head below, to Sty Head on the left, over Great End, Broad Crag and Scafell Pike to Mickledore and the great cliff-rimmed summit of Scafell itself; the descent lies down the slopes on the right.

A Traverse of the Scafell Crest

Length: 14.5 kms/9 miles
Total ascent: 1300 m/4,270 ft
Difficulty: a rugged and fairly strenuous expedition on high and exposed mountains, appropriate equipment essential: one major section of slightly exposed semi-scrambling could appear intimidating
Note: most of route National Trust property

Start: NT car-park/camp site 182075, N end Wastwater (70 m/230 ft), limited parking possible out-of-season Wasdale Green 186085.

(1) Ascend easily as described preceding walk (1) to Rescue Box, multi-path junction, summit Sty Head Pass (480 m/1,575 ft).
5 kms/3 miles

(2) Following major Esk Hause path, initially due E, 500 m, just before ford strike ½R up grassy hillside, faint path, to conspicuous block on crest whence better path zigzags L up shoulder, through trough R of The Band peaklet, to steeper craggy slope. Ascend easiest line, hands useful, to scree patch, shallow gully. Steep boulder field leads to wide plateau, two cairns GREAT END, summit SE cairn/outcrop (910 m/2,984 ft). Descend SSW to saddle, join major path continuing SW, rough, bouldery, many cairns, over shoulders Ill Crag, Broad Crag, dropping to narrow red col before climbing steep eroded rocky slope to huge cairn SCAFELL PIKE (978 m/3,210 ft).
4 kms/2½ miles

(3) Rugged path descends SW, boulder slopes, to narrow rocky saddle Mickledore (c 790 m/2,600 ft). Ascend slightly to far end, descend steeply R skirting cliff, stony, path traverses easily below cliffs 250 m till above scree slope. Now narrow cleft-like gully – Lord's Rake – rises steeply to tiny col behind pointed buttress ahead. Ascend gully **with care**, steep, rocky, loose, until 10 m below col step L onto wide easy ledge – West Wall Traverse. Path, slightly exposed, ascends into chasm Deep Ghyll, climbs RHS gully into upper bowl then bears R up red cleft, shaly, loose, hands useful, zigzagging to grassy plateau. Go R 250 m to summit outcrop, cairn, SCAFELL (964 m/3,162 ft).
1.5 kms/1 mile

(4) Retrace steps 150 m to grass, small cairn, stony path descends L near cliff edge until above scree funnel Lord's Rake (see 3.A) whence line of cairns, faint path, leads L, descending grassy hillside W. Follow path, often near RH edge, to top prominent Rakehead Crag. **Avoid** very steep path dropping directly over edge soon after crag but continue SW, intermittent path, descending across slopes then following beck to bridle-path at intake wall above wood. Go R, follow path easily to start.
4 kms/2½ miles

Alternatives

(3.A) Continue Lord's Rake beyond West Wall Traverse over two tiny cols, stony hollow, joining (4), retrace to summit. Easier, less interesting.

(3.B) To avoid Lord's Rake: stony path drops steeply L from Mickledore skirting cliff 500 m until stream in small gully ascends R to tiny pool – Fox's Tarn – sometimes dry. Ascend steep slopes R to grassy plateau Scafell.
Extra ascent 100 m/300 ft

(3.C) Wasdale avoiding Scafell: continue to start Lord's Rake gully whence drop R down scree into Hollow Stones combe, good path leads down Brown Tongue, R bank stream, to Wasdale.
Scafell Pike to start: 4 kms/2½ miles

The Carneddau Snowdonia

OS 1 50,000 Sheet 115

'The crests of solitude – the moaning wastes of the Carnedds,
The frightened curlew flying from a wrecked plane's wing.
The empty, perfect, peaceful top of Llewellyn.'

'A Boy goes Blind' from *Verses from My Country*
Roger Redfern: 1975

The Carneddau is the secret range of Snowdonia, a complex tangle of great whale-back crests cradling hidden cwms, remote tarns and several sizable lakes. This is a very extensive mountain group, a great block of country stretching from the edge of the sea into the very heart of Snowdonia. Here rises Carnedd Llewelyn, the second highest summit south of Scotland surrounded by more high ground above 3,000 feet than the rest of England and Wales put together. The climate on these high tops is virtually 'Arctic-Alpine' and in winter the range offers the best skiing in the region: in many ways the Carneddau resemble the Cairngorms.

Writing of his 1778 tour, unsuspecting Thomas Pennant reported the Carneddau as '. . . very disagreeable – dreary bottoms or moory hills . . .' and indeed at first sight the Carneddau do appear unspectacular mountains. But an apocryphal tale has it that early rock climbers discovered the great crags of Craig yr Ysfa by telescope from the summit of Scafell, and this and the other imposing cliff of Ysgolion Duon – the 'Black Ladders' – are the most famous among several noteworthy crags. Though the high tops are typically stony, the naked rock remains characteristically secluded. An aura of the unexpected, the unusual, seems to cloak the Carneddau. Wild ponies breed, for instance, in the sanctuary of Ffynnon Caseg – 'the Fountain of the Mare' – and the feathery cataract of lovely Aber Falls, plunging a clear 50 metres (170 feet), is the highest waterfall in Wales. Dark Llyn Colwyd is the most profound lake in Snowdonia and it is said that smiling Llyn Crafnant is home

Yr Elen must be the prettiest Carneddau summit: it is seen here from the west across the mouth of Cwm Llafar with the Black Ladders – Ysgolion Duon – of Carnedd Dafydd just visible on the right. A highly recommended route follows the skyline crest.

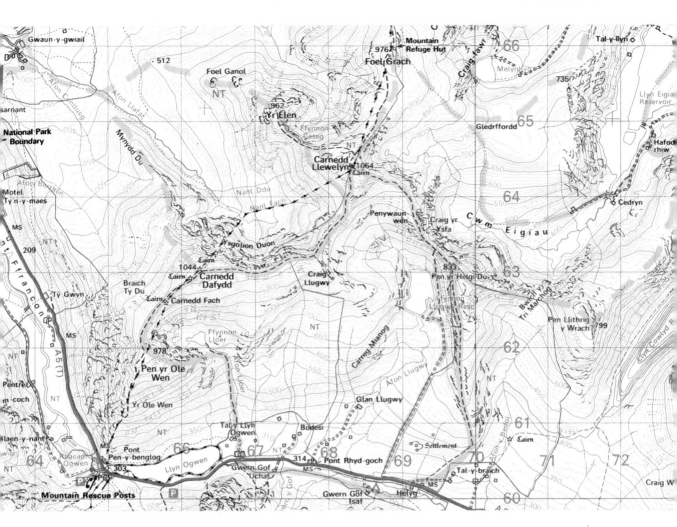

to the largest trout in the Principality. The sad ruins of a burst dam lie in Cwm Eigiau, there are aircraft wrecks scattered on the high tops while the seaward northern slopes are scattered with Bronze Age remains. Carnedd in fact means 'cairn' or 'burial mound' and the large burial cairn between Carnedd Llewelyn and Foelgrach is said to be the grave of Tristran, a Knight of the Round Table. Appropriately the two highest summits are named for Llywelyn Fawr – 'the Great' – who first united Wales and died in 1240, and for his son Dafydd who succeeded him. Certainly the Carneddau are special.

The circular walk described is not a difficult one, but the Carneddau are continuously high and lack the small-scale features so useful when navigating in all but perfect conditions: a mistake of a few degrees in mist can lead the walker miles from his destination so compass skills are a

prerequisite. Admittedly the climb up onto Pen-yr-oleu-wen, (the 'Hill of the Moonlight') is a long pull, but the mountain occupies a strategic position in the Ogwen valley; there are superb views from its slopes to Cwm Idwal and the Glyders – and from the mouth of delightful little Cwm Lloer (the 'Cwm of the Moon') a most unusual view of *aiguille* Tryfan. Once up on the tops the going is never hard and the only strenuous ascent is that of the final scree-cloaked dome of Carnedd Llewelyn – just 75 feet (23 metres) lower than Yr Wyddfa. The extensive panorama, especially northward to the sea, to Puffin Island and the Great Orme, is a just reward. This peak is the hub of the Carneddau and three great ridges spring from its summit, while a fourth lesser arete leads to strangely isolated Yr Elen, (the 'Peak of the Fawn') a rugged and imposing mountain in its own right and most shapely of the Carneddau summits. Until recently the range was considered to contain six of Snowdonia's fourteen 3,000-foot tops but with the advent of metrification Carnedd Uchaf has been promoted to 926 metres – 3,038 feet – so there are now seven 'three-thousanders' in the range, making fifteen in all. Peak-baggers will be pleased to note that there are seventeen Carnedd 'tops' of which no less than twelve are classed as 'separate mountains'.

In so extensive a range there are many other good walking routes, and notable are the Cwm Eigiau Horseshoe and the classic Carneddau traverse, some 21 kilometres (13 miles) one-way from Ogwen to the coast at Aber. However, an excellent and rather shorter alternative (13 kilometres/8 miles) to the main circuit described is the round of Cwm Llafar – the 'Valley of Sound'. Starting from Bethesda where limited laneside parking is currently possible at 634662, the route enters the lower cwm before striking up the west and north-west ridges of Yr Elen

from where there are good views across to Dafydd and forbidding Ysgolion Duon – a favourite winter climbing cliff which dominates the wide head of the cwm. Llewelyn's summit can be ascended or avoided by a col-to-col traverse path across its south-west flank, and the main Carnedd crest followed to Dafydd from where, carefully avoiding the northern crags, easy slopes fall northwestward to the grassy Mynydd Du ridge dropping to the boggy path at the cwm mouth.

A Carnedd Circuit

Length: 18 kms/11 miles
Height ascended: 1030 m/3,380 ft
Difficulty: mostly easy going on grassy or rock-strewn terrain after long initial ascent, two short semi-scrambles in section (3)
Warning: this route is continuously high and can attract fierce weather. It passes close above major cliffs of Ysgolion Duon and Craig yr Ysfa where care is necessary in bad conditions. Appropriate equipment, including map and compass, essential.

Start: good roadside parking beside A5 at head Llyn Ogwen at 667605 (303 m/994 ft).

(1) Take lane N past Glan Dena hut almost to Tal y Llyn Ogwen farm were path crosses stile to ascend easy hillside beside Afon Lloer stream. Just before Ffynnon Lloer tarn strike up steeply left, rocky couloir giving best line, onto stony E ridge ascending to PEN YR OLEU WEN summit. (979 m/3,211 ft).
3.5 kms/2¼ miles

(2) Easy going along stony ridge curving NE above Cwm Lloer leads to CARNEDD DAFYDD (1044 m/3,424 ft). Ridge continues, rocky at first, descending gradually to flat section: just before, at 678632, safe escape is possible to SSE. Flat narrow ridge now curves to NE broadening to scree-covered slopes leading to wide top of CARNEDD LLEWELYN (1064 m/3,490 ft).
4.5 kms/3 miles

(3) Descend SE ridge, initially scree then grassy and narrowing, passing above cliffs of Craig yr Ysfa to easy rocky step down onto narrow saddle (Bwlch Eryl Farchog 750 m/2,460 ft). Slender ridge now climbs via a short slight scramble to spacious crest of PEN YR HELGI-DU (833 m/2,733 ft). Path descends long grassy S ridge, avoids Tal-y-Braich cottage on W and follows track to cross main road at Helyg (280 m/930 ft). Return to start by old road along S side of the valley bottom.
6 kms/3¾ miles

Variations
(1.A) At end of flat ridge at 683639 strike left on vestigal path across stony SW face of Carnedd Llewelyn to obvious col on its NW ridge, now follow narrow crest to YR ELEN summit (961 m/3,152 ft). Retrace steps to col and ascend NW ridge to Llewelyn summit.
3 kms/1¾ miles

(2.A) From Bwlch Eryl Farchog steep rocky path descends SW to Ffynnon Llugwy lake. Ugly CEGB jeep road leads down to A5.
3 kms/1¾ miles

The familiar view from the Glyders over the Ogwen valley towards the Carneddau peaks encircling Cwm Llugwy: our route drops off Carnedd Llewelyn on the left, crosses the Craig yr Ysfa saddle and climbs again over Pen yr Helgi-du on the right.

The Glyders   Snowdonia

OS 1: 50,000 Sheet 115

'. . . a fit place to inspire murderous thoughts, environed with horrible precipices . . .'

Thomas Pennant
describing Cwm Idwal, 1778

Although Pennant was not favourably impressed, many modern mountain lovers will consider the Glyder range their favourite Snowdonian mountain group and for the same reason. With imposing Cwm Idwal cradled at its very heart and Tryfan – the most striking peak south of the Scottish Highlands rearing closeby – the diverse scenery of these most craggy of Snowdonia's mountains is unsurpassed. Excellent and characterful walking, scrambling and climbing – the latter especially so in the easier grades – together with straightforward access to its summits, ensure the attraction of the Glyders.

The chain of the Glyders (strictly speaking – Y Glyderau) forms a north-east facing arc centred on Pen y Benglog at the end of Llyn Ogwen and holds no less than eight 'separate mountains' and two 'subsidiary tops'. Five summits rise above 3,000 feet. Although the lower south-west slopes of the range above the narrow Llanberis Pass are steep and rocky and hold a succession of popular climbing crags, the southern and western flanks of the Glyders are generally rounded and grassy and the spectacular scenery is concentrated above the Ogwen Valley. Here an array of twelve hanging cwms – some among the finest in Britain – are deeply gouged into the northern flanks of the chain. Jutting northwards from the main crest is Tryfan whose triple summits and craggy shark-fin outline are familiar to all who travel the A5 Holyhead road. Reputedly it is the only British mountain outside Skye where hands are required to reach the summit, twin monolithic blocks known as Adam and Eve. For scramblers Tryfan's long north ridge provides classic sport and if continued via the seemingly intimidating yet no more difficult Bristly Ridge to the main plateau, a superb alternative start to any route over the Glyders. Continuity, perfect rock, large holds, and an airy situation ensure the popularity of both ridges though the easiest lines are not always obvious and neither ascent should be underestimated by the inexperienced or in bad conditions. Descent from Tryfan to the Bwlch and Bristly's foot is by the shorter and easier south ridge, the regular ascent route and possibly just a scramble. But bleak and windy Bwlch Tryfan is more easily reached from Cwm Bochlwyd, its moody tarn overshadowed by the cliffs of Glyder Fach, and the usual route onwards by the diagonally ascending 'Miner's Track' crosses the scree-seamed headwall of Cwm Tryfan to the marshy plateau near pretty

The jagged peak of Tryfan rises steeply above the Ogwen valley: this distinctive mountain is seen from Helyg on a winter afternoon with the North Ridge on the right and Bwlch Tryfan and Bristly Ridge on the left.

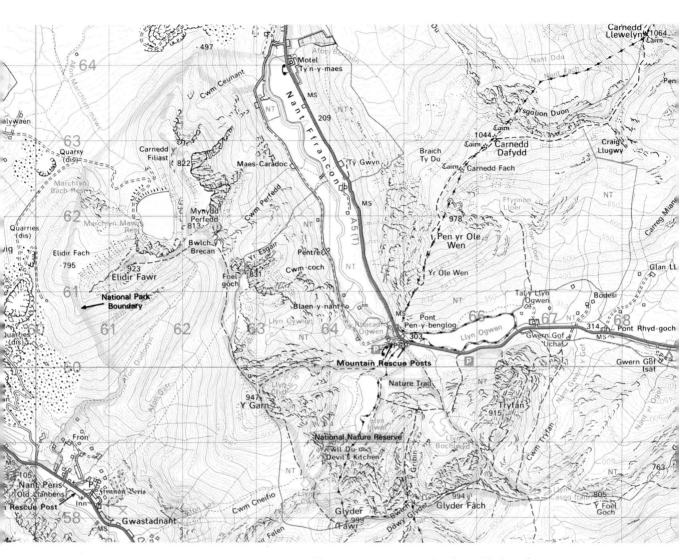

little Llyn Caseg-fraith – 'the Lake of the piebald Mare' – a superb viewpoint for Tryfan.

Charles Kingsley described the extensive stone and boulder covered summit plateau of Glyder Fach as an '. . . enormous desolation, the dead bones of the eldest born of time . . .' An apt description for here are scattered strange configurations of rocks such as the famous Cantilever Stone and the bizarre bepinnacled Castell y Gwynt – the 'Castle of the Winds'. In poor visibility navigation can be difficult for the plateau extends over 2 kilometres (1¼ miles) to Glyder Fawr, though it does narrow to a noticeable saddle between the two summits above the secret and delightful little Cwm Cneifion (known as the Nameless Cwm). The useful Gribin Ridge drops northward a little

further on. At the big Glyder the crest turns north-east and scree slopes fall steeply to the broad boggy saddle that holds tiny Llny y Cwn, where once lived peculiar monocular fish, so they say. The vertical cliffs of Clogwyn y Geifr drop abruptly from the eastern edge of the saddle into Cwm Idwal and are rent by several great gullies: Hanging Garden, the Devil's Staircase, the Devil's Appendix, and others. Most famous of all is the Devil's Kitchen – Twll Du, 'the Black Hole' – into which tumbles a fine waterfall providing a splendid view for the cautious photographer. From the saddle a wide grassy ridge leads up to the triangular summit of Y Garn, a rocky top with fine seaward views – sometimes as far as Ireland. The north-east ridge, curving round shallow Cwm Clyd with its tiny tarns, provides an excellent descent to the north lip of Cwm Idwal with its celebrated view across the lake towards the dark wall of Clogwyn y Geifr: on a moody day the legend of Prince Idwal, how he was thrown by a giant from these cliffs into the lake over which – to this day – no bird will fly, may not seem so far fetched!

The ridge onwards from Y Garn, attractive and cwm-scalloped on its eastern flank, continues over Foel Goch and Mynydd Perfedd to Carnedd y Filiast before falling away as a great shoulder towards the abandoned Penrhyn slate quarries and the village of Bethesda.

The final Glyder top however is Elidir Fawr, a shapely rocky summit on a subsidiary spur jutting over the Llanberis valley. Sadly this worthy mountain has been despoiled over the years, first by the Dinorwic slatemen whose mighty quarries hacked to within 800 feet of the summit, and more recently by the CEGB who dammed the once perfect circular tarn of Marchlyn Mawr which lies in its beautiful crag-girt northern cwm.

The summit of Glyder Fach is crowned by the extraordinary Cantilever Stone.

A Glyder Circuit

Distance covered: 10.5 kms/6¾ miles
Height gained: 1040 m/3,400 ft
Difficulty: mostly rough stony ground, paths of sorts most of the way
Warning: serious and craggy mountain country, appropriate equipment essential: in bad weather navigation often difficult and mistakes serious. Cairns proliferate, do not navigate by them. Only easy escape routes on Ogwen flank between those described are scrambly Gribin Ridge and steep screes E side Bristly Ridge.

Start: Ogwen Cottage car-park W end of lake, 649603, phone, toilets, often refreshments. (303 m/994 ft).

(1) Subsidiary path forking L from well-used Cwm Idwal track leads over boggy ground to torrent, climbing steeply beside it to Llyn Bochlwyd and round E side of lake before climbing to Bwlch Tryfan saddle (709 m/2,325 ft). After slight descent E, path ascends diagonally to Glyder crest near tiny Llyn Caseg-fraith (762 m/2,500 ft) before turning W up broad rocky flank to stony plateau and OS cairn GLYDER FACH summit (994 m/3,262 ft). **4 kms/2½ miles**

(2) Cross plateau to W, pass round Castell y Gwynt, descend to shallow saddle. Avoiding path ascending N to head of Gribin Ridge, continue W to regain ridge crest and ascend gradually to GLYDER FAWR summit (999 m/3,279 ft). Descend screes NW to wide saddle near Llyn y Cwn (637585: 715 m/2,350 ft). Grassy slopes ahead lead to rocky summit Y GARN (946 m/3,104 ft).
3.5 kms/2¼ miles

(3) Just N of summit, path descends grassy NE Ridge into Cwm Clyd before dropping steeply to Llyn Idwal N shore and main Ogwen Cottage path.
3 kms/2 miles

Variations
(2.A) Direct descent to Cwm Idwal: From Lyn y Cwn cairned path leads NE into mini canyon near abrupt cliff edge before descending ramp across cliff face, scrambly near bottom, to foot Devil's Kitchen cleft. Descend boulders to well-marked path leading beneath famous Idwal Slabs to Llyn Idwal E shore and onwards to Ogwen Cottage.
Distance from Glyder Fawr: **3.5 kms/2¼ miles**

(3.A) Continuation to Elidir Fawr: From Y Garn grassy crest leads N over FOEL GOCH (831 m/2,727 ft) to MYNYDD PERFEDD (812 m/2,665 ft). Descend SW to col above Cwm Marchlyn. Lower contour path on W avoids these summits. Ascend easily to rocky summit ELIDIR FAWR (924 m/3,030 ft).
Distance from Y Garn: **4 kms/2½ miles**
Ascent: **370 m/1,210 ft**

(4) Descent from Elidir Fawr: Contour Mynydd Perfedd N to CARNEDD Y FILIAST (821 m/2,695 ft). Go 500 m NNW then descend pronounced ridge NNE for 1 km until faint path crosses SE into Cwm Ceunant, descend to old Nant Francon road at bottom of slope. Pleasant walk up valley to Ogwen Cottage.
Distance: **9 kms/5½ miles**
Ascent: **200 m/650 ft**

It is said that no bird will fly over the moody waters of Llyn Idwal! In this view of the lake from its outfall, the Idwal Slabs are seen on the flank of Glyder Fawr on the left, ahead is the cleft of the Devil's Kitchen while the slopes of Y Garn rise on the right.

Snowdon and the Horseshoe

OS 1 : 50,000 Sheet 115

'We've the stones of Snowdon
and the lamps of heaven'

Charles Kingsley 1856

Rising to the highest summit and the most magnificent peaks south of the Highlands, the compact Snowdon massif contains surprisingly little high ground and only four tops above 3,000 feet (900 metres). But the summits are characteristically sharp and rocky and the five great ridges that spring from the central peak of Yr Wyddfa are rugged, often narrow and cradle several fine craggy cwms – two of which hold the greatest cliffs in Wales, Clogwyn D'ur Arddu and Y Lliwedd.

Snowdon predictably is a major tourist attraction and since 1896 Yr Wyddfa has suffered the indignity of a mountain rack-railway to its summit. While the antiquated little steam trains themselves are quaint and perhaps even sufferable, the obtrusive ugliness of the sordid summit terminus is unacceptable. Luckily the tourist season is short and for six months of the year visitors must walk to the summit, many by the

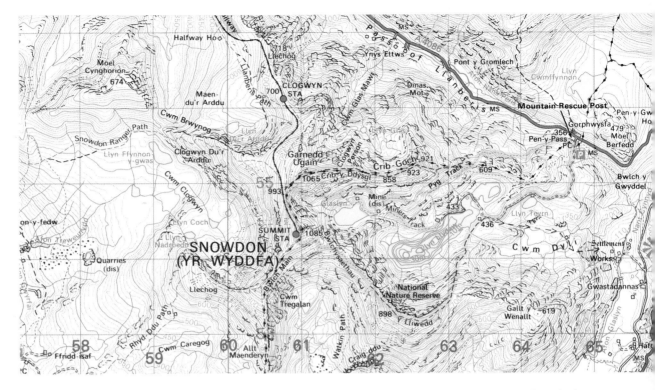

easiest way, a trudge of nearly 8 kilometres (5 miles) up the gentle flanks of the NW or 'Railway Ridge' from Llanberis. In poor conditions however the route can be deceptive, weather up high can be very different from that in the valley and when icy the track above Cwm Du'r Arddu can be very treacherous.

The classic route on Snowdon is the 'Horseshoe' – the most famous ridge scramble in Britain though many folk may find it rather challenging. The Crib Goch arete falls precipitously on the northern side and although in good conditions surefooted climbers will delight in skipping along the actual crest, most ordinary mortals will scramble along on the southern side using the crest for handholds. Under snow it can provide a superb expedition for experienced alpinists. The view from Yr Wyddfa – 'the Tomb' where they say Rhita Gawr, an early prince was buried – is justly celebrated. On the best days the panorama extends to the Preseli Hills, the Wicklows of Ireland and the Lake

District; on hazier days the silhouette of Harlech Castle beyond the glinting Glaslyn Estuary is sufficient inspiration. Five hundred metres (1,600 ft) below lies tiny Glaslyn in whose fathomless green waters is sometimes glimpsed the legendary Afanc, a monster supposedly banished from the Conway in days gone by.

Most convenient of the easier routes to the summit, the Miners Track also provides a swift descent. Derelict workings of the Britannia copper mines, abandoned before the Great War, are scattered above the northern shores of Llydaw and in Cwm Glas, the copper accounting for the colour of the 'green lake': a massive iron casting from the crushing mill still lies near the path. The miners lived in barracks beside Llyn Teyrn below. Other straightforward routes to the summit follow the south ridge, the Watkin and the Snowdon Ranger paths. The latter, ascending from Llyn Cwellyn to the west ridge of Crib-y-ddysgi and passing above the finest climbing crag in Snowdonia, awesome Clogwyn Du'r Arddu – the 'black cliff of darkness' – was the regular route before the coming of the railway. It was tramped by Thomas Pennant in the 1770s and named from the professional guide who once frequented it.

All the four summits traversed by the Snowdon Horseshoe circuit are seen in this classic view over Llynau Mymbyr: left to right they are Y Lliwedd, Yr Wyddfa, Crib Goch and Crib-y-ddysgl.

The Watkin Path, rising from lovely Nant Gwynant, was constructed in 1892 by the local proprietor to facilitate the ascent on horseback. Today only feasible on foot above Bwlch y Saethau, the final steep rubbly traverse below the top can demand caution, especially in snowy conditions. Rather more rugged, the south ridge can be reached from Rhyd-Ddu, Beddgelert or Nant Gwynant but ideally over the pretty little peak of Yr Aran. The almost scrambly ridge crosses Llechog (605537) often now considered – since metric maps show a ten-metre contour ring round its 931 m (3,054 ft) spot-height – to be a 'three-thousander'.

Bwlch y Saethau itself – the 'Pass of the Arrows' – was the site of King Arthur's last battle and it was into Llyn Llydaw that Sir Bedivere hurled the sword Excalibur. His knights lie sleeping to this day in a cave, accessible only to skilled climbers, in Slanting Gully on Y Lliwedd, awaiting again the call to arms. Surely Lliwedd is one of the great moun-

tains of Wales, through it just fails to reach 3,000 feet, and the traverse of its splendid twin summits above thousand-foot crags laced with vintage rock climbs and frowning down upon Llyn Llydaw completes the Horseshoe. Llydaw is second deepest of the Welsh lakes – nearly 200 feet – and the black pipes feed the old Cwm Dyli HEP scheme in the valley below. There is one final view of Yr Wyddfa from the shore before the Miner's Track is joined and followed round the corner towards Pen y Pass.

A Snowdon Circuit – The Horseshoe

Distance covered: 11 kms/7 miles
Height gained: 1060 m/3,500 ft
Difficulty: committing, rugged, high and susceptible to bad weather, long section of exposed but straightforward scrambling potentially hazardous in bad conditions. Route always well defined. Serious undertaking for the inexperienced

Start: Pen y Pass car-park (charge) on A4086 at 647556 (356 m/1,170 ft), telephone, refreshment and YHA.

(1) From W corner car-park take Pyg Track, rough path contouring hillside above Llanberis Pass up to grassy saddle Bwlch y Moch 633553 (570 m/1,870 ft).
1.5 kms/1 mile

(2) Ascend E ridge Crib Goch ahead, initially path then rocky steps on steep narrowing ridge leading to narrow rocky shoulder – false summit. **Easy scrambling: beware loose stones** often dislodged from above. Exposed knife-edge rock arete continues horizontally 150 m to tiny summit CRIB GOCH (922 m/3,026 ft), not difficult but **caution required.** Narrow crest continues to Pinnacles – short, steep, airy scramble avoidable unpleasantly on L. Steep descent to grassy saddle, Bwlch Coch. Narrow rocky ridge continues over short scrambly steps to widening summit plateau CRIB-Y-DDYSGL (1065 m/3,496 ft). Slopes descend to finger stone at broad saddle Bwlch Glas near railway track. Virtual highway ascends to summit YR WYDDFA (1095 m/3,560 ft).
3.5 kms/2¼ miles

(3) Descend SW ridge 150 m to finger stone, drop L onto Watkin Path descending across steep rubbly SE Face **caution loose rock** to wide saddle Bwlch y Saethau, continue easily over bluffs to Bwlch Ciliau where Watkin Path descends R. Ascend instead narrowing stony ridge ahead to sharp twin summits Y LLIWEDD (898 m/2,947 ft), exposed on L. From E summit path descends along crest 750 m before dropping L down steep grassy slopes to Llyn Llydaw (436 m/1,430 ft). Here join stony Miners Track contouring hillside to Pen y Pass.
6.25 kms/4 miles

Variation
(3.A) From Yr Wyddfa retrace route to Bwlch Glas fingerstone and drop E down steep stony zigzags into Cwm Glas. **Caution** in winter conditions. Path forks above Glaslyn, upper route – Pyg Track – contours via Bwlch y Moch to Pen y Pass **5 kms/3 miles**, or lower Miners Track returns via Llyn Llydaw **6.5 kms/4 miles**

Yr Wyddfa – Snowdon itself – appears almost Himalayan in this spring view from the east over the ice of Llyn Llydaw: the northern cliffs of Y Lliwedd rise on the left.

The Pennant Hills   Snowdonia

OS 1:50,000 Sheet 115

'Oh god, why didst Thou make Cwm Pennant so beautiful and the life of an old shepherd so short?'

Eifion Wyn

Cwm Pennant is indeed a delectable valley. A narrow lane winds some four miles into its secret depths, crossing and recrossing the tranquil Afon Dwyfor, passing scattered farms and a chapel or two. Sweeping hillsides, once the home of Bronze and Iron Age folk, hold but few conspicuous traces of the miners who toiled here after slate and copper, and are today deserted save for shepherds, their dogs and their ubiquitous sheep. Surrounded by a horseshoe of fine mountains, the valley opens southwards to the sea and the sun, and seems always to hold a smile.

The so-called Nantlle Ridge that walls Cwm Pennant on the north is notable for its series of craggy north-facing cwms, especially Cwm Silyn with its twin tarns and Great Slab which climbers hold in high regard. Deeply scarred by abandoned workings and containing the celebrated 180 metres (600 feet) deep Dorothea slate pit, the Nantlle valley strongly contrasts Cwm Pennant. Holding three shapely mountains and three subsidiary peaks, the Nantlle Ridge provides an excellent traverse, though not an obvious circuit. A single public path climbs from the Nantlle valley, and after a period of local antagonism to mountain goers, access to and along the crest is now by Courtesy Footpaths carefully negotiated by the National Park. An ancient right of way does however run to the head of Cwm Pennant, past the sad ruins of the

Ogof Owain Glyndwr – the lonely cave on Moel y Ogof, a satellite of Moel Hebog, in which the Welsh leader is supposed to have hidden for six months.

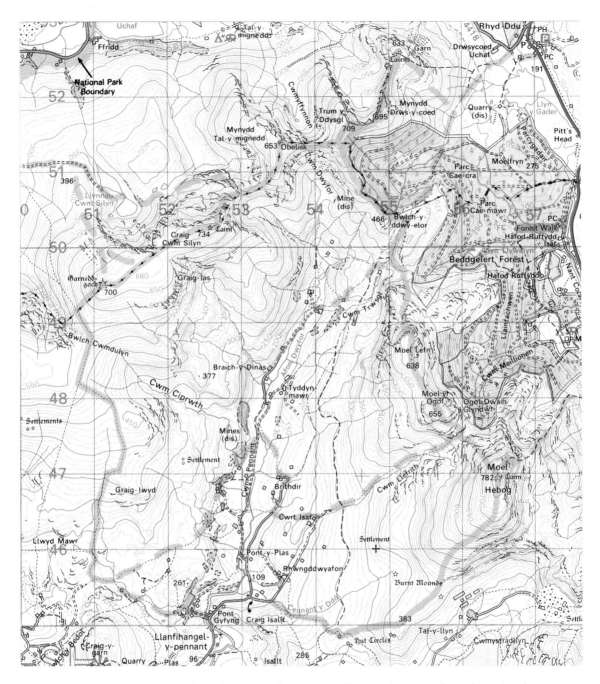

Prince of Wales Quarry abandoned in 1882 after a fatal rockfall, to narrow Bwlch-y-ddwy-elor, the 'Pass of the Two Biers', which leads over to Nant Colwyn and Rhyd-Ddu. The Bwlch is a useful and legal access point to the mountains on either side. Local tradition claims that the hill-sides between the Bwlch and Rhyd-Ddu were those most frequented by fairies in all Wales, indeed the last claimed sighting was in 1899, but now alas, regiments of sombre pine have conquered fairyland.

The regular route up the big dome of Moel Hebog, the 'Hill of the Falcon', is by its north-eastern slopes above Beddgelert but it can just as well be climbed from Cwm Pennant over the shoulder of Braich y Cornel with its scattering of prehistoric hut circles. The summit is smooth and round and a rewarding viewpoint, both out to sea and over Nant Colwyn to the Snowdon massif. Moel Hebog is associated with Owain Glyndwr. Surprised in Nantmor by his enemies he is said to have swam the then tidal Glaslyn estuary and fled up the eastern slopes of the mountain, the pursuit hard on his heels, finally escaping up a deep chimney in the summit crags. But he was still not safe and for six months he is supposed to have laid up in a cave under the rocky lip of Moel yr Ogof – the 'Hill of the Cave': hardly a comfortable retreat, it can be located at 559478. The route north from Hebog descends to strange Bwlch Meillionen – the 'Clover Pass' – lush with ferns and mossy outcrops, before climbing to the reedy pools and jumbled rocks of Moel y Ogof and onwards to Moel Lefn, Bwlch Sais – the 'Englishman's Pass' which leads nowhere – and through a complex area of bogs and bluffs to Bwlch Cwm Trwsgl and Bwlch-y-ddwy-elor.

One can return now into Cwm Pennant or continue onwards to join the Nantlle Ridge at the grassy table-mountain summit of Trum y Ddysgl – the 'Dished Ridge'. It is worth diverting here to visit little Y Garn, via the airy arete of Mynydd Drws-y-Coed – 'Mountain of the Wooded Gap' – before returning to descend over a narrow green *mauvais pas* and climbing to the conspicuous Victorian Jubilee pillar, over 6 metres high (20 feet), which crowns Mynydd Tal-y-mignedd – the 'Mountain at the Bog's End'. A useful but ill-defined path strikes down from the deep saddle beyond and contours to the twin lakes of Cwm Silyn. However the rocky arete above rises to the major peak of the Nantlle Ridge – Craig Cwm Silyn – and although intimidating at first sight, a straightforward scrambly route a little right of the actual crest leads to the stony summit plateau.

Easy ground leads onward to the final top, Garnedd Goch, from where the normal route descends northward to the Cwm Silyn road-head. To return to Cwm Pennant however, without trespassing, one must join an ancient right of way on the next saddle and follow its gradual convoluted descent back into the peaceful valley below Moel Hebog.

A steep climb leads up from Bwlch Dros-bern towards the top of Mynydd Tal-y-mignedd. The rocky ridge leading to Craig Cwm Silyn is seen across the saddle.

The Pennant Horseshoe

Distance: 24 kms/15 miles
Height gained: 1540 m/5,050 ft
Difficulty: rough mountain country, several rocky, airy – but avoidable – sections: a long and strenuous route that can be conveniently shortened. Appropriate equipment essential
Warning: concealed workings Bwlch Cwm Trwsgl vicinity
Note: visitors to Cwm Pennant should be tactful and especially considerate of local sensibilities
Parking: approved only at lanehead 540492 (140 m/460 ft) – parking fee payable Braich y Dinas farm, customary but unapproved at Dwyfor bridge 532476 (110 m/360 ft) and 504512 below Cwm Silyn (330 m/1,100 ft)

Start: because parking is difficult and varied, route is described from lane junction at 531454 (chapel + phone box).

(1) From junction follow narrow lane 400 m E, then footpath branching R towards Cwm Ystradllyn. After 1200 m at highest point, strike NE on faint path up spur to Braich y Cornel shoulder, continue to MOEL HEBOG summit (782 m/2,567 ft).
5 kms/3¼ miles

(2) Path descends NW flank R of wall to deep col, climbs through rocky outcrops to MOEL Y OGOF (655 m/2,150 ft), over MOEL LEFN (638 m/2,094 ft) and descends N to Bwlch Trwsgl, before bearing W to join Pennant track by old workings (340 m/1,115 ft).
4 kms/2½ miles

(3) Ascend track R to Bwlch-y-ddwy-elor crest then climb boggy path past forestry edge to grassy ridge leading to summit plateau TRUM Y DDYSGL (710 m/2,329 ft). (To include MYNYDD DRWS-Y-COED (695 m/2,280 ft) and Y GARN (634 m/2,080 ft) follow path contouring NE 150 m (500 ft) before summit plateau. **Extra 3 kms/2 miles; 175 m/575 ft return**.) Descend ridge E from S end plateau, over narrows, ascend to stone pillar on MYNYDD TAL-Y-MIGNEDD (655 m/2,148 ft). Follow boggy path S to steep shaly ridge, descend to Bwlch Dros-bern (500 m/1,640 ft) and climb steep rocky ridge beyond to summit plateau CRAIG CWM SILYN (734 m/2,408 ft). Continue SW, via walls and stiles, to GARNEDD GOCH (700 m/2,297 ft).
6.5 kms/4 miles

(4) Descend bouldery slopes SSW to Bwlch Cwmdulyn. Legal route follows grassy/heathery rights of way S and E to reach Cwm Pennant N or S of starting point.
7.5 kms/4¾ miles

The Moelwyn – Melancholic Mountains

Snowdonia

OS 1 : 50,000 Sheets 115, 124

'By fair Festiniog, mid the Northern Hills,
The vales are full of beauty, and the heights,
Thin set with mountain sheep, show statelier far
Than the tamer South.'

Sir Lewis Morris Songs of Britain: 1887

These are strange hills. They rise at the southern extremity of a wild inland region of high rumpled moors, rocks and lakes of which Moel Siabod is the northern bastion, yet with their faces to the sea they seem almost maritime mountains. Indeed, until William Madocks MP built his embankment across the Glaslyn estuary in 1811 and reclaimed the sands of the Traeth Mawr, the Moelwyn peaks stood literally with their feet in the waves.

Standing beyond the high central massifs of Snowdonia, the Moelwyn lack somehow the assertiveness of the real peripheral ranges such as the Rhinogs or the Arans and exude an aura of melancholy. Probably this is the fault of history, of the once frenzied slate industry that hacked and tunnelled into their flanks, changing the face of the landscape and then disappearing to leave a plaintive legacy of deserted quarries, roofless barracks and grey mountains of spoil. The Moelwyn are certainly intriguing, their mood is compelling and they offer excellent hill walking.

Seen from the heights of Snowdonia to the north-west, the Moelwyn appear as a knot of distinctively shaped peaks. This itinerary traverses the three major summits by their most challenging routes, sampling meanwhile much of the unique atmosphere of the area. It starts at the tiny village of Croesor, perched at its lane-

Cnicht has been dubbed 'the Matterhorn of Wales' – a title which belies its gentle nature. The south-west ridge of this graceful mountain, our line of ascent, is seen straight-on from the water-meadows beside the Afon Glaslyn. Cwm Croesor on the right.

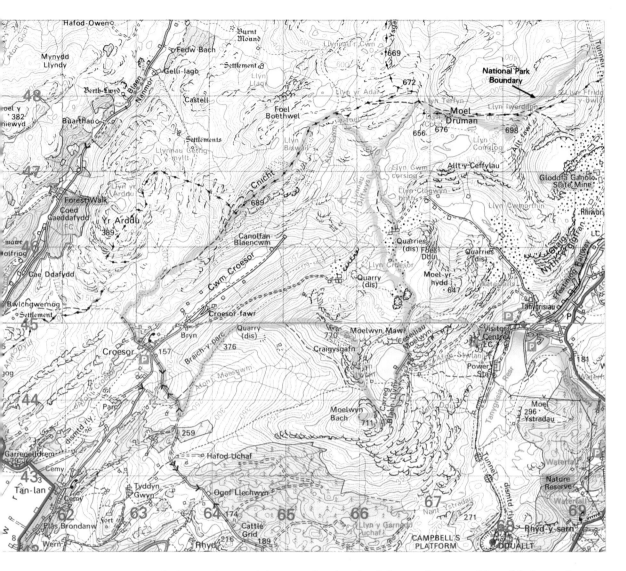

end high above the lush meadows of the Traeth Mawr and dominated by the beautiful cone of little Cnicht rising steeply behind. Perversely Cnicht is not a Welsh name, it is middle-English for knight and to medieval sailors in Tremadog Bay its sharp outline no doubt recalled the pointed bascinet helmet then worn by chivalry. After ascending its shapely little south-west ridge, Cnicht is discovered to be a sham – merely the butt end of a long moorland crest – but none the worse for that as the moorland is wild and lonely and scattered with small tarns, its rumpled surface broken by rocky outcrops and unfrequented tops. Beside Llyn yr Adur – the 'Lake of the Birds' – the old path from Nant Gwynant to Ffestiniog is joined, leading boggily around the

head of Cwm Croesor. The old slate mines in this deep defile between the flanks of Cnicht and Moelwyn Mawr, though never a commercial success, are notable for being the repository of the treasures of the National Gallery during the Second World War. The path leads onward to the wide saddle of Bwlch y Rhosydd.

When the extensive quarries closed in the 1920s the Bwlch must have been an industrial wasteland but time and weather have mellowed the acres of grey slate, and surrounded by grey-green hillsides the incongruity is now one only of shape rather than colour. Among the eyeless buildings the inquisitive will discover rusted machinery, old shafts and dripping adits: one adit is said to emerge eventually at workings a mile away beyond the mountain but exploring it is for experienced cavers only. Old and carefully constructed quarryman's paths lead onwards into Cwm Stwlan. One can continue thus directly to the rather sinister looking defile of Bwlch Stwlan between Moelwyn Bach and Moelwyn Mawr, but it is better to descend to the dam, visiting *en route* the rocky knob immediately above its northern end from which an interesting view unfolds. Although it extends to Cader Idris, the Rhinogs and the nuclear power station at Trawsfynydd, probably most intriguing is the valley immediately below with its hydroelectric station, the tiny steam trains of the quaint Festiniog Railway puffing along the shores of Tanygrisiau Lake, and the magnificent Vale of Ffestiniog beyond. The wild goats that roam these hillsides might also be glimpsed. Though purists will resent its existence, the engineering of the dam is impressive and it does impart some scale to the cwm: it was commissioned as the upper reservoir of the Ffestiniog Pumped Storage system in 1963, though there was a small lake here before.

Moelwyn Bach, the 'Little White Mountain', ringed with crags and with its well-known nose appearing actually to overhang Bwlch Stwlan, appears almost inaccessible from this eastern flank until close scrutiny reveals several steep grassy breaches in its defences. Whatever route through the cliffs is chosen, it is wise to take careful note of the diagonal descent path that leads from the shoulder left of the summit down to the Bwlch. The panorama from the summit itself, reached across a peculiar plateau of narrow pools between rocky spines, is superb, particularly down the twisting Dwyryd estuary and over the glinting sea to St Tudwal's Islands off the distant Lleyn.

The well-trodden route up Moelwyn Mawr rears steeply up from Bwlch Stwlan. There are two short rocky steps – almost scrambling – before the angle eases along the shoulder of Craig ys Gafn: soon the path steepens again and zigzags up the final rounded grassy ridge to the airy summit and OS cairn. Now the circle is almost closed and the north-east ridge, at first quite narrow in places and then becoming a sweeping grassy crest, provides a delightful descent back to Croesor.

A Moelwyn Horseshoe

Length: 16 kms/10 miles
Height gained: 1150 m/3,770 ft
Difficulty: a fairly committing circuit with some strenuous walking – mostly grassy, often boggy, sometimes rocky. Both Moelwyn peaks involve a little easy scrambling
Warning: some confusing ground where detailed navigation is not easy in poor conditions, beware old quarry workings with loose rock, pits and shafts. Craggy Moelwyn Bach deserves respect

Start: good SNP car-park in Croesor village at 631447. (157 m/515 ft)

(1) Follow main lane leading NW through village, over brow, through gate/stile and woods to 628451 where path leads off right just before next stile, occasional waymarks. Fork right at ruin to stile/wall on crest 150 m above and continue on L flank of ridge over scree section to grassy saddle. Now follow good path – scrambly alternatives to left and right – up prominent SW ridge to CNICHT summit (690 m/2,265 ft).
3 kms/2 miles

(2) Continue NE descending gradually on vague path to wide boggy plateau by Llyn yr Adur. At path junction (657478, flattened cairn) turn SE onto twisting undulating path leading to large abandoned quarry on wide saddle. Behind prominent ruin ascend inclines, etc to moor where well-marked path leads off left of first large quarry pit towards lowest point of skyline ahead – shallow col at 666449 with path junction and cairn. Follow good path contouring R round hillside for 400 m, then descend left on vague path to N end of Llyn Stwlan Dam. (500 m/1,640 ft).
5.5 kms/3½ miles

(3) Cross dam and ascend broken ground into shallow cwm below NE flank of Moelwyn Bach. Pass left below prominent quarried cave to reach stepped rib on left skyline. Scramble up steep grass and rocky bluffs to summit plateau, cross glacis and pools NW to cairn of MOELWYN BACH (711 m/2,334 ft). If unsure of route or ability on scrambly ground, use (3.A).
1.5 kms/1 mile

(4) Strike ENE 150 m to vague marshy saddle above cliffs where narrow path descends diagonally left across steep scree-covered hillside to Bwlch Stwlan (585 m/1,920 ft). Ascend rocky ridge N, two easy scrambly steps, to shoulder then zigzag up steep grass ridge to MOELWYN MAWR summit (770 m/2,527 ft). Descend grassy ENE ridge to metalled lane 0.5 km S of Croesor village.
5.5 kms/3½ miles

Variations
(3.A) Do not descend to dam from the contour path but follow it easily to Bwlch Stwlan. From here ascend MOELWYN BACH by descent route used in (3) above. Bwlch also reached easily from S end dam.
1.5 kms/1 mile

(4.A) From MOELWYN BACH summit descend easy grassy W ridge to metalled lane 1.5 kms S of Croesor, thus avoiding Moelwyn Mawr.
4.5 kms/2¾ miles

Moelwyn Bach displays its most rugged flank to Llyn Stwlan, dammed in 1963 by the CEGB. Our route crosses the dam and ascends the mountain virtually by the left skyline and the descent route to Bwlch Stwlan is also well seen.

Cader Idris   Gwynedd, North Wales

OS 1: 50,000 Sheet 124

. . . the polished peak . . . where God had sat on the seventh day to bless the Mawddach estuary.

Huw Jones 'Cadir Idris' from the *Anglo Welsh Review*

The walls of Dolgellau, they say, are a mile high. Actually Cader Idris with its 6 miles (10 kilometres) of northern crags rears to only 2,928 feet, a little over half a mile above this little grey town at the head of the beautiful Mawddach estuary. But certainly this magnificent mountain dominates the country hereabouts and is a magnet for mountain lovers of all kinds.

Cader Idris: the name means Chair – or Stronghold – of Idris. Was Idris a giant, or a poet, or a prince? Was he Arthur himself? No one is sure. Certainly Cwm y Gadair (Gadair = Cader), scooped deep from the northern crags below the summit, appears like a gigantic chair when seen from afar. More of a range than a single mountain, the 20-kilometre (12-mile) ridge of Cader springs from the sea above Tywyn and rises to nine tops above 2,000 feet (600 metres). The valleys to north and south, the one a striking tidal estuary with wooded shores, the other a deep and tranquil lake-floored glen, are among the finest in Wales. The glory of Cader however is its succession of sculpted cwms, five holding tarns, of which Cwm Cau –

Mynedd Pencoed rises a thousand feet over the tranquil waters of Llyn Cau on the southern flanks of Cader Idris.

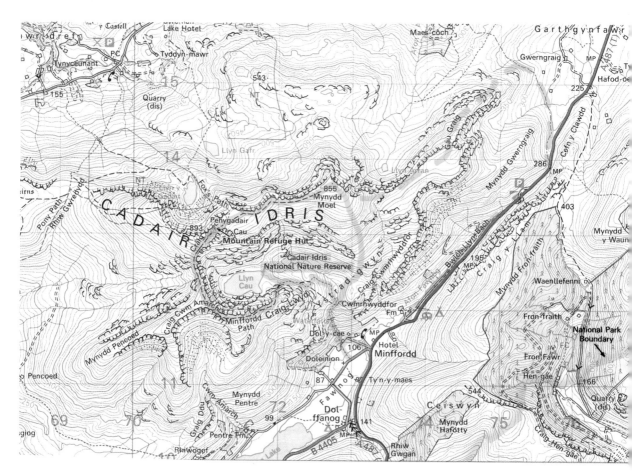

the 'Hollow Cwm' – is famed as a perfect example and with its surrounding hillsides and the ferny woods below is now an NCC Nature Reserve.

The regular tourist route to Penygadair, Cader's summit, ascends the broad easterly ridge – the so-called Pony Path – but discerning hill walkers will find the more rugged route suggested here far more interesting. Craggy bluffs and enchanted woods through which the Nant Cader plunges in a series of continuous cascades and waterfalls, provide a truly dramatic start and before beginning the steep ascent from the cwm above to the ridge of Craig Lwyd it is worth diverting along the grassy floor to visit the shores of Llyn Cau, invisible until almost the last moment. The view across the dark waters to the brooding crags is an imposing one. Owen Glyn Jones, greatest of Victorian rock climbers, cut his teeth amid this great phlanx of gullies and buttresses but such climbs are not really fashionable today. Meanwhile, the main path traverses the ridge above and shortly before reaching Mynydd Pencoed the now sparkling waters of the lake can be glimpsed through the forbidding cleft of Great Gully, one of Jones's classic climbs, and for years a major *tour de force* until rock fall destroyed its crux.

From Bwlch Cau beyond connoisseurs can continue their ascent around the steeply rising cwm lip rather than remaining on the main trail. Crouching among the boulders below the rocky summit is a little refuge shelter, successor to a refreshment hut erected here by Dolgellau guide Richard Pugh in the 1830s, when the ancient belief that those who spent the night alone on the summit would descend either blind, mad or a poet already seemed rather far fetched! The wide summit panorama includes most of the mountains of North and Central Wales but the proximity of the sea is part of Cader's charm and the closeby lip of Cwm y Gadair provides a foreground for the splendid vista down the glinting estuary to the sands of Barmouth and the wide ocean. This cwm is hardly less impressive than Cwm Cau and the jagged rib rising above its little lake is the celebrated Cyfrwy Arete on which Sir Arnold Lunn met with the near fatal accident that switched his destiny from rock climbing to be the founding father of modern skiing.

Descending eastward the route passes the head of the Fox's Path, the steep, shaly and unpleasant descent into Cwm y Gadair, and continues along the precipitous northern edge of a wide ridge carpeted with short wiry grass and patterns of small stones. On this airy upland the rise to Mynydd Moel is hardly noticed. Just past the cairn the ridge drops steeply round the secluded little Cwm Aran with its tiny tarn then runs flat to the more broken ground of Gau Graig. One can continue along this ridge and return beneath the unfrequented south-east face of the mountain – in summer a maze of rocky ribs and bilberry-hung hollows – but it is a long route and the recommended descent strikes directly down steepening grassy slopes to rejoin eventually the ascent route at the lip of Cwm Cau.

From Mynydd Moel the main crest of Cader Idris stretches westward towards Pen y Gadair, the main summit of the mountain. Little Llyn y Gafr is visible on the right.

Over Cader Idris

Length: 10 kms/6¼ miles
Height gained: 960 m/3,150 ft
Difficulty: in ascent good paths, often on steep and rocky ground, on descent rough ground and steep slopes
Warning: this is a large isolated mountain taking full force of bad weather, paths often run close to cliff edge, take care in windy or bad conditions
Note: much of route lies within NCC Reserve, respect by-laws posted at Idris Gate. Path erosion is occurring, avoid such areas especially on descent route
Start: good SNP car-park at 732115 just W of junction A487 with B4405, or on foot 300 m along B4405 at iron gates bearing legend Idris Ltd. Good campsites and B&B at two cottages closeby. (94 m/308 ft).

(1) From either start follow signed paths that cross river and meet at edge of woods. Badly eroded path now climbs steeply through woods above stream gorge to open ground and cwm lip. Easy path continues to shore of Llyn Cau. (470 m/1,540 ft).
2.5 kms/1½ miles

(2) At prominent shark-fin rock 400 m before lake (720123) fork left to rocky path zigzaging steeply up to ridge and continuing over minor top of CRAIG LWYD (686 m/2,251 ft) to fence and stile at summit of MYNYDD PENCOED (798 m/2,617 ft).

Short descent N near cliff edge leads easily to Bwlch Cau before path zigzags up wide 'final slopes to meet 'Pony Path' among rocky tors close to PENYGADAIR (893 m/2,928 ft) – summit of CADER IDRIS, refuge shelter 30 m N of trig point.
2.5 kms/1½ miles

(3) Descend NE over boulders to long wide ridge, follow easily edge of N cliffs over slight eminence of Twr Du to stile in fence and MYNYDD MOEL summit and shelter-circle (863 m/2,831 ft). Descend SE down wide steepening slopes keeping well L of NCC fence and eroded traces of path closeby. Avoid scree band to L or R. When angle eases stile leads W into shallow re-entrant, cross brackeny hillside to NW corner of fir plantation where stream is easily crossed and ascent route rejoined.
5 kms/3¼ miles

Alternative
(3.A) From Mynydd Moel path descends steeply SE round head of Cwm Aran, continuing NE over several stiles along wide undulating ridge to Gau Graig. Descend long spur, indistinct traces of path and some broken ground, to strike bridle path at 754152 continue S to A487 road. At 751133, 300 m SW of large layby, fork right to follow old road descending to valley floor eventually rejoining highway 500 m NE of Minffordd junction close to start.
10.5 kms/6½ miles from Penygadair

The Llangollen Escarpments

Clwyd, North Wales

OS 1: 50,000 Sheets 116, 117, 125

The first real landmark in Wales as the traveller hurries up the A5 road towards Snowdonia is the sharp cone of Dinas Bran above the Dee, and with luck the arched ruins on its summit might even be silhouetted against the evening sun. Before reaching the outskirts of Llangollen our traveller might briefly glimpse behind Dinas Bran a broad hillside topped by tiers of white limestone. This is Eglwyseg Mountain, not really a mountain, more the impressive edge of a domed moorland plateau.

Eglwyseg – a name likely to confuse an English tongue – is pronounced 'egloosik' and means 'church lands': presumably it once belonged to the medieval Cistercian Abbey of Valle Crucis whose ruins still stand beside the Eglwyseg river a couple of kilometres below the mountain. The Llangollen area has a long history, the town with its fourteenth-century bridge is one of the traditional 'Seven Wonders of Wales' while the fortress of Dinas Bran itself – 'Castle of the Crows' and surely all but impregnable – was the eighth-century stronghold of the Princes of Powys. Until the designation of the 270-kilometre (168-mile) Offa's Dyke Long Distance Footpath in 1971, Eglwyseg Mountain and the beautiful valleys beneath it were comparatively unknown to other than local walkers. The definitive route however follows an old and narrow path – known locally as the Cow's Path – below the western scarp of the hill, and the magnificent sequence of gleaming limestone crags that line the edge above has become more familiar. Indeed this is probably the most

The great limestone prow of Craig Arthur rears over the Eglwyseg valley in this view northward along the Cow's Path that runs along the base of the escarpment.

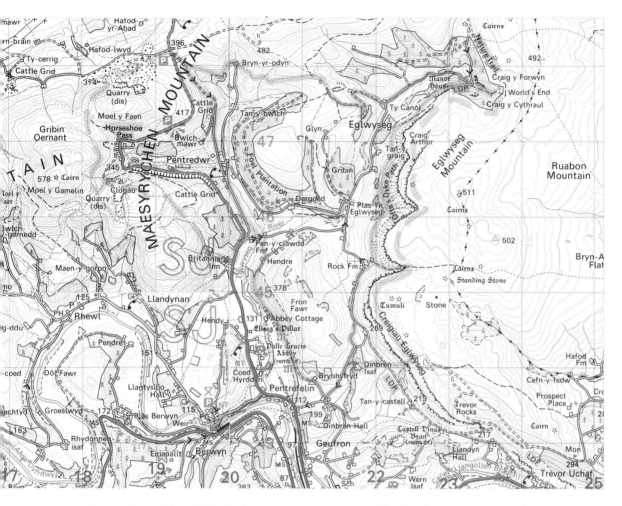

spectacular section of the Offa's Dyke route.

The delightful valleys of the Eglwyseg River and its tributaries are deep and narrow and H-shaped – and must have been even more beautiful before the modern road, the A542, was constructed over the Horseshoe Pass. The first leg of our suggested route follows an ancient grassy track around the lonely head of the western valley, over a gorsey saddle, down a green lane from where there are excellent views of the imposing cliffs ahead, and into the secluded eastern valley – Eglwyseg Valley itself. This tranquil glen beneath the white cliffs is traversed only by the burbling kingcup-bordered stream and a narrow lane set about with hazel, hawthorn and tall ash trees. At the head of the valley stands an ancient manor house, a jewel in a sylvan setting. Perfect proportions and geometrically patterned black and white timbering emphasize the date above the door

–1563. The furthermost recess of the valley is appropriately known as World's End and here our route joins the 'Cow's Path' traversing the base of the cliffs. At first a low line, the cliffs rapidly grow higher and the first major bastion is Craig Arthur, over 30 metres high (100 feet), the largest unbroken crag on Eglwyseg Mountain and a favourite modern rock-climbing area. The path crosses patches of scree and areas of greens-ward dotted with stunted thorn bushes and passes the remains of old lime-kilns: ravens circle overhead.

Above Rock Farm a rugged and popular path leads up beside waterfalls through a cleft in the cliffs to the wide moorland above. Strictly speaking – and inexplicably – this path is not a right of way although 500 metres beyond the cliff top it becomes one and continues for some 5 kilometres (3 miles) over the managed grouse moor of Ruabon Mountain to the village of

Penycae. Neither is our suggested route south-ward along the cliff top a right of way – though traversing 'common land' and well frequented – and the entire cliff-top section can be bypassed by continuing the Offa's Dyke route along the lane at the cliff bottom. Nevertheless the limestone moorland along the cliff edge is delightful walking country and the splendid views from it over the smiling vale extend to the distant mountains of Snowdonia.

It is important, but not too difficult, to locate the correct gulch down which the next path – this time a right of way – drops through the crags to the lane below. A rural section follows, descending to what was once an old tramway running through the woods along the edge of the Valle Crucis meadows – a meander of the Dee abandoned long ago – where a path leads off

to the closeby abbey, a worthwhile diversion. The final section of the route takes the quiet lane up the western branch of the Eglwyseg Valley, once the old road over the Horseshoe Pass, and climbs steeply back to the start. A more strenuous alternative crosses the steep moorland of Maesyrchen Mountain with its grey slate quarries, a very different landscape from the limestone mountain across the valley.

Eglwyseg Scarps

Length : 18 kms/11¼ miles
Total height gained: 800 m/2,650 ft
Difficulty : a fairly gentle route on good paths or metalled lanes, but moorland section trackless though easy going with rocky outcrops to negotiate and two steep sections
Warning : exercise caution when walking above vertical cliffs especially in windy or bad conditions

Start : large parking area at 192482 opposite Ponderosa Café. 396 m/1300 ft.

(1) 100 m SE down Pentredwr Lane grassy track forks L descending gradually to Bryn-yr-odyn, path continues behind cottage, contouring hillside to broad saddle and green lane, descend taking L fork at each junction via hairpin into deep valley on L, past cottage to lane at Ty Canol. Follow lane L to woods and ford at World's End (233477, 310 m/1,017 ft).
5.5 kms/3½ miles

(2) Follow 'Offa's Dyke' waymark S from lane through wood onto open stony hillside, good path contours steep slopes below cliffs to stream at 220454 (255 m/837 ft) in cwm above Rock Farm. Rough path leads steeply E up narrowing valley through cliffs to re-entrant in moorland above, at c 225453 strike up R off path and contour above upper tier of cliffs (425 m/1,395 ft) W then S to 2nd deep re-entrant in cliff top (225441) with straggly pine trees beyond. Descend steep rocky path N side stream, dropping diagonally R below cliffs to lane.
6 kms/3¾ miles

(3) RoW opposite descends W across fields to Dinbren Isaf farm and lane beyond, descend lane steeply L, bridle path leads off R 60 m before junction, passes Brynhyfryd and contours N through woods to Hendre. Neglected RoW cuts corner across fields L to lane by bridge (204457: 140 m/460 ft). Ascend lane L 60 m, RoW cuts corner R to lane leading N up valley through Pentredwr hamlet and steeply up to start.
7 kms/4¼ miles

Variations
(2.A) From World's End ford follow FC Nature Trail up valley E through woods to open moorland, strike R along forest boundary until above cliffs and contour S above Craig Arthur to join (2) at path above Rock Farm in 3rd large re-entrant in cliff top (225453).
Extra 1 kms/½ mile

(3.A) From bridge 204457 continue W to main road then S 250 m to Britannia Inn. RoW leads NW behind Inn up steep moorland slopes Maesyrychen Mountain. Pass abandoned quarry on first summit (450 m/1,475 ft) to saddle and follow contour path N above Horseshoe Pass to extensive abandoned quarry on Moel y Fan, descend NE to start.
Extra 2.5 kms/1½ miles, +65 m/213 ft

Seen westward from Offa's Dyke footpath, the cliffs of the Eglwyseg escarpment look down on the strange peak of Dinas Bran, crowned with its ruined fortress.

The Gentle Berwyn Clwyd, North Wales

OS 1:50,000 Sheet 125

'Aren't they the hills on the left just past Llangollen?' The Berwyn is just a name to the majority of English mountain lovers heading up the A5 to Snowdonia, and its northern flanks seem unremarkable as they rise steeply above the twisting Dee. But the Berwyn is actually quite an extensive range, its single ridge stretches almost 30 kilometres (18 miles) from Llangollen to Lake Vyrnwy and twenty-one summits top 2,000 feet (600 metres), no less than ten of them classed as separate mountains. And only one road crosses the Berwyn near its southern end at the little pass of Milltir Gerrig. The Berwyn range is not the border but it is the final crest of Wales before the Shropshire plain. Holding its beauty close to its heart, the Berwyn is best approached from the head of the Rhaeadr valley above the sleepy little 'waterfall village in the pig glen' –

Llanrhaeadr-ym-Mochnant. Rhaeadr – 'water-fall' – is the operative word here for at the very end of the valley stands Pistyll Rhaeadr, the 'spout waterfall' and one of the traditional Severn Wonders of Wales: it is certainly the jewel in the heart of the Berwyn with the highest summits and most impressive scenery standing to the north within easy reach. Any walk on the Berwyn should include a close look at the waterfall, the ferny spray-damp wood at its foot easily reached by a short public path from the lane end. The water pours over the lip of a dark crag 75 metres (240 feet) above and falls as a white column to explode behind a natural arch

Little Llyn Lluncaws lies below the eastern flank of Moel Sych. The most interesting ascent route is by the east ridge from where Cadair Berwyn is seen rising across the cwm.

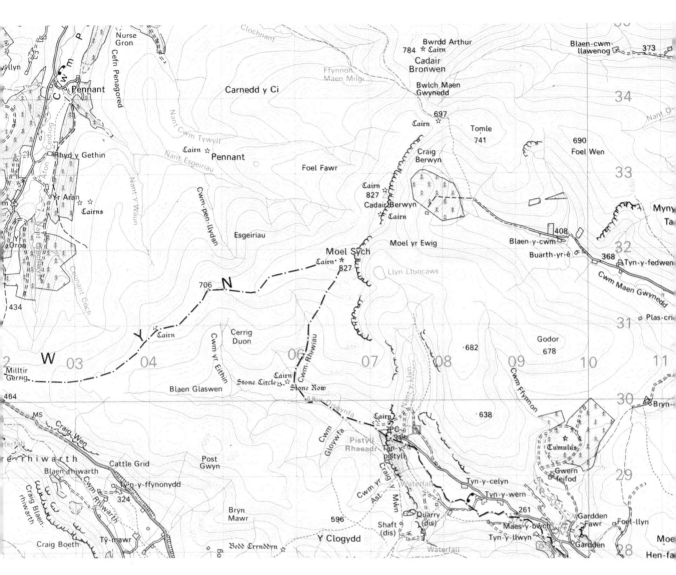

two-thirds of the way down. Dr Johnson, who came here in the 1770s, is said to have remarked 'Very high and in rainy weather very copious', an accurate if unimaginative comment on such a beautiful and imposing place.

A path zigzags steeply up above the falls where the Afon Dysgynfa flows down a wide green valley and into a series of pretty cataracts among the trees before surging over the cliff edge. Another path leads northwards from Tan-y-pistyll up an attractively desolate little glen towards Llyn Lluncaws, the only tarn in the range, lying beneath the craggy eastern face of Moel Sych. At 827 metres (2,713 feet) Moel Sych is the highest point in the Berwyn and its east ridge, cradling the little lake like a protective arm, provides the most interesting ascent. Unfortunately the top is flat and unprepossessing, just a small cairn and a junction of fences, though the view is excellent round a full 340 degrees encompassing both Snowdon and the Long Myndd, while the little lake below, its surface covered with strange wide-leaved pondweed, appears in certain lights as a pool of molten metal. Cadair Berwyn, a kilometre northward along the grassy but sharp-lipped ridge, is a more imposing summit with a rocky edge, a stone shelter-circle and an OS pillar, unfortunately in real terms it is just one foot lower than Moel Sych although its metric height is the same. The ridge continues easily northward to Bwlch Maen Gwynedd, crossed by an ancient trackway

Pistyll Rhaeadr, where the Afon Dysgynfa plunges over a high crag on the southern flanks of the Moel Sych massif, is the highest waterfall in Wales.

and presumably once the border of the medieval principality of Gwynedd, before rising again to Cadair Bronwen whose actual summit is known as Bwrdd Arthur – 'Arthur's Table' (78 metres/2,572 feet). Northward now the ridge flattens out and loses height, and though still good wide walking country its character becomes one of moorland hills rather than gentle mountains. However the long eastern spur that springs from the ridge just south of Bwlch Maen Gwynedd is not without interest and its second top, Foel Wen (690 metres/2,265 feet), is a worthy little summit and a 'separate mountain'. From Moel Sych the main crest falls away southward as a flat heathery ridge to Milltir Gerrig but its grassy southern shoulder drops to the Disgynfa valley not far above the falls and provides a convenient descent route.

Like so much of Wales, the Berwyn is sheep country, in fact no fewer than ninety-six farmers hold grazing rights on the western flanks alone, a large part of which has recently been acquired by the Nature Conservancy Council. Although the range is well frequented by walkers, well-used paths traverse the main ridges, and a major fell-running event is held every September, the only rights of way to approach the high tops are the ancient track over Bwlch Maen Gwynedd and the path leading almost to Llyn Lluncaws, all other access is only on the acquiescence of the local landowners though happily an atmosphere of tolerance and reason currently prevails. Starting from Tan-y-pistyll several circular routes will suggest themselves, both short and long, and nothing that has been described is in any way difficult or dangerous – except the abrupt lip of the Falls: the discerning hill-walker can safely make his own arrangements to explore these airy ridges and lonely recesses.

Berwyn Circuits

Difficulty: easy going on all obvious routes, grassy hillsides, bracken, several short steepish sections. This is high isolated ground, appropriate equipment should be worn/carried

Start: good parking beside the narrow lane at Tan-y-pistyll 076293, or beside the swiss chalet-style tea room beyond for modest charge

Routes: as legal access here is not formalized, walkers should seek permission locally, as necessary, for the itineraries they plan

Pumlumon – the Heart of Wales

OS 1 : 50,000 Sheet 135

Raising its crest almost to 2,500 feet, just above the level of the great upland plateau of Central Wales and the convoluted valleys that cut into it, Pumlumon has been variously described as a 'sodden weariness' by one ancient traveller and as 'probably the best viewpoint in Wales' by the great geologist Sir Arthur Trueman. To most people the truth will lie somewhere in between.

Pumlumon, often Anglicized to Plynlimon,

would appear to mean 'five tops' – there are certainly four definite summits above 2,000 feet (600 metres) besides several points which might appear as tops. Pumlumon is in fact a series of smooth hills covered in peat bog and poor grassy pasture strung out along a broad flat-topped ridge that runs south-west to north-east for some 14 kilometres (9 miles). A dozen cwms cut into the ridge flanks, most of them shallow and

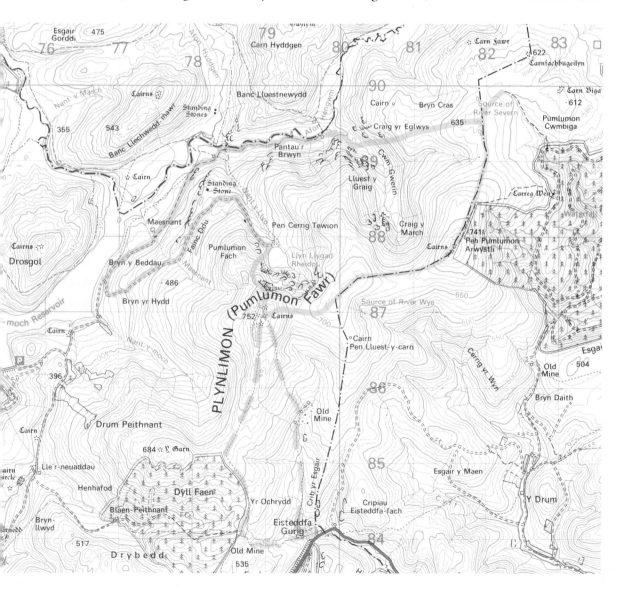

unremarkable, although three – which our route will visit – are of interest.

Pumlumon's claim to fame, besides being virtually in the centre of Wales and the highest point between Cader Idris and the Brecon Beacons, is that two of Britain's great rivers – the Wye and Severn – rise high on its eastern flanks; for several centuries travellers have ascended the mountain to visit their sources. Most of the upland area of the mountain is common land belonging to the Crown Estates to which free public access was granted in 1932, thus with its generally gentle contours and straightforward terrain Pumlumon offers excellent walking in a fine situation under a wide sky. Both the two popular routes approach the summit from the south: the shorter waymarked route leaves the A44 road at Eisteddfa Gurig farmhouse café (a small charge is made for parking) on the pass between Wye and Rheidol, the main watershed of Wales at 415 metres/1,360 feet. A longer ridge route leaves the A44 at Dyffryn Castell hotel 4 kilometres ($2\frac{1}{2}$ miles) further west. Linking the two routes gives a circuit of about 7.5 kilometres ($4\frac{3}{4}$ miles).

A more interesting circuit leaves the narrow road above the twisting and not unattractive Nant-y-Moch Reservoir to follow a good access track up to what might be termed the 'Jewel of Pumlumon', the little Llyn Llygad Rheidol – the Source of the Rheidol – nestling beneath steep craggy hillsides in a dark and moody cwm, surely the most spectacular scenery on Pumlumon. The lake itself is the Aberystwyth water supply and is guarded by a notice threatening dire penalties to '... persons found poluting same by bathing or other acts ...' Steep but easy green hillsides lead to the small grassy summit plateau, where ugly fences intrude on the magnificent view which on a good day encompasses the entire width of Wales from the Marches to Cardigan Bay and the two headlands of Lleyn and Preseli. The route onwards is well scarred by passing feet and leads easily to Pumlumon's third highest and least inspiring summit, Pen Pumlumon Llygad-bychan – 'Pumlumon of the Little Source' – where adjacent to the small cairn

Llyn Llygad Rheidol has been called the 'Jewel of Pumlumon' and lies under the mountain's northern face surrounded by the most rugged scenery in the area.

is a slate slab bearing the enigmatic inscription '1865 ↑'. Blaen Gwy – the Source of the Wye – lies some 400 yards due east across a plateau of short windblown grass, over a fence and down into a green gulch which frames the distant hills of the Radnor Forest. It is a worthy birthplace for a famous river.

Stretches of easy path and a fence line continue along the ridge, over a scabby saddle where the overlying peat has eroded away, to the two cairns and several stone shelter-rings that mark Pen Pumlumon Arwystli, Pumlumon's second summit. Now a long gradual descent and a little compass work leads to a wilderness of peat hags, colourful in summer with heather, moss, and bog plants. Here, amid a maze of small trickles, a white post proclaiming 'Tarddiad Afon Hafren' stands over a reedy pool. Here rises the mighty Severn. It is pretty perhaps but hardly impressive. The route now descends into Cwm Gwerin, a fine rugged little valley which leads down to a sizable river, the Afon Hengwyn, where the melancholy ruins of a remote farmstead – Pantau'r Brwyn, the 'Hollow of the Rushes' – stand in an overgrown crag-girt dell beside the water. The boggy track along the river makes heavy going as far as a second ruined cottage below Llyn Llygad Rheidol. Just across the river in the wide green flats beside the Afon Hyddgen two standing stones mark the site of Owain Glyndwr's decisive victory over a small English army in 1401. Gathering his men in this secluded valley, Glyndwr had found himself suprised by superior forces, and the ensuing bloody engagement initiated his bid to create a united and independent Wales.

A dryer and easier trail leads past Maesnant, now an outdoor pursuits base, back to the start.

A Pumlumon Crossing

Length as described: 16 kms/10 miles
Height gained: 600 m/1,970 ft
Difficulty: easy walking on high bleak plateau mostly above 650 m/2,000 ft

Start: careful parking is possible on the roadside verge near track junction at 768874. (350 m/1,150 ft).

(1) Follow jeep-track up and across hillside to Llyn Llygad Rheidol at 510 m/1,675 ft. Ascend steep hillside above W end of dam to obvious shallow re-entrant leading to small grassy col. Climb knobly shoulder to summit plateau where trig point and stone shelter-ring mark summit of PEN PUMLUMON FAWR (752 m/2,468 ft).
4.5 kms/2¾ miles

(2) Descend E on peaty path alongside fence to broad saddle then ascend to plateau and small cairn of PEN PUMLUMON LLYGAD-BYCHAN (723 m/2,372 ft) (not named on map). Source of Wye lies at head of gulch 400 m. E. Follow wide flat ridge parallel to fence, occasional path, over saddle and stony areas to large cairns at summit of PEN PUMLUMON ARWYSTLI (741 m/2,427 ft). Descend N past two small tarns to white cairn at 819899, post 400 yds E over stile marks source of Severn. Retrace steps to first tarn then strike E down wide ridge before descending steeply past rocky outcrops into lower Cwm Gwerin, follow stream to ruin at 797893. (375 m/1,230 ft).
8.5 kms/5¼ miles

(3) Very boggy riverside track leads W to second ruin at 783891 then good path leads to Maesnant. Continue 1 km along road to start.
4 kms/2½ miles

High on the eastern flank of Pumlumon Fawr lies this little hollow – Blaen Gwy – the source of the River Wye.

Lonely Elanydd

Central Wales

OS 1 50,000 Sheet 147

'All that I heard him say of (Wales) was, that instead of bleak and barren mountains, there were green and fertile ones;'

James Boswell *Life of Samuel Johnson*: 1774

The Elan Valley cuts deeply into the wide plateau of empty moorland and smoothly domed hills that separates Pumlumon from the Brecon Beacons, an upland so remote that it has been called 'the desert of Wales' but is more generously known as Elanydd. This ancient name was applied loosely by Giraldus Cambrensis, the twelfth-century Welsh traveller, to the southern mountains of Wales, as opposed to Eryri, the northern mountains, but in context he clearly meant this particular upland. Elanydd was the final refuge of the Romano-British chieftain Vortigern from the Saxon invader and from here Owain Glyndwr waged his guerilla campaigns in the fifteenth century. Here too were early Celtic monastic communities and later an important satellite of the famous Cistercian abbey of Strata Florida whose ruins stand on Elanydd's western extremity. Lead, silver and copper were mined here from Roman times until the late nineteenth century and important hordes of bronze axes and Romano-Celtic gold jewellery have been discovered locally. Even the extensive bogs were once celebrated and the local peat was said to be '... scarce inferior to coal ...' But sheep were the real wealth of Elanydd – as they are today – and in the Middle Ages wool was exported to the Continent after a special customs exemption had been granted by King John. Eventually communications improved the romantic appeal of the rugged hillsides and green valleys attracted tourists, among them

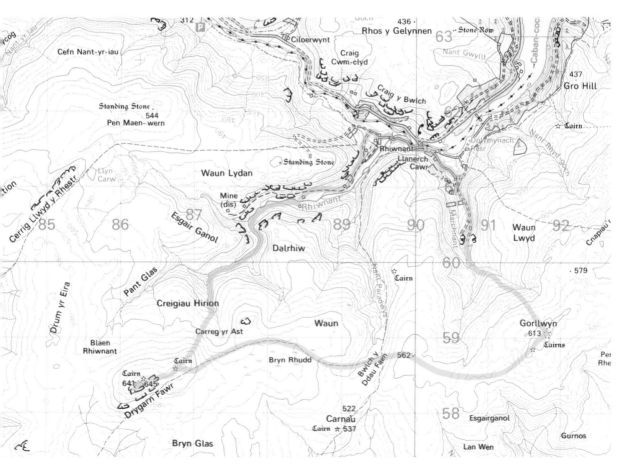

the poet Shelley who stayed near Llanerch in 1810.

However, these hills suffer an annual rainfall of seventy inches and in 1904 three great dams were completed for Birmingham Corporation Waterworks, flooding over 1,200 acres of valley bottom. Parliament meanwhile guaranteed free public access to the entire seventy-one square miles of the Elan watershed. A fourth dam was commissioned in 1952 and today good roads lead along the wooded shores of a chain of attractive lakes into the heart of Elanydd. The Welsh Water Authority, landlord to some hundred people and 45,000 sheep, has created in a low-key but farsighted way, the nearest approach to an American-style National Park – one actually owned by its administrator – in Britain. Recreational use such as walking, pony trekking, fishing and bird watching is en-

couraged, an interesting visitor centre is open daily below the Caban-coch dam and there is a helpful ranger service.

The freedom to roam at will – always respecting the rights of the farmers – gives scope for several interesting walks especially among the rugged lesser hills either side of the Elan 'portal' or over the ancient drove roads which once linked the Wye Valley to West Wales. The circuit described traverses the two highest of Elanydd's three 2,000-foot tops. It has a rare lonely quality, for these unfrequented hills are virtually trackless and rippling purple moor grass sets off distant vistas of cloud-shadowed plateaux shared only with semi-wild ponies, the circling red kites and the ubiquitous sheep. Easy going leads to the summit of Gorllwyn from where there are superb views southward over the patchwork field of the Irfon valley to all four

massifs of the Brecon Beacons National Park. At first Drygarn Fawr with its twin tower-like cairns is visible in the distance only to disappear as the wide swell of the ridge becomes broken by peat hags eventually fading into a desert of awkward tussocky moorland slashed by the deep gash of Bwlch y Ddau Faen. Then a cairn reappears and firmer ground leads to the rocky bilberry-hung crest that links these two strange drum-shaped constructions. Typically the mountain streams of Elanydd are deep-cut and the Afon Rhiwnant followed on the descent route is no exception. Presenting an unexpected contrast to the moorlands above with its twisting tumbling course and pretty cataracts, some intriguing pot-holes, a fine waterfall and isolated rowans overhanging deep pools, it makes a fitting final stage to an unusual excursion.

A Circuit in Elanydd

Length: 16 kms/10 miles
Total ascent: 490 m/1,600 ft
Difficulty: strenuous but never steep walking over trackless, rough and often boggy country. Confusing terrain, map and compass useful even in good conditions
Note: patrolling rangers ask that walkers out overnight leave a note on their car or more securely on the ranger ansaphone tel: 810-880

Start: small car-park at 901616 near Llanerch Cawr phone box. (260 m/850 ft).

(1) Cross bridge opposite car-park following lane SE past bungalow, across stream bridge then up R on wide track to old quarry (907603). On trackless hillside ahead ascend rib between streams, continuing upwards to summit GORLLWYN, low rocky cairns, OS pillar (613 m/2,009 ft).
4 kms/2½ miles

(2) From tall cairn 300 m SW, follow high ground W to Pt 562, peaty hollows, ponds, stony patches. Irregular sequence small concrete posts, useful for navigation, marks watershed. Descend to marshy Bwlch y Ddau Faen (510 m/1,670 ft), cross stream to gain boggy plateau Bryn Rhudd. Continue WSW, featureless, rough, to conspicuous 6 m (20 ft) white-topped cairn on rocky outcrop DRYGARN FAWR and on to OS pillar at second cairn (641 m/2,104 ft).
6 kms/3¾ miles

(3) Descend easily NE from first cairn into stream defile, continue past cataracts, join Pant Glas stream at 872598. Take S bank path through narrow glen, past major confluence, waterfall, into Rhiwnant valley. When possible cross stream to join mine track descending N side valley, best place probably near old workings 884607, track continues to Rhiwnant Farm then E to start.
6 kms/3¾ miles

The strange tower-like cairn that crowns the remote summit of Drygarn Fawr. This is desolate, open moorland dotted with peat bogs.

The Beacons Crest South Wales

OS 1 : 50,000 Sheet 160

'Brecknockshire is a meer inland county
...' The English jestingly call it
Breakneckshire, Tis mountainous to an
extremity...'

Daniel Defoe:
*A Tour through the Whole
Island of Great Britain*: 1727

The Brecon Beacons National Park, a group of
four adjoining upland massifs, contains the most
splendid mountain country in southern Wales.
There are other mountains more lonely or
perhaps more atmospheric but these are the
steepest, the highest and the least gentle mountains south of Cader Idris. Each flaunts, in one
form or another, great north-facing scarps of
Old Red Sandstone, yet their character is very
different. Pen y Fan, the culminating point of the
massif that lends its name to the entire Park, is
just 94 feet short of the magic 3,000-foot mark,

its name aptly meaning 'Top of the Beacon' for
its summit can be seen from deep into Central
Wales, from the Cotswolds and even from the
Exmoor coast. Five other tops rise above 2,500
feet (760 metres) and this large area of high
ground displays the harsh environmental conditions that go with it.

From the Vale of Usk these seem shapely
peaks but from elsewhere the truncated main
tops appear disappointing and suggest a comic
strip rendering of minor lunar volcanoes. Their
glory however is in their northern flanks where
steep and sometimes craggy faces rise from a
sequence of deep and attractive glacier-carved
cwms. Elegant ridges divide the cwms and their
meeting points with the scalloped northern scarp
form the main summits – a classic formula. With
their typically grassy yet steep enough slopes and
real mountain ambience the Beacons offer many

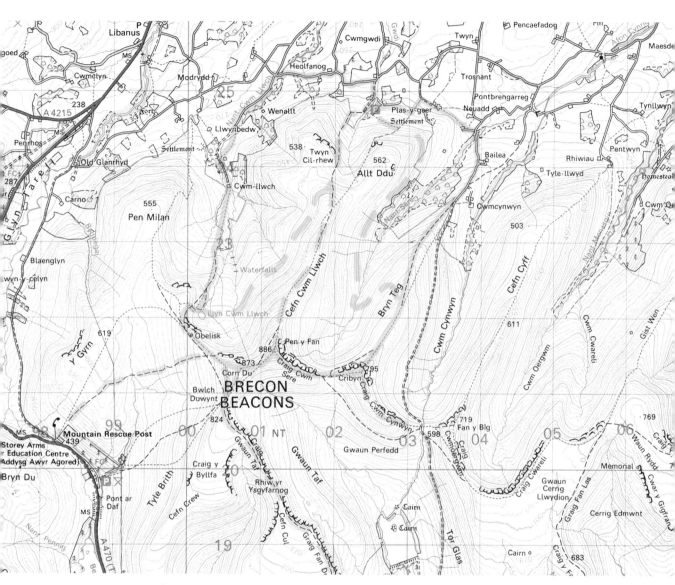

worthy and challenging routes to discerning hill walkers. The heavily eroded 'tourist' route to Pen y Fan ascending the western flank from the Storey Arms – once an inn now an outdoor centre – on the A470 Brecon to Merthyr Tydfil road, is of little interest.

Routes from the south, typically gentler than those from the north, start from the mountain road traversing the attractive Taf Fechan valley. A pleasant 'horseshoe' of about 12 kilometres ($7\frac{1}{2}$

From the steep final section of the north-east ridge of Y Cribyn there are impressive views across Cwm Sere to the precipitous face of Pen y Fan – the Beacon's highest peak. The truncated summit of Corn Du can be seen in the distance.

miles) round the upper reaches of the valley follows the ancient trackway – thought to be a Roman Road – to Gap, the lowest pass over the Beacons at 032205, before crossing the four highest tops: a convenient start is the forest car-park at 036171 below the Neuadd – or 'Zulu' – reservoir. The challenging east-west traverse of the entire range crosses the peaty plateau east of Gap keeping to the easier terrain of the scarp edge, to link Talybont to Libanus, a distance of some 18 kilometres (11 miles). But the classic circuit from the north detailed here includes the highest summits and the most spectacular scenery.

The grassy Bryn Teg ridge – which translates

as 'beautiful hill' – surely lives up to its name, for it sweeps up steeper and steeper in smooth symmetry to the seemingly sharp summit of Cribyn. But there is a good path and the final rocky step is hardly a scramble. Across Cwm Sere rears the 400-foot (120-metre) north-east face of Pen y Fan – the largest crag in the Beacons. The red rock layered with green ledges and slashed by dark gullies is an impressive sight but the sandstone is poor and too broken to hold any attraction for the climber; although under a plastering of ice and snow it has provided some excellent sport. From Cribyn the path onwards is fairly steep but badly eroded and carves an ugly scar up a grassy and otherwise graceful hillside. Cliffs fall abruptly from the flat summit of Pen y Fan but the view northward over them, across the Vale of Usk with its little fields and white cottages to the Mynydd Eppynt and the distant blue tablelands of Elanydd must be the best in the Beacons. On the summit, and also on the tops of Cribyn and Corn Du, there are traces of Bronze Age cairns: the latter summit was excavated in 1978 and contained pottery cremation urns dated to around 1,800 BC. It is believed that folk then lived high on the Beacons – hunting, herding and subsistance farming – until overgrazing, soil exhaustion and deforestation interacted with a wetter colder climate and forced them to lower ground. Steep at first, the descent from Corn Du leads down to the dark little lake cradled in the green head of Cwm Llwch past the Tommy Jones obelisk marking the spot where in the summer of 1900 after a month long search the body of a missing child was found, dead from exposure. Tommy was a miner's son who disappeared while visiting his grandfather at Cwm-llwch farm. A tragic tale.

Some good waterfalls on the eastern fork of the Nat Llwch are worth visiting on the way down the valley and before reaching the hill fence. Then pleasant lanes and pretty woods complete the circuit back to the starting point.

A Brecon Beacons Circuit

Distance covered: 15 + kms/9½ miles
Height gained: 825 m/2,700 ft
Difficulty: grassy hillsides and well-marked paths except for steep semi-scramble below summit of Y Cribyn
Caution: on steep edges in high winds or winter. Conditions often unexpectedly severe high up, appropriate equipment essential

Start: car-park on lane 500 m S of Blaen-Gwdi farm at 024248. (297 m/975 ft).

(1) Strike E above fence line 600 m to track, 200 m N lane leads E via Plasgaer to minor road and Nant Sere bridge at 039244, continue S to lane end at 036235.
3 kms/2 miles

(2) Good footpath ascends open hillside SW onto Bryn-teg ridge. Path steepens to final short very steep stony section leading directly to small summit Y CRIBYN (795 m/2,608 ft). Easy path leads W along scarp edge, via pronounced saddle, to broad summit PEN Y FAN (886 m/2,906 ft).
4 kms/2½ miles

(3) Continue easily to wide summit CORN DU (873 m/2,863 ft). Descend NW Ridge, initial steep section avoidable by traverse path from next saddle to S (extra 0.5 km). At Tommy Jones obelisk (000218) strike N along scarp then descend to Llyn-cwm-llwch (580 m/1,900 ft). Easy path descends valley to lane head at Cwm-llwch farm (005238) (305 m/1,000 ft). Follow RoW then lane N to crossroads at 012252, minor road leads E to Blaen-Gwdi.
7.5 kms/4¾ miles

Alternatives
(1.A) From car-park contour above hill fence into Cwm Sere ascending to join Bryn Teg ridge at c 600 m/2,000 ft. Occasional path.

(3.A) From Pen y Fan summit good path descends initially steep N Ridge directly to start, white markers indicate lower section.
3.5 kms/2¼ miles

(3.B) From Llyn-cwm-llwch contour hillside to NE to join (3.A) path near 019238, rough going, no path.
Saves 2 kms/1¼ miles

Steep crags fall northward from close beside the summit of Pen y Fan, the highest point in Wales south of Snowdonia. In the distance lies the Vale of Usk.

Carmarthen Fan – The Black Mountain

South Wales

OS 1:50,000 Sheet 160

Mynydd Ddu the Welsh call it – the Black Mountain. And so it seems even on balmy summer days when skylarks sing and cloud shadows dapple its swelling moorland plinth, while this long wedge of mountain broods dark and mysterious against the sky.

The most westerly massif in the Brecon Beacons National Park and also the most desolate, for the connoisseur the Mynydd Ddu is also the most beautiful. The spectacular scenery is concentrated at the north-eastern corner of the 20 kilometres (12 miles) of upland which bears the name Black Mountain on the map, while the extensive limestone moors to south and west are windswept, almost featureless and very remote – and of considerable ecological interest. Under the moors lies the famous Dan-yr-Ogof cave system. Yet at night from the summit the whole southern sky glows orange from the lights of the villages and towns that cluster along the valleys beyond the moors, a reminder that Swansea is but twenty miles away.

There are five 2,000-foot summits on the Black Mountain, the two highest standing either side of the distinctive north ridge of the main massif and either side of the boundary between the ancient counties of Brecknockshire and Carmarthenshire – now Powys and Dyfed – hence their names. Bannau Brycheiniog – the 'Horns of Brecon' – is also known perversely as the Carmarthen Fan and is the higher at 802 metres (2,632 feet) while Bannau Sir Gaer, at 750 metres (2,460 feet), is the 'Horns of Carmarthenshire'. Indeed, from the north the mountain does appear to rise to two shallow but sharp tops. Perhaps the Mynydd Ddu is best seen from the western heights of the Fforest Fawr, from above the rumpled moorland that from lower altitudes tends to mask its stature. The precipitous eastern

The view westward at dawn from near the summit of Bannau Brycheiniog along the lip of the 'scarp to Bannau Sir Gaer: the dark waters of Llyn y Fan fach can be seen beyond.

scarp, narrow at first, rises gradually higher and higher to run unbroken for more than 5 kilometres (3 miles) over the slight hump of Bannau Brycheiniog with its graceful prow to the more gentle sweep of the north ridge. Below the prow lies dark Llyn y Fan fawr, lonely and unspoilt, the source of the River Tawe and – through 200 yards of moraine – also a major feeder of the infant Usk. In the valley below and close beside the Tawe and the bleak mountain road that links Trecastle to Glyntawe, stands Cerrig Duon, a strange stone circle, one of the few in Wales. Many would claim that Cerrig Duon reflects the mood of Bannau Brycheiniog – and of Brycheiniog himself who is said to have been a local prince during the Dark Ages.

At the head of the north ridge the escarpment turns sharply back on itself and runs south for a short way before curving round westward and rising again to Bannau Sir Gaer. The impressive scarp edge runs for another $3\frac{1}{2}$ kilometres (2 miles) and holds a few narrow bands of red cliff before fading out in the green ridge that cradles Llyn y Fan fach – the source of the Sawdde which feeds the Tywi. There is a change of

mood on this side of the mountain and this little lake is a smiling one: possibly it holds the sun longer. Anyway, the lake is known to be the home of the Tylwyth Teg – the fairy folk. Tradition has it that a local herd boy met one of the fair ladies of the lake, wooed her and won her. Her fairy father, though he provided a rich dowry of sheep and oxen, cast an unfair spell on the marriage that should he strike her thrice she would vanish. Eventually he did, gently to be sure and under great provocation, and she disappeared again into the lake. But not before they had raised three remarkable sons who, steeped in the secrets of fairy medicine, became the celebrated Physicians of Myddfai, the first of a line of medical men that seems to have lasted in that village until the mid-nineteenth century!

Fairies or not, it is fitting perhaps that the National Park has defined the Black Mountain as a special 'remote area' and has decided not to promote and formalize access to it. The only

Here Bannau Brycheiniog is seen to the west from the heights of the Fforest Fawr some four miles distant. The ascent route climbs to the shallow saddle left of centre past Llyn y Fan fawr which is hidden in a fold of the moor below the scarp.

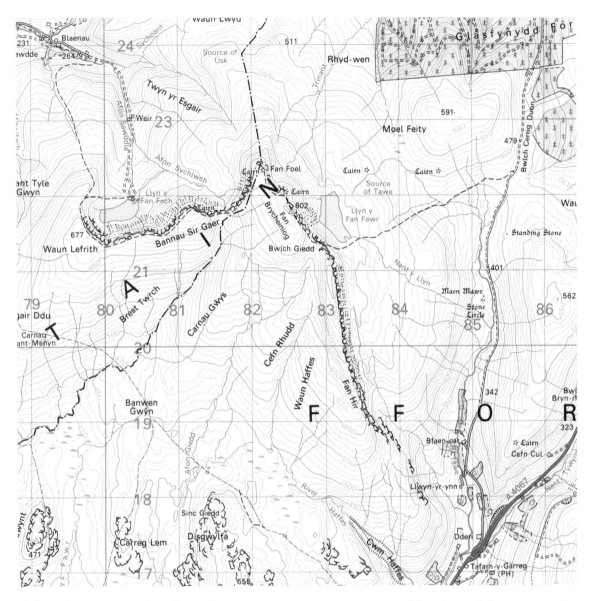

rights of way are ancient long distance routes that cross the moors from south to north linking the Swansea Valley to the Vale of Llandovery: all other access is, strictly speaking, 'unofficial' yet apparently tolerated. Thus we suggest no routes on Mynydd Ddu and leave it to the enthusiastic hill walker to taste the delights of exploration and find his or her own way over the mountain armed only with a map, compass and experience.

The Eildon Hills

Scottish Borders

OS 1: 25,000 NT 53 (OS 1: 50,000 Sheet 73)

'I was but three days in Scotland, and was glad to get back to my own dull flat country, though I did worship the . . . Eildon Hills, more for their Associations than themselves. They are not big enough for that.'

Edward Fitzgerald, letter 1874

Small the Eildon Hills may be but they are as shapely as any in Britain besides being, as one might say, 'well-connected'. These are connoisseur's hills, and though hardly justifying more than an afternoon's expedition their ascent can be conveniently combined with other attractions in the area or used to break a journey to the real mountains of the north. The Eildons are indeed a *bonne-bouche*. Dominating the entire Melrose region, the triple summits of these hills are unequalled as viewpoints in all the Border Country. Their steep cones, cloaked with heather and wiry grass, are the remnants of a great dome – or laccolith – of volcanic lava which invaded the bedding planes of the surrounding old red sandstone some 300 million years ago to be exposed only when the softer sandstone was eventually worn away.

The Eildon Hills are closely associated with Sir Walter Scott who lived at Abbotsford, the Tweedside mansion in their shadow, from 1811 until his death twenty-one years later, writing meanwhile a stream of celebrated works, several of them stimulated by his 'delectable mountains' as he dubbed them. 'Scott's View' – his favourite – looks to the Eildons over the horseshoe bend of the Tweed below Bemersyde Hill a short way from Dryburgh Abbey where he is buried among the ruins. Another ruined abbey lies immediately at the foot of the Eildons: the Gothic splendour of Melrose Abbey, where traditionally the heart of Robert the Bruce is interred. It is one of the treasures of the Borders and is an important Cistercian foundation dating to 1136 whose great wealth was based largely upon wool: standing upon the ancient route into Scotland it was regularly sacked by the English. But the Hills were important as early as the Iron

The Eildon Hills belie their modest height in this dusk view
from the east near Dryburgh Abbey.

Age when a large fortified village some forty acres in extent on the summit of North Hill was the chief settlement of the Selgovae, a Pictish tribe: archaeologists have located over 300 houses within the still clearly discernible twin ramparts. But in AD 79 the Roman legions marched up the Tweed and the inhabitants fled. The invaders built a fort called Trimontium on the river bank at Newstead below the hill's north-eastern flank and established a signal station on its summit.

These are popular hills and the route sugges-ted is a short and simple one which traverses all three summits and the less-frequented eastern flanks of the range. Though all summit paths are steep and stony, only on the southern flanks of Wester Hill and Mid Hill is the going at all 'sporting' – and easily avoidable by other paths obvious on the map. But climbing these short steep slopes of scree, heather, grass and rock does add a flavour of the mountains to the expedition.

It is easy to see how the Eildon Hills command the surrounding countryside in this view from the summit of North Hill towards Mid Hill (right) and Wester Hill.

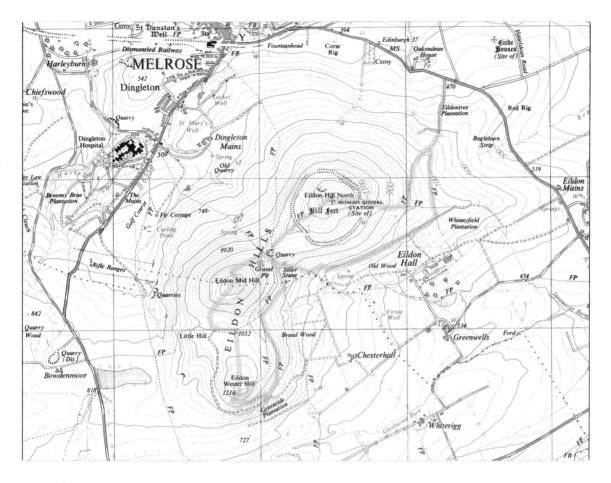

An Eildon Traverse

Length: 7.5 kms/4½ miles
Total ascent: 510 m/1,675 ft
Difficulty: lower paths perhaps muddy, upper paths steep, rough; trackless sections scree, heather, avoidable by paths elsewhere
Note: military firing ranges below W flank Mid Hill, red flags and sentries guard limited dangerous area: territorials may shoot on Sundays

Start: limited vergeside parking on N side A6091 at 563336. (140 m/460 ft).

(1) Across road farm track ascends S, becoming narrow stony trail to gate on to open hillside, several paths diverge. Go L 150 m along plantation edge, find well-defined path leading steeply up vague ESE ridge of EILDON HILL NORTH (404 m/1,325 ft).
1.5 kms/1 mile

(2) Obvious path descends SW to wide northern saddle, descend track L 300 m then strike R on narrow contour path along forest edge, keep L at junctions until below SE flank Wester hill where vehicle track emerges from Greenside Plantation, follow to end at 'quarry', vague contour path continues on scree 100 m across S face. Strike straight up very steep hillside to small cairn EILDON WESTER HILL (371 m/1,217 ft).
3.5 kms/2 miles

(3) Path descends gently N to wide southern saddle, go L to join steep scree path ascending vague SW ridge to topograph and summit trig pt EILDON MID HILL (422 m/1,385 ft). Descend steep path to northern saddle, drop SE again to forest edge, follow wide track just inside wood 800 m ENE until path strikes L across open moorland to rejoin ascent route near gate.
2.5 kms/1½ miles

White Coomb and the Grey Mare's Tail

Southern Uplands

OS 1:50,000 Sheets 78, 79

The traveller driving up Moffatdale towards Birkhill Pass and Selkirk is unlikely to enthuse at the scenery, though he may recognize the dale as an excellent example of a U-shaped glacial valley perhaps more Welsh in character than Scottish. Where the dale starts to steepen he will pass a National Trust for Scotland parking area set between two humped bridges and here he should stop and take a short stroll, for folded into the hillside closeby and unseen from the road is one of the most spectacular sights in southern Scotland – the Grey Mare's Tail – one of Britain's finest waterfalls.

A few minutes ascent up a steep path provides a good and very popular glimpse of this graceful plume of water pouring from the lip of a hanging valley some 60 metres (200 feet) clear into a narrow defile. A series of smaller cataracts above more than double the total fall. The best

view is seen from the depths of the defile itself but the approach path has collapsed and the route is now accessible only to those with mountaineering skills: the waterfall itself has been climbed in winter when frozen solid. However, few panting tourists will follow the regular path above the falls and the jewel of the Tweedsmuir Hills is fortunately left for those prepared to continue upwards, albeit easily, for a further $1\frac{1}{2}$ kilometres (1 mile). It appears quite suddenly almost at your feet as you emerge from a maze of heather-cloaked moraines. Loch Skeen, shimmering water and rippling reeds: a blue boulder-ringed lake studded with tiny islets and cradled by handsome swelling hills. It is a new unsuspected world up here, a gentle world of heather, grass and sky and the valley below is invisible and forgotten. The craggy spur of Mid Craig rises above the western shore of the loch and offers a stylish route to the crest of the hills behind, though not necessarily a shorter circuit. Meanwhile the suggested route follows a fading path along the opposite shore before climbing to the tight windswept grass of the Lochcraig Head plateau. A few metres north of the cairn the junction of stone wall and wire fence marks the meeting point of three counties, Dumfries, Peebles and Selkirk, as well as the boundary of the National Trust's 2,800-acre Loch Skeen property.

After the initial steepish descent to the saddle above Lochcraig – the raven-haunted rocky slopes that arc round the head of Loch Skeen – the boundary wall leads onwards over undulating dun-coloured moorland to Firthhope Rig. A lower boggy alternative avoids the crest of the hills but visits the impressive little gorge of the Midlaw Burn cutting deep in the plateau lip below Donald's Cleuch Head. From Firthhope Rig the most scenic route to White Coomb now follows the southern edge of the plateau

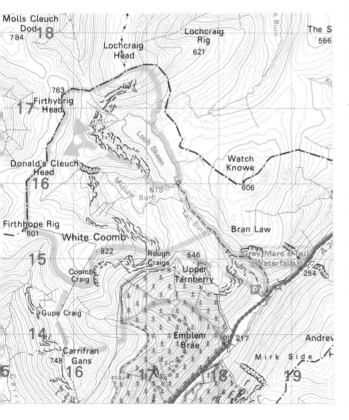

Flowing from Loch Skeen, the Tail Burn plunges over the famous waterfall of the Grey Mare's Tail: the route to Loch Skeen crosses the hillside at upper right.

with good views along the craggy edge of Raven Craig as it sweeps round above the deep trench of the Carrifran glen to shapely Saddle Yoke. Providing transport can be arranged, a traverse round this edge with a descent down the beautiful south ridge of Saddle Yoke, or even onwards over Hart Fell and round the imposing Blackhope glen, provides a fine continuation for energetic walkers.

In bad conditions however the tumbledown wall offers the surest route to White Coomb the small and as yet invisible summit cairn standing just one hundred metres south-west of the first sharp bend in the wall. White Coomb is the fourth highest summit in southern Scotland and like its neighbours it is an unexciting yet strangely tranquil hill surrounded by an ocean of rounded tops and flowing ridges reaching, like waves, an almost consistent height. A second cairn rises a hundred metres further across the broad plateau and provides better views, though the best viewpoint is the plateau edge where the spur of Coomb Craig makes a impressive foreground. The wide pano-

rama extends from the Eildon Hills and the Cheviots to the Lake District and the Mull and hills of Galloway while a keen eye can discern Annan power station fifty miles distant.

The easiest return route follows the wall down through an area of broken slopes to the lowest reasonable crossing point of the Tail Burn above the cascades. A more elegant but rougher descent continues down the long east ridge before dropping through a craggy band to the steep hillside south of the Grey Mare's Tail and the final return to Moffatdale.

White Coomb from Loch Skeen

Length: 13 kms/8 miles
Total ascent: 770 m/2,530 ft
Difficulty: high trackless moorland, usually easy going but occasionally boggy, rarely steep. Map and compass skills desirable

Start: large NTS car-park below Grey Mare's Tail at 187145. (230 m/755 ft)

(1) Ascend steep tourist path above true L bank of Tail Burn, above Falls muddy path continues beside burn to Loch Skeen (510 m/1,675 ft) take rough E shore to small tributary burn near NE corner of loch. Now follow burn to steepening grassy slopes near wall, bearing L ascend to wide summit plateau, near junction wall and fence is small cairn LOCHCRAIG HEAD (800 m/2,625 ft).
4.5 kms/2¾ miles

(2) Descend wide ridge steeply SW and follow broad crest curving to S, usually marked with wall over FIRTHYBRIG HEAD (783 m/2,569 ft) and DONALD'S CLEUCH HEAD (775 m/2,543 ft) to FIRTHHOPE RIG (801 m/2,621 ft). Descend E to shallow saddle then contour S and W round White Coomb plateau to steep shoulder of Coomb Craig, strike N to 2nd small cairn WHITE COOMB summit (822 m/2,695 ft).
5 kms/3½ miles

(3) Go NE 100 m to wall, follow it R, occasional faint path, descending 500 m to rocky step, wall continues down to crossing place Tail Burn above highest cataract, now return down ascent route.
3 kms/2 miles

Variations
(1.A) For shorter circuits: from S end Loch Skeen poor path ascends prominent nose of Mid Craig then traverses ridge above W shore Loch to plateau near Firthybrig Head; continue L to White Coomb or R to Lochcraig Head

(3.A) Descend E ridge White Coomb over rough ground to poor path descending steep shoulder S of waterfall.
2.5 kms/1½ miles

(3.B) From White Coomb descend SW past Coomb Craig to saddle, ascend broad ridge S to CARRIFAN GANS (748 m/2,454 ft). Descend well-defined E ridge breaking L when convenient to join burn at forestry edge, path follows burn to road 1 km below start.
5.5 kms/3½ miles

White Coomb is surrounded by an ocean of rounded tops and flowing ridges. This is the view south-west over the spur of Coomb Craig towards Carrifan Gans with Loch Fell, in the Ettrick group, in the left distance.

Loch Enoch and the Merrick Galloway

OS 1:50,000 Sheet 77

Galloway is the far south-western corner of Scotland, a region of grand upland country all too often ignored by the hurrying Sassenach to whom Glencoe is the next stop beyond the Lakes. This was the Stewartry from which sprung the Scots royal line, the home of Black Douglas and Young Lochinvar, here was the setting for John Buchan's *Thirty Nine Steps* and the wilderness sanctuary of Robert the Bruce. Beyond a periphery of pastoral prosperity the rugged Galloway heartland is an area of rolling mountains, tangled granite hills, scattered lakes and spreading forests far more akin to the Highlands than to the rest of the genteel Southern Uplands, more the haunt of red deer and wild goats than of people. Jutting into the Gulf Stream, Galloway is wetter and lusher than the adjoining Borders and boasts the most extensive peat bogs outside Sutherland and Caithness. Here rises the Merrick, at 843 metres (2,764 feet) the highest point on the Scottish mainland below the Highland Line.

Enjoying easy access, beautiful surroundings and a top-of-the-world summit, the Merrick is a walker's mountain among the best, though it is not a particularly conspicuous one. The culminating point of the range known as the Awful Hand – a fanciful description of its western outline – its feet stand among the serried conifers of Glentrool Forest, part of the huge Galloway Forest Park, the second largest woodland in Scotland, which dates only to the 1920s: the

From Glen Trool our route passes Loch Neldricken on its way to the Merrick, seen here rising to the north beyond the Loch.

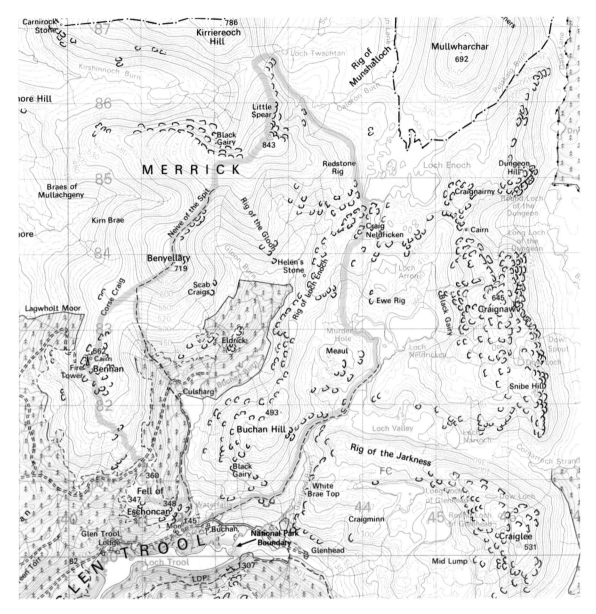

natural oak, birch and pine of the ancient Forest of Buchan are mostly long gone. The waymarked regular Merrick ascent strikes north from a popular car-park above the attractive shores of sinuous Loch Trool where a memorial stone nearby commemorates Bruce's 1307 victory over English troops on the opposite bank: Trool derives from the Gaellic *t'struthail* meaning 'river-like'. Our recommended route however continues eastwards to a good path climbing away towards Loch Valley and the spectacular granite wilderness at Galloway's heart.

In primeval times three great granite batho-liths intruded into the shaly sedimentary rocks of present-day Galloway. The original rocks forced up to roof this massive intrusion have worn away, remaining only as crests of higher ground – the Rhinns of Kells ridge to the east and the Åwful Hand chain to the west – overlooking the now exposed central granite mass where heavy glaciation has left a line of peculiar, low and extremely rocky granite hills with strange names such as Mullwharchar (692 metres/2,270 feet), Rigg of the Jarkness and Dungeon Hill. On one flank of these hills lies the dangerous quaking bog of the Silver Flowe, on the other the chain of enchanting lochs linked by our route, first the shallow lily-scattered Loch Valley and then Loch Neldricken where the so-called Murder Hole at its western extremity is a curious circular rush-fringed lagoon featured in *The Raiders*, a tale by the Edwardian novelist SR Crockett. Surrounded by glacis slabs and erratic boulders and fringed with beaches of silver sand, the third loch, Loch Enoch, fills an ice-scooped rock basin, deep, remote and splendid. It is said that originally its name was 'Loch-in-Loch' because one of its three small islands holds a tiny tarn of its own, equally implausible is the legend that because of the rough rock of the lake bed Loch Enoch trout have evolved without ventral or lower tail fins.

Fairly strenuous going over tussocky slopes leads now below the sculpted eastern flank of the Merrick to a well-defined col between it and Kirriereoch Hill, the adjoining summit, and the ridge rising to the Merrick, with its final narrow shaly crest, is surely the most elegant line on the mountain. The summit, a domed plateau of sparse stony grass and the occasional granite erratic dumped by the departing ice, is the meeting place of no fewer than six ridges, Merrick aptly meaning 'branched finger'. A fascinating viewpoint, the wide prospect stretches not only from nearby Loch Doon – Burns' 'Bonnie Doon' – to spiky Arran, bizarre Ailsa Craig and the long finger of the Mull of Galloway; but on a clear day even to Ben Lomond, the Mountains of Mourne, the Isle of Man and the Cumbrian summits: a shadow on the southern horizon could be Snowdonia. It is worth looking over Black Gairy into the lonely north-western corrie before joining the faint path and following the dry stone dyke which crosses the gentle grassy saddle known as Neive of the Spit, to Benyellery – 'Eagle Hill'. Those anxious to stay high to the bitter end will continue over Bennan and some extraordinarily rough ground to the rocky lip of Eschoncan Fell, a superb eyrie perched over Loch Trool and a worthy final top.

The granite heartland of Galloway: in this view below the eastern flank of the Merrick, Mullwharchar (left) and Dungeon Hill rise beyond remote Loch Enoch.

A Circuit over the Merrick

Length: 17 kms/10½ miles
Total ascent: 840 m/2,750 ft
Difficulty: part easy going on paths, part trackless and a little extremely rough. No scrambling, exposure or crag dangers

Start: good FC car-park at Glen Trool roadhead 416804. (145 m/476 ft).

(1) Follow track E, at bend 200 m past bridge fork L up good path leading to Loch Valley, continue N along shore and onwards to Loch Neldricken. Faint path follows W shore, past Murder Hole, to 2nd burn descending from crags to N, strike N up L bank continuing over rocky ground to SW corner Loch Enoch (494 m/1,620 ft).
6 kms/3¾ miles

(2) Traverse glacis terraces then boggy ground below steeper hillsides, round NE face Merrick to 3rd burn – that descending to tiny Loch Twachtan. Steep ascent leads to hummocky saddle below Kirriereoch Hill. Climb steep grassy slopes S over shoulder Little Spear to narrow shaly crest and summit plateau, OS cairn, THE MERRICK (843 m/2,764 ft).
3.5 kms/2¼ miles

(3) Descend W to follow corrie lip to southernmost point, strike S down wide grassy slopes to join path descending SW to wall, follow wall along grassy ridge and up to large cairn summit BENYELLARY (719 m/2,360 ft). Follow path 500 m SW until it strikes down S, thence continue SW along wall then S to cairn, radio mast, THE BENNAN (562 m/1,844 ft). Rocky shoulder, rough ground leads S then SE to trees, cross forestry track, continue across flat shoulder to OS cairn FELL OF ESCHONCAN (347 m/1,138 ft) and viewpoint SW 200 m. Descend steep craggy slopes to start, easiest to E.
7.5 kms/4¼ miles

Alternative

(3.A) From Benyellary continue on regular path dropping S into forestry, then down beside Buchan Burn to start.
4 kms/2¼ miles

The Arrochar Alps Southern Highlands

OS 1:50,000 Sheet 56

This is virtually sacred country for Glaswegians. Easily reached by both rail and road from the great conurbations of the Clyde, the group of rugged mountains clustered around the head of Loch Long has been a mecca for hill-lovers since the end of the last century. Here was rugged, scenic and relatively wild mountain country – containing the best rock-climbing in the Southern Highlands besides several real Munros – accessible on a day trip from Glasgow long before car ownership became universal. In the Depression years of the Thirties many folk escaped to Loch Lomondside and the Arrochar Alps from industrial squalor and the dole queue and discovered for the first time the freedom and camaraderie of the mountains. *Always a Little Further*, Alastair Borthwick's delightful anecdotal account of those days, recently republished, is essential reading for those interested in Scottish mountaineering.

Chief among these mountains is the extraordinary three-peaked Cobbler. By no means the highest of the Arrochar Alps – and not even a Munro – it must be considered one of Scotland's more important mountains if only because of its character and steep crags. 'This terrific rock forms the bare summit of a huge mountain' wrote John Stoddart nearly two centuries ago, 'and its nodding top so overhangs the base as to assume the appearance of a cobbler sitting at

work ...' (*Local Scenery and Manners in Scotland* 1799.) Contrary therefore to most modern descriptions the frowning North Peak is traditionally the Cobbler himself, the highest point, Centre Peak, is the Cobbler's Last while the sharp South Peak is the Cobbler's Wife. More prosaically the mountain is known also as Ben Arthur and its bizarre shape is due to the highly contorted and folded mica-schist rocks of which it is composed.

The route up from Loch Long beside the cascading Allt a'Bhalachain – the 'Buttermilk Burn' – is an old favourite and in dry conditions it is fun to pad up the smooth water-worn slabs of the stream bed. Little now remains of the celebrated 'doss' – or bivouac – of the Thirties beneath one of the twin Narnain Boulders from where the view of the Cobbler cirque really opens up. Several paths diverge nearby, one directly onwards to the Bealach a'Mhaim and another, the Cobbler regular route, winding

upwards to the ridge just left of North Peak: our more sporting route however takes us round the base of the formidable South Peak and along the narrow connecting ridge to the summit. In good conditions intrepid scramblers may decide to traverse the crest of both via the south-east ridge, a fairly long and exposed scramble graded 'moderate', followed by a steep and slightly awkward thirty-metre descent to the ridge beyond whose actual crest, falling sheer into the coire on the right, is straightforward except for one short crack at about 'difficult' standard.

Though it looks intimidating, the little rock tower that is the Cobbler's true summit is easily ascended by crawling through the window from left to right and scrambling up a short gangway on the western face: but it stands on the edge of all things and is not for the faint hearted particularly when the rock is damp. Thereafter the route onwards to North Peak is a walk and the slabby summit above the huge overhanging

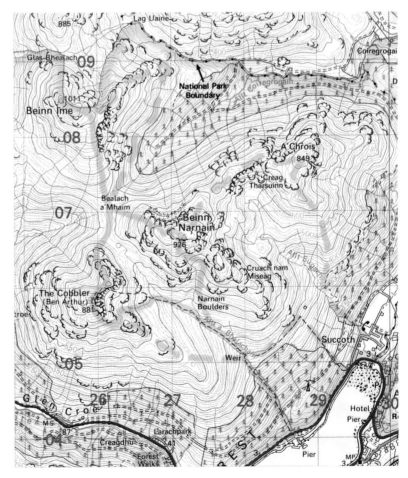

Beinn Ime commands a wide view: beyond its East Top the summit of A'Chrois is just visible with Loch Lomond and Loch Arklett in the left distance and the cone of Ben Lomond on the right skyline.

prow is worth gaining for its spectacular views across the cirque.

Beinn Ime – the 'Butter Mountain' – the highest of the Arrochar Alps, is shapely and quite rugged though unfortunately it presents its least interesting flank to the Cobbler. However, the well-defined north-east ridge, quite narrow near its rocky top, offers an excellent if considerably longer route to the summit, itself an excellent viewpoint especially eastwards over Loch Lom-

ond to Loch Katrine and the Trossachs. Now easily reached, the craggy final mountain, Beinn Narnain, is perhaps the most prominent of the Arrochar Alps with a characteristic flat top looking right down the bright fjord of Loch Long towards the distant ocean. Winding down between rocky outcrops and past waterfalls the intricate descent provides an entertaining finish to the day but if energy permits a delightful return may be made northwards over A'Chrois:

the superb panorama from this fine little peak – 'The Cross' – standing at the heart of the Arrochar Alps includes the most impressive flanks of the surrounding mountains rising over the deep recess of wild Coire Grogain.

Though it appears intimidating, the summit tower of the Cobbler proves a simple scramble; it looks down, past the South Peak, to Ardgartan at the mouth of Glen Croe and Loch Long.

The Arrochar Alps

Length: 14.5 kms/9 miles
Total ascent: 1600 m/5,300 ft
Difficulty: rough hillsides, some steep and rocky ground: all difficulties avoidable but serious scrambling is involved, rope useful, if Cobbler taken direct. These are real mountains, area known for poor weather, rock slimy when damp. Easy escape possible after each stage
Note: route lies within Argyll National Forest Park

Start: limited vergeside parking 284039 at S junction of MoD Torpedo Station road with A83, larger laybys at 294049. (10 m/30 ft).

(1) 300 m E along A83 at W side bridge narrow path enters scrubby woods, follow path uphill near burn, unrelenting, muddy, after climbing 300 m (1,000 ft) emerge from pines onto open hillside. Muddy path crosses small dam to N side burn continuing to conspicuous Narnain Boulders. After 300 m cross burn L soon striking off path aiming L across upper coire for obvious skyline saddle L of Cobbler S Peak. Go R at saddle then L of big buttress on scrambly well-defined path below vertical cliffs, zigzag up R to gain narrow ridge between S and Centre Peaks. Path leads just L of arete to small plateau below 5-metre summit tower COBBLER (884 m/2,900 ft).
4 kms/2¼ miles

(2) Path descends near ridge to broad saddle whence easy scrambly slabs gain exposed summit NORTH PEAK (c 850 m/2,790 ft). Path, steep in parts, drops N to wide boggy saddle Bealach a'Mhaim (620 m/2,040 ft). Ascend broad grassy S slopes Beinn Ime ahead, path soon disappears, keep R near coire edge for best terrain, to trig pt summit BEINN IME (1011 m/3,318 ft★) on 2nd rocky kopje.
3.5 kms/2¼ miles

(3) Retrace route to Bealach a'Mhaim, ascend steeper grass slopes NW ridge Beinn Narnain, best going far LHS, rocky near top, to summit plateau BEINN NARNAIN (926 m/3,036 ft★).
3 kms/2 miles

(4) Immediately S summit cairn grassy couloir leads down through craggy band to wide grassy ramp descending L into shallow corrie above Narnain Boulders. Retrace (1) to start.
3.5 kms/2¼ miles

Variations
(1.A) Do not cross dam on burn above forest but bear W up boggy slopes to join long SE ridge of South Peak, rejoining (1) at skyline saddle.

(2.A) From Bealach a'Mhaim make descending traverse N into Coire Grogain, contouring L between crags and forestry to base NE ridge Beinn Ime below Ben Vane. Ascend ridge easily round rocky steps, potential scrambling if desired, to Beinn Ime plateau.
Extra 2.5 kms/1½ miles, plus 460 m/530 ft

(3.A) Descend easily NNE from summit to traverse knobbly NE ridge to sharp peaklet A'CHROIS (849 m/2,785 ft). Descend initially 400 m SSW to reach grassy SE ridge descending to path beside Allt Sugach burn and Succoth Farm.
Extra 3 kms/2 miles, plus 170 m/560 ft

Ben Cruachan Argyll

OS 1 : 50,000 Sheet 50

'We thought it the grandest mountain we had seen . . .'

Dorothy Wordsworth:
Journal 1803

'For elevation, magnitude and magnificence, I do not recollect a mountain superior to Cruachan.'

Thomas Wilkinson:
Tours to the British Mountains 1824

In medieval times it was thought to be the highest point in Britain. Ever since then this isolated and distinctive mountain rising above the shaggy and accessible shores of lovely Loch Awe has been celebrated in story and song, as a tourist 'sight' and even as one of the few Scottish mountains whose name appears on large-scale maps. Its correct gaelic name – Cruachan Beann – meaning 'Mountain of Peaks', is an apt description, for its main ridge, fashioned from coarse diorite and granite, extends some 8 kilometres (5 miles) and with its two subsidiary southern spurs rises to no less than seven summits about 3,000 feet (900 metres), two of them Munros.

Charmingly dubbed 'Queen of the Southern Highlands' and certainly a commanding height, Cruachan dominates Mid Lorne and its characteristic shape is easily recognized from a distance: from the north, from the Blackmount peaks or Ben Nevis, the sharp twin western summits linked by a gracefully arcing ridge rise above the horizon, while from Mull or out at sea

High and stately, Ben Cruachan dominates the Firth of Lorne in this view from Duart on the north-eastern point of Mull.

the 'Red Peak' – Stob Dearg – also known as Taynuilt Peak because it rises behind that village, is seen as a single shapely pyramid. Because of their form, their character, certain mountains demand attention and Cruachan is one of them. The traverse of its ridges is a classic expedition along an exhilarating and predominantly rocky crest that in winter can be truly alpine. While fairly long and strenuous the route is uncommitting and escape southwards is possible from many places: it is most aesthetically taken from east to west to enjoy to the full the splendid and ever changing vistas over Loch Awe and Loch Etive that almost moat the mountain, and beyond to Loch Linnhe, the Firth of Lorne and the hills of Mull.

Loch Awe points its 35-kilometre (22-mile) finger through the rolling landscape of Nether Lorne to the foot of Ben Cruachan, where our route starts above a wooded shore with rich historical associations. Kilchurn Castle, an imposing fifteenth-century pile at the eastern corner of the loch, is perhaps the finest castle ruin in Scotland and on small islands stand the remains of another castle, a nunnery and a crannog – an ancient Celtic lake dwelling. The rugged slopes of Meall Cuanail drop steeply into the gloomy defile of the Pass of Brander where the loch becomes the River Awe, a strategic narrows where Wallace defeated the men of Lorne in 1298 and Bruce overcame the MacDougalls in a bloody engagement ten years later.

Technically our route is a straightforward one. The first summit, Beinn a'Bhuiridh – 'ben a vuie', the 'Peak of the Bellowing' (... stags) – gives a good overview of the circuit and the

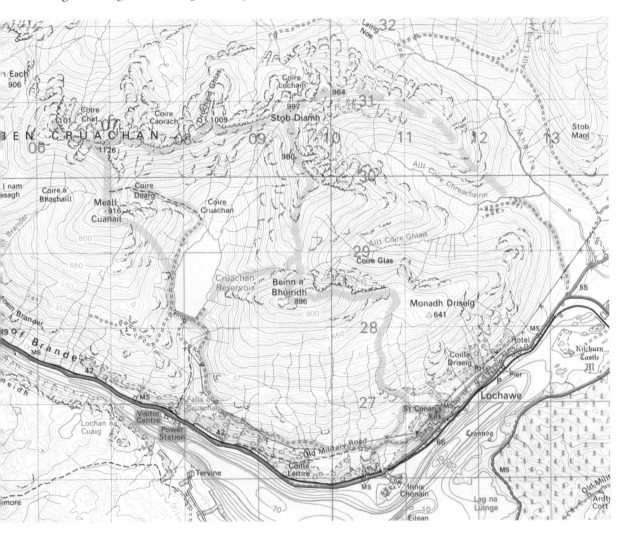

return route. A steep descent over broken slopes, sometimes awkward in winter, leads to the Larig Torran, the col over which Wallace is said to have outflanked the enemies challenging him in the Pass of Brander. Stob Garbh, the 'Rough Peak', leads on to Stob Diamh – pronounced 'daff' – the 'Peak of the Stags', from where the ridge starts to become narrow and stony. Drochaid Glas the next summit – in English the 'Grey Bridge' – demands careful navigation in mist for it stands a little proud of the ridge northwards at the head of a steep spur dropping towards remote Glen Noe, a flank of the mountain rarely frequented. The main summit is quite small and sharp and the final approach over steep and slightly exposed blocks can be another winter 'crux', while Stob Dearg, the far western peak ringed by redish granite slabs to north and west, is a viewpoint not to be missed.

A swift descent into Coire Cruachan leads to

the lake. Pent up behind a hideous 45-metre high (150-foot) concrete dam, the lake, entirely artificial, is almost the only outward manifestation of the huge 400 megawatt pumped-storage power station buried in a massive cavern hewn into the heart of the mountain nearly 300 metres (900 feet) below. Completed in 1965, it was a great feat of engineering, but surely the corrie could have been less brutally raped? The dam access road, though hard on the feet, gives an easy four-kilometre descent to the starting point.

A Traverse of Ben Cruachan

Length: 18 kms/11½ miles
Total ascent: 1700 m/5,500 ft
Difficulty: a long rugged route on a continuously high mountain chain, careful navigation essential in mist. A serious though not difficult expedition in winter conditions
Note: the hydro-scheme Visitor Centre at 077268 is interesting

Start: limited parking at 112266 beside Hydro Board access road immediately before locked gate.

(1) From access road climb N up long steep hillside to wide grassy crest Monadh Driseig, ascend W to summit BEINN A'BHUIRIDH (896 m/2,940 ft). Descend steep rocky flank N – hints of poor path – continuing across grassy saddle to easy ridge leading N to summit cairn STOB GARBH (980 m/3,215 ft) whence short descent, ascent leads to summit cairn STOB DIAMH (997 m/3,272 ft★).
7 kms/4¼ miles

(2) Descend easily W to saddle and follow narrow rocky ridge upwards fading out into wider bouldery slopes, ascend R to narrow rocky summit DROCHAID GLAS (1009 m/3,312 ft). Go SW to regain main ridge, descend to low point whence long narrow rocky crest ascends, finally steepening to summit BEN CRUACHAN (1126 m/3,695 ft★) trig pt. Descend W to col and short steep ascent to summit STOB DEARG (1101 m/3,611 ft).
3.5 kms/2¼ miles

(3) Retrace route E until easy ground leads R across SW face Ben Cruachan to S ridge, descend to narrow col whence short ascent reaches summit MEALL CUANAIL (916 m/3,004 ft). Grassy slopes lead to lakeside, cross dam and follow undulating road back to start.
7.5 kms/4¾ miles

Variations
(1.A) Avoid Beinn a'Bhuiridh by following access road to hydro dam and ascending grassy slopes NE to saddle below N flank.
Extra 1 km/½ mile: saves 180 m/600 ft ascent

(1.B) Reach Stob Diamh by E ridge: start at 132284 junction on A85 road, follow old rail track 1.5 kms NW until bridge crosses Coire Chreachainn burn, ascend NE onto long curving ridge leading over SRON AN ISEAN (964 m/3,163 ft) and Stob Diamh 500 m beyond.
6 kms/3¾ miles from road: 1010 m/3,300 ft

(3.A) Avoid Meall Cuanail by descending easily E from narrow col N of peak to lake.
Extra 1 km/½ mile: saves 80 m/250 ft ascent

February snow swirls from the main ridge below the summit of Ben Cruachan. The westernmost top, Stob Dearg, is seen beyond with the Isle of Mull in the far distance.

Bidean nam Bian — Glencoe, Central Highlands

OS 1 : 50,000 Sheet 41

'Glencoe itself is perfectly terrible . . .
It is shut in on each side by enormous rocks
from which great torrents come rushing
down . . . On one side of the pass there are
scores of glens, high up, which form such
haunts as you might imagine yourself
wandering in, in the very height and
madness of a fever.'

Charles Dickens: letter 1841.

'The Anvil of the Mist' the MacDonalds called
it, a flat-topped rock beside the old road at the
head of the glen. In dialect it became the Stiddie
– the Anvil – and later 'The Study', a famous
viewpoint where Queen Victoria herself enjoyed a picnic in 1873 and surely gazed down the
desolate defile of Glencoe. As a connoisseur of
Highland scenery she would have appreciated
the wild view rather better than did Mr Dickens

and a multitude of other hyperbolic Sassenach
travellers. She would have noted the triple great
glowering buttresses – the Three Sisters of
Glencoe – that wall the glen on its southern side
but she could not have glimpsed the great
mountain from which they spring, Bidean nam
Bian. The monarch of Glencoe stands well back
from the glen, a reclusive ruler, withdrawn,
aloof and accessible only to those who work
hard for an audience.

Bidean nam Bian is a shapely summit, the
highest in Argyll, and best seen rising above its
satellites from a distance, from the Mamores, the
Blackmount or from Loch Linnhe. Bill Murray
suggests that its name in English means 'Sharp
Peak of the Bens' for it is the culminating point
of four great ridges which rise to nine separate
summits and cradle three deep and distinctive
hanging corries. Uncompromisingly precipi-

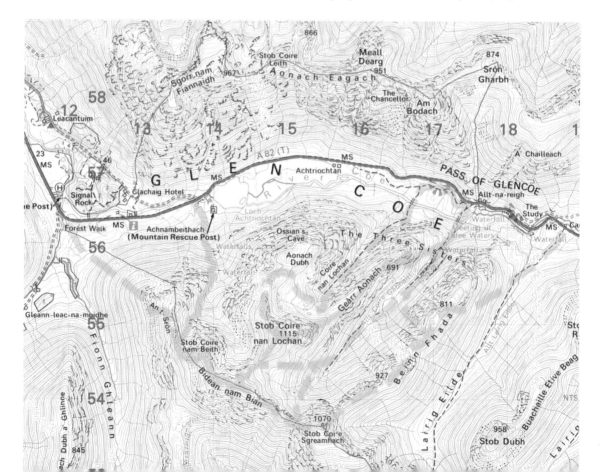

The celebrated view down Glen Coe from The Study: on the left rise the Three Sisters. The zigzag route up the great buttress of Gearr Aonach is clearly seen with the sharp summit of Stob Coire nan Lochan just visible to the left above: the 'Lost Valley' is the first valley on the left.

tous, its rock largely firm volcanic rhyolite and with plenty of accommodation at its foot served by excellent communications, the massif is among the most frequented in Scotland in both summer and winter. Glencoe itself, scene of the treacherous massacre of some forty of its MacDonald inhabitants by soldiers under Campbell command in February 1692 – it was not so much the doing as the manner of the doing that earned disapprobation in those more savage times – attracts a steady stream of tourists in its own right.

Such a complex massif offers a wide variety of routes. The one described here gives a good introduction within a reasonable day's expedition though it involves some straightforward scrambling which may appear from its imposing location a little intimidating to some. Several alternatives are suggested, both as easier variations or as itineraries for a subsequent visit.

Before commencing the climb up Gearr Aonach it might be interesting to divert a short distance into the Lost Valley – the popular name for Coire Gabhail. Pronounced 'Gyle', the name means 'Capture' for this was the sanctuary where the MacDonalds, notorious cattle rustlers, would hide their plundered herds. The inner corrie, a flat and charming fairy meadow, is sealed off by a great maze of gigantic boulders that fell from the cliffs above in the distant past and is thus invisible and unsuspected from the glen below.

Route-finding on the zigzag ledges of Gearr

Aonach – the 'Short Height' – is fairly obvious and the scrambly section just a few easy moves: the flat ridge top, a different and airy world from the forbidding glen below, proves easy going. Soon there are good views of the elegant cliffs of Coire nan Lochan above three tiny tarns, a renowned winter climbing venue, before the ridge climbs entertainingly round the lip of the corrie to the Stob above. The next steep ascent is to Bidean itself and passes above the famous crags of the Diamond and Churchdoor Buttresses, the latter immediately under the small summit. The junction of three sharp ridges, this can be the perfect mountain top in ideal winter conditions.

Stob Coire Sgreamhach – the 'Peak of the Rocky Corrie' – and twin topped Beinn Fhada – the 'Long Mountain' – can provide an excellent continuation around the head of the Lost Valley besides returning to the road nearer the start, but the westward descent will take us over the great cliffs of Stob Coire nam Beith – the 'Peak of the Birch Tree corrie' – and provide fine views back to Bidean over the craggy depths. The final path

down the lower corrie leads past conspicuous waterfalls, below the beetling and strangely symmetrical western cliffs of Aonach Dubh – the 'Black Height' – and finally down to the road at about the one place in the glen from which the summit of Bidean is visible: and the Clachaig Inn is but a stone's throw distant.

Two climbers follow our route up the north-east ridge of Stob Coire nan Lochan, the flat crest of Gearr Aonach is seen below. The twin summits of Beinn Fhada on their long ridge rise from the shadow across Coire Gabhail.

Bidean nam Bian

Length: 9.5 kms/6 miles + 3.5 kms/2¼ miles on road
Total ascent: 1200 m/4,000 ft + 55 m/180 ft
Difficulty: well-frequented rocky slopes and ridges, several short scrambly sections, route finding, map/compass skills essential: this is serious, high, very rugged mountain country demanding respect, particularly in winter, snow often remains into summer
Note: interesting Visitor Centre at 127564 operated by NTS who own area

Start: large car-park S side A82 at 171568 (170 m/560 ft): several similar car-parks nearby. Useful parking Achtriochtan junction 138567

(1) Paths descend S to cross 'Meeting of the Three Waters' footbridge (145 m/480 ft) whence muddy path ascends towards Coire Gabhail. Soon strike up R, faint path climbs hillside to base lowest crag L of Gearr Aonach. Better path leads up diagonally L along bottom of cliff to small cairn where obvious rake, initially steep, rocky, then grassier, leads back R below vertical blank wall to exposed nose where obvious route leads steeply back up L, short easy scramble before angle eases. At easier ground ascend rocky heather direct, or ledge ascending R, to flat ridge top. Go L to small cairn GEARR AONACH (691 m/2,267 ft).
2.5 kms/1½ miles

(2) Grassy undulating ridge continues SW eventually rearing into rocky ridge, easy scrambling over blocks, short walls, small gap, exposed on RHS, leads to steep final slopes STOB COIRE NAN LOCHAN (1115 m/3,657 ft).
2 kms/1¼ miles

(3) Descend easily SW to col whence steep easy rocky ridge, exposed on RHS leads via 2 false tops to summit BIDEAN NAM BIAN (1148 m/3,766 ft★).
1 km/¾ mile

(4) Descend W over subsidiary top then rocky ridge curves N to small cairn STOB COIRE NAM BEITH (1104 m/3,621 ft), drop steeply W to rejoin ridge. At lowest point before An t-Sron descend R down steep scree, trending R to join rough path near stream junction, path descends near W bank stream, steep in places, to road just W of Achtriochtan bridge.
4 kms/2½ miles

Variations

(1.A + 2.A) From footbridge below Coire an Lochan ascend well-used path to small lochans upper corrie. Strike NW to ascend easy N ridge, exposed on LHS, to Stob Coire nan Lochan.
4.5 kms/2¾ miles

(3.A) From col S of Stob Coire nan Lochan descend easy slopes directly L into Coire Gabhail trending L to avoid upper stream gorge. Follow path to Meeting of the Three Waters.
5 kms/3¼ miles

(4.A) From Bidean take easy stony ridge SE to STOB COIRE SGREAMHACH (1066 m/3,497 ft). Straightforward descent possible to Coire Gabhail from col immediately W of peak, Bealach Dearg – avoid gorge (3.A). Or continue ridge NE, several short, narrow, scrambles, over two summits of BEINN FHADA (S top 951 m/3,120 ft). Descend steeply L from col beyond N top into Coire Gabhail or more easily R into Lairig Eilde from pt 811 m beyond.
6 kms/3¾ miles to road + 2.0 kms/1¼ miles on road to start

Ben Nevis and the Carn Mor Dearg Arete
Lochaber, Central Highlands

OS 1 : 50,000 Sheet 41

'Read me a lesson, muse, and speak it loud
Upon the top of Nevis blind in Mist
I look into the Chasms and a Shroud
Vaprous doth hide them :'

John Keats
On Ben Nevis, 1818

Climbers know it affectionately as the 'Ben'. It's a mountain of superlatives, the highest summit with the biggest cliffs and the worst weather in Britain: mean, ugly and treacherous into the bargain. But these very qualities make it a very special mountain attracting not only top-class international alpinists intent on the superb winter climbing found on its northern flank, but also hundreds of ordinary summer tourists to whom the zigzag path on the whale-back western flank leads to the high point of their holiday. Every September fell-runners race up and down – their record stands at less than eighty-seven minutes – sometimes the mountain is descended by hang-glider or balloon and occasionally even insulted by such stunts as 'ascents' by car, motorcycle or even bedstead. Nevertheless to the keen hill-walker this magnificent mountain and its only close neighbour Carn Mor Dearg provide one of

The cliffs of Ben Nevis rear above the hanging corrie of the Allt a'Mhuilinn in this view over the Great Glen from the north-west. Our route is seen almost in its entirety, with the Carn Mor Dearg Arete as the skyline crest linking Carn Mor Dearg on the left to the Ben itself.

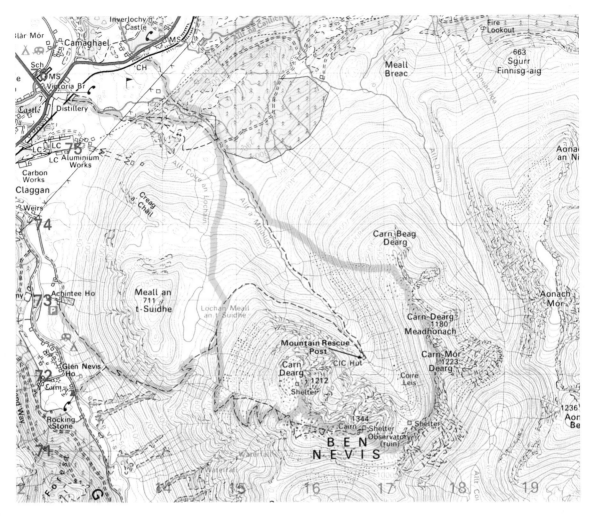

the finest – and certainly the highest – ridge traverses in these islands.

Nevis is an appropriate name, apparently derived from a Gaelic compound word which translates loosely as 'head in the clouds', indeed on less than one day in three is the top clear. Readings taken at the old summit observatory record an average of 261 gales a year and wind speeds often rising well over one hundred miles per hour besides a mean temperature of **minus** 0.3°C! (31.4°F). Snow may fall in high summer and névé patches usually persist until winter at the base of the great northern cliffs. Rising straight from the sea and almost alone, the Ben stands right in the storm track of North Atlantic hurricanes and it has been calculated that were the mountain but a couple of hundred feet higher it would hold a small glacier.

Although the vast southern flanks above Glen Nevis are not devoid of interest, they encompass for instance the longest hillside in Britain rising over 1200 metres (4,000 feet), attention naturally focuses on the precipitous northern flanks which rear above the rugged glen of the Allt a' Mhuilinn (pronounced 'voolin') – the 'Mill Stream'. Our route climbs viciously boggy yet attractively sylvan slopes to the lip of the glen where suddenly the serried spurs of the Ben come into view facing the smoothly curving slopes of Carn Mor Dearg across the defile ahead. The ascent of the latter – a full 600 metres (2,000 feet) – will appear daunting, but starting from the first scattering of boulders to approach the path, and following a series of shallow depressions and hollows in the hillside, the going is surprisingly good and the granite screes of the rounded summit ridge are gained without undue effort.

A handsome mountain in its own right with craggy eastern slopes and an arcing snow-wreathed crest, the twin summits of Carn Mor Dearg – the 'Big Red Cairn' (pronounced 'Jerrak') – provide good walking with everchanging views of Britain's grandest mountain wall. The north-east faces of the Ben and Carn Dearg extends over 6 kilometres (4½ miles), rising in places over 600 metres (2,000 feet) and sculpted into an array of famous ridges and buttresses, walls, gullies and corries carved from smooth dark porphyry, an igneous rock which provides excellent rock-climbing when dry.

The arete that sweeps round the secluded hollow of Coire Leis towards Ben Nevis is the crux of the expedition; in summer merely a sustained but easy and entertaining scramble, though quite exposed and potentially a serious undertaking in winter conditions. The southern end of the arete merges into the slopes of the Ben and can be approached from the corrie but route finding through the broken cliffs is awkward, hence the abseil posts which facilitate a safe winter descent. A rough path now winds up steep rocky slopes to the summit plateau giving the corrie edge a wide berth: the series of marker posts was placed here after a multiple accident in winter some years ago to indicate a safe descent line.

The summit, a flat stony desert surrounded on three sides by the abrupt cliff edge, is graced by several cairns, an emergency bivouac shelter and the ruins of the Observatory occupied between 1883 and 1904. One of the famous climbing gullies ending closeby is named Gardyloo after the old street cry 'Gardez l'eau!' because this was where Observatory staff used to tip their rubbish. In clear weather the panorama is incredible, ridge after rumpled ridge of hills stretching

away in every direction: from Torridon to Ben Lomond; from Barra to the Cairngorms; the sparkling pathway of Loch Linnhe leads south-west to Mull, the Paps of Jura – and on the very clearest of days even to Ireland.

Even in early summer the snow cornices can be immense and several profound gullies cut deeply into the plateau edge so the route onwards towards Carn Dearg along the plateau rim must be followed warily, but there are continuous exciting views of the jagged ridges and buttresses beneath against a backdrop of Loch Eil and the Great Glen. The stony desert rises to Carn Dearg where another emergency bivouac is sited and where the cliff edge just south – supposedly rising just above 4,000 feet and thus higher than the official summit – provides a last glimpse of Ben Nevis. The Tourist Track zigzags steeply down beside the cleft of the Red Burn and back to the valley.

Ben Nevis and Carn Mor Dearg

Length: 19.5 kms/12 miles
Total ascent: 1620 m/5,300 ft
Difficulty: rough ground with section of sustained but easy scrambling, straightforward in good weather: these are very high serious mountains with notorious weather, in bad conditions accurate navigation crucial. Route is quite committing especially in winter when it can become a serious alpine expedition

Start: Ben Nevis Distillery at 126757, parking currently on adjoining lot W. Golf Club currently threaten £3 fee at 137762 but convenient layby 500 m W on A82

(1) Cross Distillery yard then railway following streamside path E over old tramway, go L then steep, boggy path leads to stream dam at lip of Mhuilinn glen. Or from Golf Club take track under railway, arc L round greens to fence/stile across old tramway, boggy path leads steeply to dam. Easy path continues above R bank of burn until glen starts to narrow after 1 km/½ mile, now strike L up hillside, easiest line working R via series of shallow hollows to broad shoulder, ascend easily S to rocky summit CARN DEARG MEADHONACH (1180 m/3,870 ft), after short descent, ascend along edge to CARN MOR DEARG (1223 m/4,012 ft★).
7.5 kms/4½ miles

(2) Descend ridge S, angle eases to almost level narrow rocky arete, easy scrambling, difficulties avoidable. After 500 m ridge steepens, pass metal abseil sign (for descent into Coire Leis) and ascend wide broken slopes NW, stony path passing marker posts to summit plateau, emergency shelter, etc. BEN NEVIS (1344 m/4,406 ft★).
2 kms/1¼ miles

(3) Follow well-used Tourist Route path S then W along deeply indented cliff edge, **beware cornices**, bear R off path, descend slightly to low point and ascend gradually NW following edge past No 4 Gully marker post and across stony plateau to summit cairn CARN DEARG (1221 m/3,961 ft).
1.5 kms/1 mile

(4) From nearby shelter strike S 500 m to rejoin main stony path, descend steep zigzags to flatter ground above Lochan Meall an t-Suidhe, at path junction continue R 500 m until small cairn indicates poor path dropping L over moorland towards lake outlet, nearby drop N over lip descending grassy slopes to Allt a' Mhuilinn dam. Retrace route to start.
8.5 kms/5¼ miles

Alternative
(4.A) At path junction above Lochan Meall an t-Suidhe fork L to descend regular Tourist Route direct to Achintee roadhead.
6.5 kms/4 miles from Ben Nevis summit.

The summit of Carn Mor Dearg is seen from its northern top, Carn Dearg Meadhonach. On the right the great spur of North-East Buttress falls from the flat summit of Ben Nevis. Tower Ridge is the buttress on the far right beyond snow-filled Tower Gully with Gardyloo Gully at its head. Part of the Carn Mor Dearg Arete is seen above the figures.

Ben Macdhui and the Cairngorm Plateau

Eastern Highlands

OS 1:50,000 Sheet 36

'Nothing could be grander and wilder; the rocks are so grand and precipitous, and the snow on Ben Macdhui had such a fine effect'

Queen Victoria:
describing Loch Avon, 1861

The Cairngorms are unique. Once known as the Monadh Ruadh – the 'Red Hills' – from their bare red granite, they rise between the broad straths of the Dee and the Spey. These are mountains carved from a high plateau, the largest area of high ground in Britain with no less than 150 square miles (240 square kilometres) above the 2,000-foot contour (610 metres) and nine of the dozens of tops reaching about 4,000 feet (1220 metres). They appear featureless from a distance except in early summer when snow wreaths hint at the outline of cliff and corrie, but an actual visit reveals a wealth of unsuspected grandeur: great deep-gouged corries, a graceful rolling plateau, jagged crags and remote lochs, tumbling torrents and stately pines, all forming a rare 'arctic-alpine' environment nurturing a specialized flora and fauna. The climate is extreme, here are the largest snowfields in the country with snow patches lingering throughout the summer: this is the home of Scottish skiing.

In such a wide area it would be invidious to specify a particular itinerary to introduce the Cairngorms, rather one should select a sequence of the best characteristic features and link them by an interesting route. Any expedition among these mountains is governed by the weather, in winter it may be impossible to venture onto the plateau where experienced well-equipped mountaineers, unable to escape, have died of exposure: a week later it may be shirt-sleeves on the summits. Not even in high summer should the Cairngorm traveller let down his guard – he must be prepared for anything.

The unsightly ski-road zigzagging up from Loch Morlich gives a head start to any expedition from the north and some entertaining but easy scrambling up the blocky arete of the Fiacaill Ridge of Coire an t'Sneachda – pronounced Corrie an'Treck and meaning 'Toothed Ridge of the Snow Corrie' – ascends to the open plateau. So easily accessible, this is possibly the most popular winter climbing venue in Scotland. A slight ascent along the plateau edge leads to the vague summit of Cairn Lochan perched close to the lip of Coire an Lochain. Typically the impressive vertical cliffs here hold harder climbs while the long slopes beneath are famous for the thick neve that accumulates on them in winter; forming a miniature glacier which avalanches in spring to obliterate the tiny lochan below with huge ice blocks.

Across the wide plateau of broken rock and gravel the going is easy all the way to the large cairn on the rounded summit of Ben Macdhui, the second summit in Britain and held to be the highest until the 1847 survey. The name has been variously translated as 'MacDuff's Mountain', 'Dark Hill' or even 'Hill of the Black Pig'. Ferlas Mhor, the Great Grey Man, is reputed to haunt Macdhui in misty conditions and Professor Collie, the noted mountaineer and distinguished scientist, was just one of several reputable people to have encountered this frightening apparition. Nevertheless in clear weather the views extend from Caithness to the Southern Uplands and across the great defile of the Lairig Ghru into the Garbh Coire where glaciologists claim relict glacial ice still lingered well into the eighteenth-century.

A descent past the moody waters of Loch Etchachan leads down over an edge to the head of Loch Avon. Surrounded by a horseshoe of beetling cliffs over which white cataracts foam down from the plateau, this is one of the most

There is a fine view up Loch Avon from the path below the Nethy Saddle. The hanging valley followed by our route from Loch Etchachan can be seen on the left between the dark crags of Beinn Mheadhoin and the twin cliffs of Carn Etchachan and Shelter Stone Crag which rise above the head of the loch.

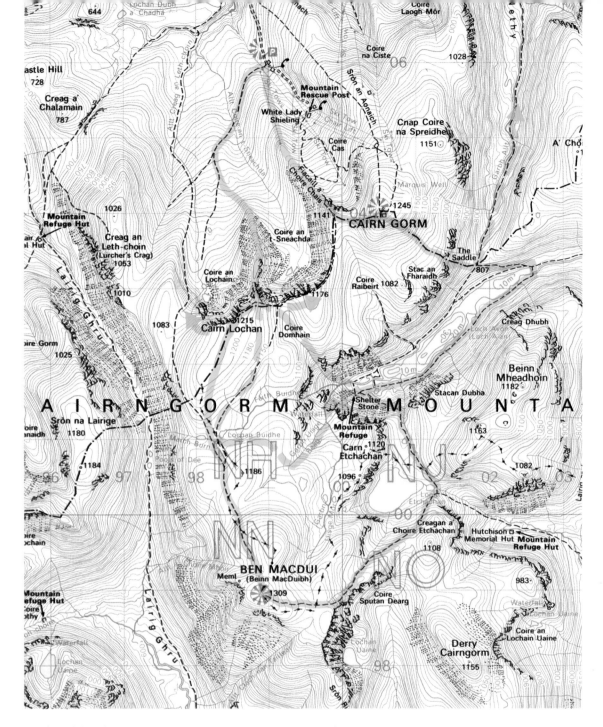

inaccessible places in the Cairngorms, indeed one of the most awesome sanctuaries in Britain. The path passes below the peaked crags of Carn Etchachan to the renowned Shelter Stone, a huge boulder lying beneath the 250-metre (800-foot) monolith of Shelter Stone Crag. Under it is a large and excellent cave, described in 1794 as 'accommodating eighteen armed men' – though only half that number can sleep in modern comfort. It probably weighs some 1,400 tons.

They say that a milk-white water-horse ranges brooding Loch Avon, a hardy beast for the waters are usually frozen half the year. A considerable river flows from the loch and crossing it near the outflow may be hazardous or even impossible, in which case one must decide whether to try again at Fords of Avon nearly two kilometres downstream or to play safe and retrace ones steps round the head of the loch.

Above the eastern end of the loch is the Nethy

Saddle, a low col at the head of Strath Nethy, a long valley which leads 13 tedious kilometres (8 miles), to Glen More via the pretty Pass of Ryvoan: this is the easiest low-altitude escape from Loch Avon. Gravelly slopes above the Saddle lead onto the great dome of Cairngorm, – the 'Blue Mountain' – its summit crowned by a little radio controlled met' station and easily accessible to tourists from the top station of the chairlift. The prospect northwards over Loch Morlich and the Glen More forests to miles of low hills sweeping towards distant Ben Wyvis and the Moray coast is an exciting one marred only by the ugly developments in Coire Cas – the 'Steep Corrie', the heart of the ski area – around which leads the final descent.

A Cairngorm Circuit

Length: 22 kms/14 miles
Total ascent: 1340 m/4,400 ft
Difficulty: very committing route but generally good going on straightforward ground, one easy scrambly section. In dubious weather less experienced parties should take shorter alternatives. Proficient compass navigation, stamina, essential. In winter a major expedition
Note: 100 sq miles of highest terrain is National Nature Reserve, Loch Avon basin belongs to RSPB, access not affected

Start: huge chair-lift car-park at head of ski road 989061, fee usually payable.

(1) Muddy path contours SW round heathery hillside, beyond first burn strike S to prominent stony ridge, ascend to rounded summit, short descent to rocky arete, easy scrambling up to plateau edge, turning difficulties on RHS. Follow plateau lip R to summit cairn CAIRN LOCHAN (1215 m/3,983 ft).
4 kms/2½ miles

(2) Shallow ridge leads SW across plateau, gradual descent joins path near Lochan Buidhe, gradual ascent leads to large cairn trig pt BEN MACDUI (1309 m/4,296 ft★).
4 kms/2½ miles

(3) Descend easily ESE 1 km (½ mile), traces of path, to head 2nd shallow valley, burn. Avoid cliff edge ahead, descend NE by burn to outflow Loch Etchachan (925 m/3,035 ft). Levelish path leads NW, at lip LHS of burn descend steep rocky slopes diagonally L to boulder fields, Shelter Stone. (755 m/2,475 ft).
5 kms/3¼ miles

(4) Path descends E to Loch Avon S shore, continue to outflow. Cross to N bank, (**danger** – see text) path climbs diagonally W to Nethy Saddle whence strike up steep hillside ahead, avoid crag band, continue easier angle NW up dome to summit CAIRNGORM (1245 m/4,084 ft★).
6 kms/3¾ miles

(5) Descend W to flat area lip Coire Cas, cairn Pt 1141, descend narrow rounded ridge NW above ski area, continue direct to car-park.
3 kms/2 miles

Variations
(2.A+3.A) Direct route from Cairn Lochan to Shelter Stone: descend gradually E from summit into shallow basin Coire Domhain, follow LHS of stream steeply through gap in cliffs to head Loch Avon.
2 kms/1¼ miles

(2.B+3.B) To Shelter Stone via plateau: from Lochan Buidhe contour round NE flank – or cross – low hump Pt 1186 to shallow valley Garbh Uisge Beag whence scrambly descent RHS of burn over lip leads down R to Shelter Stone.
5 kms/3¼ miles

It needs little imagination to realise how difficult navigation can be and how fierce the weather on the wide arctic Cairngorm plateau in this April view towards Ben Macdhui from the slopes above Coire an t'Sneachda. Just right of centre appear the twin summits of Cairntoul and 'Angel's Peak' beyond the Lairig Ghru.

The Ladies of Kintail   Western Highlands

OS 1 50,000 Sheet 33

"We passed through Glen Shiel . . .
One mountain I called immense.
'No' said he 'but 'tis a considerable
protruberance.'"

James Boswell:
Journal of a Tour to the Hebrides, 1773.

Walled on either side by a high chain of
imposing peaks, its foot lapped by the salty
waters of beautiful Loch Duich and with a
modern highway running from end to end, Glen

We look back in this picture from Sgurr nan Saighead along
the narrow ridge towards Sgurr Fhuaran, highest of the Five
Sisters.

Shiel is the showpiece of the Western Highlands. The two great mountain crests to the north of the glen comprise the Kintail Forest, owned by the National Trust for Scotland thanks to the generosity of a past president of the Scottish Mountaineering Club, and there can be few mountain-lovers who are not familiar with the classic outline of the Five Sisters of Kintail, the stately crest forming the northern flank of the glen. Best seen from the Mam Ratagan, the steep pass to the west linking the head of Loch Duich to Glenelg, the ridge rises as five summits but the seaward top is shapeless and considerably lower than its sisters while a handsome sixth summit, with a distinct family resemblance, remains obscured at the far end of the crest. Should there not be Six Sisters of Kintail?

Notwithstanding their number, the traverse of these peaks is one of the very best ridge-walks in the entire Highlands. While hardly long and certainly not difficult, the expedition is sustained and fairly strenuous and the configuration of the six summits does not favour a circular trip. Public transport and taxis are virtually non-existent hereabouts but it is usually possible to arrange a lift or hitch-hike the eleven kilometres up the glen. An energetic party however could make a circular trip from Morvich using the good track up Gleann Lichd, whence an unrelenting climb of over 650 metres (2,200 feet) leads to the Bealach na Lapain: the penalty is an extra 11 kilometres (7 miles).

West Highland ridges are usually best traversed east to west, facing seaward for the views, and the Five Sisters is no exception. Bealach na Lapain is reached more easily than expected and from its grassy saddle views open up northwards to remote country at the head of Gleann Lichd. The first summit, Sgurr nan Spainteach – the 'Spaniards Peak' – is the outcast sister, rearing high above Telford's old bridge in the glen and the 1719 battlefield on the surrounding slopes. This engagement marked the end of a minor Jacobite uprising when a thousand MacKenzies aided by three hundred Spanish regulars were trounced by Government forces advancing from Inverness. The defeated clansmen and the Spaniards were driven up the hillside by bayonets and burning heather – and so the mountain got its name.

Sgurr na Ciste Duibhe – the 'Peak of the

The Five Sisters of Kintail

Length: from road 12 kms/7½ miles
Total ascent: from road 1500 m/5,000 ft
Difficulty: tough walking often over rough ground, some steep ascents, traces of path most of the way
Note: this route is **not** described as a circuit. Area belongs to NTS, Ranger's tel: Glenshiel 219

Start: good parking N side A87 at 009136 (180 m/590 ft).
Finish: limited parking on verge A87 beside Loch Shiel 9418, or by Shiel Bridge campsite 938187.

(1) At conspicuous gap in forest, narrow path, faint at first, climbs steep hillside to Bealach na Lapain (723 m/2,372 ft). On grassy crest go L following tenuous ridge path W rising to summit SGURR NAN SPAINTEACH (c 990 m/3,129 ft). Short rocky descent leads to twisting crest and complex saddle. Main path circles R round hollow before ascending L to rocky slopes and summit SGURR NA CISTE DUIBHE (1027 m/3,370 ft★).
4.5 kms/2¾ miles

(2) Descend wide grassy shoulder, ridge falls N to col (c 850 m/2,790 ft), stony ascent leads to SGURR NA CARNACH (1002 m/3,270 ft). Rocky path descends steeply to saddle (c 860 m/2,820 ft) before long steep climb continues to large cairn SGURR FHUARAN (1068 m/3,505 ft★).
2.5 kms/1¼ miles

(3) Path descends W ridge c 200 m before descending traverse R across NW face joins N ridge above lowest point (810 m/2,660 ft). Narrow ridge bends NW, grassy path ascends to SGURR NAN SAIGHEAD (929 m/3,050 ft), descending thin ridge to NW summit. Descend NW ridge to wide boggy shoulder, contour R around knoll to lower saddle, drop L down steep slopes towards Loch Shiel, aiming for footbridge at 947181 to reach road.
5 kms/3 miles

Alternatives
(3.A) From NW ridge Sgurr nan Saighead follow L bank Allt a'Chruinn to path above rocky narrows, descend to Morvich road.

(3.B) From Sgurr nan Saighead cross narrow col NE to SGURR NA MORAICH (876 m/2,874 ft). Steep grassy NW shoulder descends to Morvich road.

In this classic view from the Mam Ratagan pass, the Five Sisters are seen above the head of Loch Duich and the mouth of Glen Shiel. The traverse virtually follows the skyline from right to left – the pointed peak at the centre is Sgurr Fhuaran.

Black Coffin' – is the next top and a line left of the curious hollow at its base gives a little scrambling *en route* to its chunky bosom-shaped summit. The huge slope dropping almost unbroken into Glen Shiel was described by a traveller in 1803 as 'an inclined wall, of such inaccessible height that no living creature would venture to scale it.' Obviously a tedious flank not recommended in descent? Now the ridge broadens, swinging northwards over the 'Pass of the Tree' – Bealach na Craoibhe – to Sgurr na Carnach and Bealach na Carnach beyond, the 'Stony Place': the grassy spur dropping west from this summit is a good escape route. Peculiar spines of rock decorate the slopes of Sgurr Fhuaran, the path avoids them but they offer some scrambling to enliven the long pull up the 'Peak of the Spring'; loftiest and most handsome

of the sisters and a superb viewpoint, its long northern flank hung with a succession of wild corries, sanctuary for both deer and wild goats. Here the route descends a little way west – down another potential escape line – to avoid a rocky step on the main north ridge, before crossing the shaly flank of the mountain to reach the 'Yellow Saddle', Bealach Bhuidhe. Spectacular cliffs of rotting schist fall eastward from the narrow crest of sharp Sgurr nan Saighead beyond: possibly these narrow slabs, bundled together like quivered arrows, account for its name 'Peak of the Arrows'. The way onwards depends on whether one considers this to be the fourth or fifth sister but the best is now over and the ugly sister, squat little Sgurr na Moraich – the 'Shellfish Peak' – can only be an anticlimax.

The Falls of Glomach and the Green Mountain Western Highlands

OS 1:50,000 Sheet 33

'O Caledonia!...
Land of the Mountain and the Flood...'

Sir Walter Scott: 1805

Eas a'Ghlomaich – 'The Falls of the Chasm' – are the second highest in Britain and surely the most spectacular. They plunge nearly 150 metres (500 feet) into a rocky cauldron at the back of a deep ravine in a remote hillside in Kintail. Known sometimes as the Hidden Falls, they are accessible only to those prepared for a stiff walk and even then a view of their full majesty demands basic mountain skills and a steady head.

The shortest way to the falls lies up Glen Elchaig, reached by a narrow road from Ardelve on Loch Duich, but beyond Killilan the track is private and permission to drive to Loch na

The Falls of Glomach: this viewpoint on the lip of the chasm can be reached with great care by steep and exposed slopes below the path that descends the flanks of the gorge.

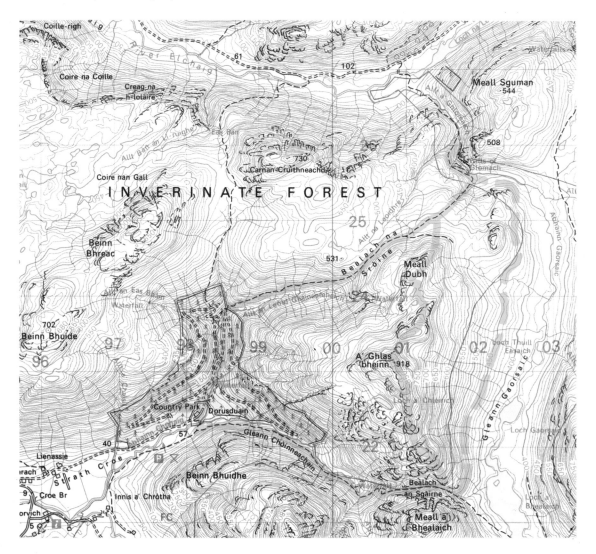

Leitreach must be sought from the Killilan Estate. From there a boggy ascent of some 250 metres (800 feet) leads to the head of the falls. But this is hardly a worthy expedition for a healthy hill-walker and the circular route described here, traversing a Munroe to boot, makes a more interesting approach. Gleann Choinneachain may mean the 'boggy Glen' but it is an especially fine one and a good path leads up it below the steep north-western slopes of the huge massif of Beinn Fhada – the 'Long Mountain' – to the narrow Bealach an Sgairne. Once known as St Duthac's Pass from the eleventh-century cleric who often used it, the present name translates as the 'Pass of Murmuring' and the eastern side falls to the barely perceptible Glen Affric watershed and a chain of shallow lochs which birth the Glomach, indeed the falls are sometimes reached this way, albeit rather boggily.

A'Ghlas-bheinn is a complex little mountain with a long and knobbly crest which rises directly from the Bealach, but the rocky outcrops are easily bypassed. It has been claimed that the mountain has sixteen tops, certainly the ridge is a fine grassy switchback with a succession of false summits and passes close above a charming little loch before climbing at last to the real summit. This aptly named 'Green Mountain' is a splendid viewpoint, both into the impressive corries of Beinn Fhada nearby and over Loch Duich to the pinnacled Cuillin, while Glen Elchaig points towards the Applecross hills rising beyond Loch Carron. Meall Dubh, the final shoulder on the descent northwards, presents a craggy flank to the Bealach na Sroine so the modest ridge dropping towards the falls should be carefully located.

There is little to be seen at the lip of the falls except boiling water disappearing into the void. But as the path leads across the steepening grassy flanks of the ravine the water can be seen plunging into a narrow chasm. There is nothing more to be seen as the main path winds down steep slopes to the ravine end, but with care a natural balcony of rock on the extreme edge of the chasm just beyond the base of the fall can be reached. The zigzag route to this vantage point is well used and will be fairly obvious but although not a scramble it is very steep and exposed and the ground is always slippery from the continual spray. From here the torrent is seen to drop in a single wild plunge before exploding on a great rock pillar and thundering down into an unseen cauldron of spray far below. It is possible for climbers to scramble to a still lower viewpoint from which the cauldron itself is visible, but this is hazardous ground. The waterfall has been climbed in winter when frozen hard.

The return route, following the excellent path over the wide Bealach na Sroine – the 'Pass of the Shoulder', no doubt that of Meal Dubh above – leads easily back to the dark pines and the car-park.

Over A'Ghlas-bheinn to the Falls of Glomach

Length: 16 kms/10 miles
Total ascent: 1400 m/4,600 ft
Difficulty: excellent path except on mountain itself, straightforward terrain, sometimes steep. **Caution** steep exposed wet grass surrounding Falls
Note: Dorusduain is Country Park, area surrounding Falls belongs to NTS, Ranger's tel: Glenshiel 219

Start: Forestry Commission car-park at Dorusduain 981224, reached from Morvich via Strath Croe (60 m/200 ft).

(1) Cross footbridge S over river, follow good path E up Gleann Choinneachain, zigzagging steeply to narrow Bealach an Sgairne. Now ascend N, avoiding rocky outcrops, to knobbly ridge NNE, continue to summit cairn A'GHLAS-BHEINN (918 m/3,006 ft★).
6 kms/3¾ miles

(2) Descend NW over narrow col, minor summit, to twin lochans. Avoiding cliffs to N and W, descend NE ridge to shallow boggy slopes, strike N to good path, continue NE to Falls of Glomach (c 340 m/1,100 ft). Steep exposed scrambly descent R below path gives best views from rock balcony. **Caution.**
4.5 kms/2¾ miles

(3) Reascend path crossing boggy ground to Bealach na Sroine (520 m/1,706 ft) before descending easily to Inverinate Forest. Forestry track S returns to start.
5.5 kms/3½ miles

The Great Corries of Applecross

Wester Ross, Northern Highlands

OS 1: 50,000 Sheet 24

The Applecross road, a narrow ribbon of rough tarmac, flings round a tight corner and into a deep square-cut valley running far up into the mountain. On the left tiered red cliffs rear above the green receding valley floor, the road ahead, an incongruous ledge, climbs across a steep hillside of broken crags and grey scree. Then the cliffs close in to sweep round the blind headwall of the valley. A tight bend, a quick glimpse of blue sea framed by dark cliffs, a vicious hairpin – pink slabs curling back from the road – another hairpin and another and another. Suddenly the

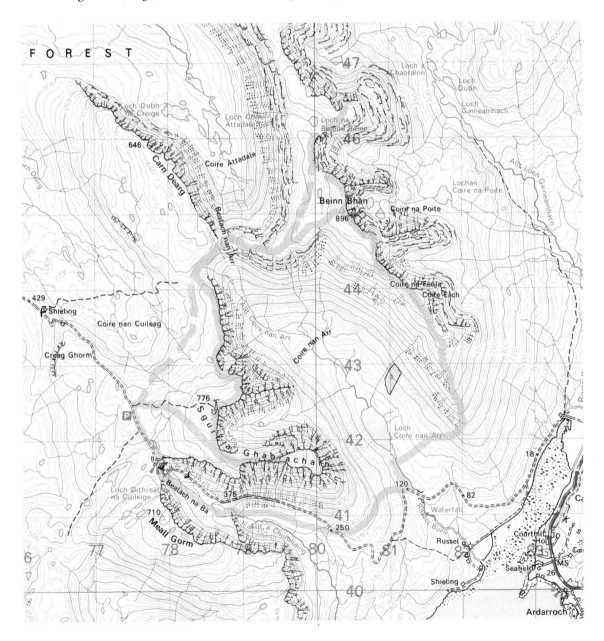

top, desolate boulder-strewn slopes and a couple of tiny lochans. This is the Bealach na Bà, one of the highest road passes in Britain – the ancient Pass of the Cattle.

Until the early Seventies this tortuous highway, often blocked by winter snow and with grades of one in four, was the only road into the remote Applecross peninsula, jutting into the Minch between Lochs Torridon and Duich. But Applecross village, a line of white cottages along the shore of a shallow bay looking out towards Skye, is now linked to Shieldaig and Torridon by a new road joining the scattered crofts of the western and northern coasts. Applecross is a corruption of Aber Crossan, the mouth of the Crossan – the ancient name for Applecross River – but to the Gael the peninsula is known as A'Comaraich – 'the Sanctuary'. St Maelrubha, second only to Columba in the history of Scottish Christianity, established a sanctuary here in 673 as refuge for all manner of fugitives, and so it remained, under the aegis of the Church, until the Reformation, though Maelrubha's monastery was eventually destroyed by the Vikings.

The Applecross mountains, southernmost of the Torridonian sandstone summits, rise gently from the coast before hunching into an array of whale-back ridges which plunge eastward into a sequence of stupendous corries. Our suggested route, which traverses both the major peaks, starts unusually by descending the spectacular valley below the Beallach na Bà for over 500 metres (1,600 feet) to the mouth of Coire nan Arr – avoiding the road is no problem. A short walk to the sandy shore of Loch Coire nan Arr brings the great Cioch of Sgurr a'Chaorachain (pronounced 'Hoorichan') into view: Cioch means a breast or nipple, often used in Gaelic to describe such upstanding features, and its intimidating 300-metre (1,000-foot) skyline gives a famous rock climb of great character which many claim is the best anywhere on Torridonian sandstone.

Across the glen the ascent onto Beinn Bhan presents no difficulty and the lip of the first of the

From the South Top, sheer cliffs over 200 metres high – more than 700 feet – can be seen falling from the summit plateau of Beinn Bhan into the deep hollow of Coire na Feola.

five eastern corries is reached just before the South Top. From here the most exciting route lies closely and carefully along the abrupt cliff edge for the views down into the next two corries, Coire na Feola (Corrie of the Flesh) and Coire na Poite (Corrie of the Pot – pronounced 'potch') are sensational. In the latter, almost enclosed by two prodigeous castellated spurs, sheer walls drop over 300 metres (1,000 feet) from the mountain's summit to two tiny lochans. It is worth continuing north from the summit for the views into Coire nan Fhamair –

Corrie of the Giant – and the wider northern corrie which again cradles two small tarns.

The summit of Beinn Bhan – the 'White Mountain' – is a broad curving plateau with an extensive view stretching from Ben Nevis to Ardnamurchan, Rhum, South Uist and the Harris peak of Clisham. Set with craggy bands, areas of boiler-plate slabs and several tiny ponds, the west ridge leads to the Bealach nan Arr, a grassy saddle from which a rough path heads directly back to the road beyond the crest of the low ridge ahead. This is the long north ridge of

Sgurr a'Chaorachain, a rugged plateau of tangled rock, grassy dells and several small lochans. Its eastern lip should be followed past the North Top, with exceptional views over the Inner Sound towards the saw-toothed Cuillin, above the deep corrie below the jutting spur of the Cioch to the true summit on the massive southern spur. From here the controversial oil-rig construction yard on the Kishorn shore, dwarfed by the Cyclopean cliffs of Meall Gorm, is the only small scar on a wide vista of lochs and islands. The return to the Beallach na Bà is easy.

An Applecross Ambulation

Length: 19 kms/12 miles
Total ascent: 1100 m/3,600 ft
Difficulty: generally easy straightforward circuit, some going quite rough, paths poor or non-existent
Note: stalking information from Estate office, tel Applecross 209

Start: large parking area 775423, highest point Kishorn/Applecross road 1 km N Bealach na Bà. (626 m/2,053 ft).

(1) Descend SE from Bealach, cut corners R of hairpin bends, descend corrie floor, at rock-band go L of burn into lower corrie, make descending contour to road at Pt 250, continuing over hillside above and drop to road again at Russel Bridge (110 m/360 ft).
5 kms/3¼ miles

(2) Follow path R bank burn NW to Loch Coire nan Arr, cross burn, head ENE to long rounded S ridge Beinn Bhan, sustained ascent leads to SOUTH TOP (763 m/2,505 ft), continue easily round exposed corrie lips, short ascent to summit BEINN BHAN (896 m/2,938 ft).
5 kms/3¼ miles

(3) Faint cairned path descends long curling W ridge, wide stony slopes become rockier, glacis, rocky bands usually avoided near L edge. From obvious Bealach nan Arr (600 m/1,970 ft) path curves L to broad ridge crest, don't continue to car-park, but instead strike L over broken ground along corrie lip to radio mast NORTH TOP (776 m/2,545 ft) continuing S around lip, then E along narrow ridge to summit SGURR A'CHAORACHAIN (792 m/2,600 ft). Retrace steps to plateau, descend diagonally NW to join jeep track descending to road.
9 kms/5½ miles

The famous 'Nose' of Sgurr a'Chaorachain and the pinnacled arete connecting it to the main mountain look impressive from the west ridge of Beinn Bhan as it drops towards the Bealach nan Arr. The Cuillin of Rhum can be seen in the far distance behind the figure.

The Diadem of Torridon – Beinn Alligin

Wester Ross, Northern Highlands

OS 1 : 50,000 Sheet 24

From the lower slopes of Tom na Gruagaich, Beinn Alligin appears more a range than a single mountain. The traverse follows the crest of the three Rathains of Alligin on the right before ascending the sharp main top, Sgurr Mor, distinguished by the great 'Gash' below the summit.

Beinn Alligin is best seen from the south, across the sheltered waters of Loch Torridon when the water is calm, the tide is low and golden sea-wrack rings the shore. It is a perfect marriage of two elements, the mountains and the sea, that so often embody the glory of Highland scenery. Most shapely of the three famous Torridon mountains, Beinn Alligin is also the smallest and most compact: an isolated tight-curving crescent of sandstone that rises to six distinct tops, a mountain range in microcosm. But do not underestimate Beinn Alligin, little it is not, it rises almost from the sea like a fortress, its slopes are steep and craggy, its crest narrow and its architecture imposing. Its name means jewel but when its arcing crest glistens with winter snow it

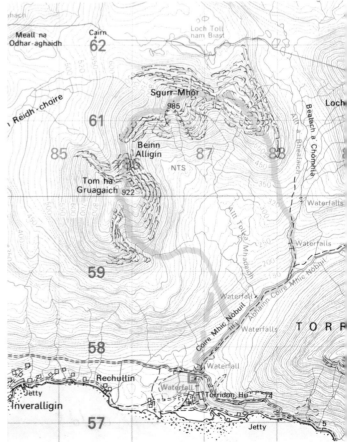

might well mean the Diadem of Torridon.

There is one obvious route on the mountain, a perfect – and popular – horseshoe above the elegant double-headed eastern corrie, which ideally should be followed north-east to south-west so that all difficulties are tackled in the ascent and the island-spread ocean is always ahead. The route starts on an excellent stalker's path leading at first through aromatic woods of Scots pine and rhododendron above the chasm of the Abhainn Coire Mhic Nobuil, the tumultuous river that drains the northern flank of Liathach. Passing a footbridge, deep pools and several waterfalls, the path eventually crosses the river at a second bridge and forks, the right fork continuing right round Liathach to the road – an easy walk through fine scenery if transport allows – the left climbing steadily northwards to a second fork where a climber's path leads up towards the looming eastern shoulder of Beinn Alligin. Ahead the badly eroded scar of the path can be seen winding up a succession of short scrambly rock steps and heathery ledges. This eastern peak of the mountain rises to three separate summits, the Rathains or 'Horns', and their entertaining and airy traverse involves some mild scrambling: the second Horn just appears the highest. Meanwhile Sgurr Mhor rears ahead resembling a snowless Monch with Tom na Gruagaich its neighbouring if emasculated Eiger.

A long but easy ascent, the only slog on the circuit, leads to the tall cairn of Sgurr Mhor, well named 'the Great Peak', a summit from which the free-standing isolation of Beinn Alligin is well appreciated. In perfect weather the view extends from Ardnamurchan to Cape Wrath, but especially impressive is the wild landscape immediately northward, a tangle of rugged outcrops, serpentine rivers and lochs of all shapes and sizes from which jut handsome blade-like peaks – the Shieldaig Forest. Some 200 metres beyond the summit the path descends past the yawning Great Cleft, a prodigious gully so deep and awesome and cutting back so far that it might have been slashed into the mountain's spine by a Cyclopean axeman. On close inspection its slabby floor is actually scramblable and a jumble of huge boulders in the corrie below – Toll a'Mhadaidh, the 'Fox's Hole' – appear to have fallen from it. Tom na Gruagaich is only

the second summit of Beinn Alligin though it bears the OS cairn, and as the 'Maiden's Hillock' it is appropriately graced with a gentle grassy top, though terraced crags fall from it and the ridge leading up to it is the rockiest on the mountain. Narrow but never really exposed, it provides some scrambling if the crest is tackled direct. Below the summit the path plunges from a sandy saddle into the narrow Coire an Laoigh – the 'Corrie of the Calves' – a V-shaped defile with one flank grass, the other scree, the floor steep and the path unrelenting. Eventually heathery moorland drops to the first footbridge over the river close above the beautiful waterfall of Eas Rob, and the stalker's path is rejoined.

The Beinn Alligin Traverse

Length: 11 kms/7 miles
Total ascent: 1400 m/4,600 ft
Difficulty: well-defined path throughout, direct route involves sections of mild but avoidable scrambling. Short expedition but a serious, steep and fairly committing mountain
Note: Rathains can be avoided by traverse path across steep S flank, escape possible S from col E Sgurr Mhor. Area owned by NTS, Ranger tel: Torridon 221

Start: NTS car-park 869576, river bridge 3 kms W Torridon village. (35 m/115 ft).

(1) Good path ascends E bank of river 2 kms to cross footbridge at stream junction. At fork go L, ascending N, cross burn, cairn LHS indicates rough path breaking L towards mountain, up steep spur on scrambly rocky steps, easier slopes lead to rocky tor, summit first Horn. Scrambly descents and ascents lead on over second Horn, highest of RATHAINS OF ALLIGIN

(c 866 m/2,840 ft) and over longer crest third Horn to col whence long grassy climb to SGURR MHOR (985 m/3,232 ft★).
5.5 kms/3½ miles

(2) Path descends ridge SSW past Great Cleft to flat grassy saddle. Cross grassy hummock to lower saddle, ascend steep narrow rocky ridge, scrambling avoidable, to OS cairn TOM NA GRUAGAICH (922 m/3,024 ft) on lip grassy plateau.
1.5 kms/1 mile

(3) Descend easily SW to wide saddle, drop L into narrow corrie, steep path descends grass, scree, to moorland, boggy slopes lead to footbridge, rejoins ascent path.
4 kms/2½ miles

The celebrated 'Gash' or 'Great Cleft' that splits the south ridge of Sgurr Mor close below the summit: it can provide a loose scrambly route up the mountain.

Liathach, the Grey One

Wester Ross, Northern Highlands

OS 1 : 50,000 Sheets 24, 25 (19)

'Liagush, rising sheer
From river-bed up to the sky,
Grey courses of masonry, tier in tier,
And pinnacles splintered on high.'

Cairngorm Club Journal: 1908

As the road from Kinlochewe down Glen Torridon swings west you will suddenly see Liathach. A bold blunt buttress rears skyward curving to a sharp peak, its tip glinting white in the sunshine, with another, sharper and whiter, beyond. Great slopes of tiered grey sandstone sweep down to dun-coloured hummocks on the glen floor. Liathach will be with you now for the next 12 kilometres (7 miles), steep, riven, and seemingly summitless, its massive flanks walling first the glen and then beyond to where the little white cottages of Fasag village find scant room to huddle between the mountain side and the tidal waters of Loch Torridon. Highest of the three mountains which line the northern side of glen and loch, and facing diffident lesser peaks to the south, arrogant Liathach dominates Torridon.

Liathach – pronounced 'Leeagach' – 'the Grey One': typically the upstanding mountains of terraced pinky-grey Torridonian sandstone that so characterize the North-West Highlands form complex massifs with several summits, and Liathach is no exception. Its 8-kilometre (5-mile) crest rises to no less than seven named tops,

Although a relatively straightforward scramble in summer, the winter traverse of the Fasarinen Pinnacles leading towards Mullach an Rathain, the second 'Munro' of Liathach visible beyond, can be quite formidable.

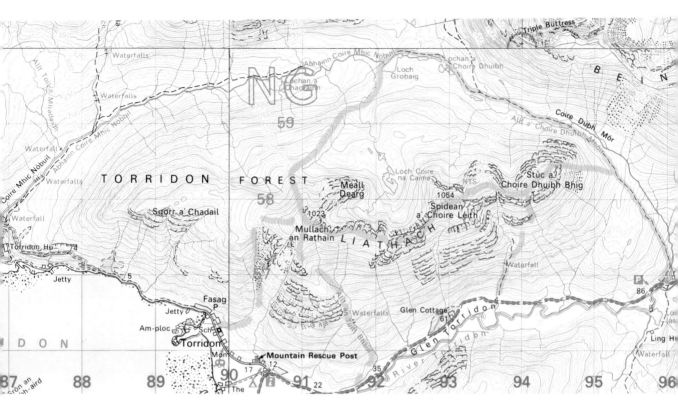

two of them classified as Munros, besides clusters of innominate pinnacles. Although it holds several high shallow corries, the southern flank appears as a continuously steep wall, leaving the northern side of the mountain, hung with five fine corries, to flaunt its real grandeur. Torridonian sandstone is an extraordinarily old rock, but older still – around 1,500 million years, the oldest known – is the Lewisian gneiss on which Liathach and its neighbours stand. Four of the Liathach summits are capped with white quartzite, rather younger than the sandstone, and from a distance they can seem plastered in glinting verglas, a bewildering sight in high summer, but the mountains themselves are of similar age to the Alps, were carved from an earlier plateau some thirty million years ago, and owe their detailed structure to more recent glaciation.

Some years ago a survey conducted by one of the mountain magazines indicated that Liathach

Stuc a'Choire Dhuibh Bhig is the most easterly summit of Liathach, and the ridge from it over Bidein Toll a'Mhuic beyond to the main summit – Spidean a'Choire Leith in the distance – appears deceptive for the going is not at all difficult.

was considered one of the two most magnificent mountains in Scotland (An Teallach was the other) and indeed its traverse is probably the best of the three great ridge scrambles on the Scottish mainland. It is usually taken east to west, a one-way outing necessitating pre-arranged transport or a road walk of at least four kilometres, but a far finer circuit can be made by using the excellent path that links the wide glens of Coire Mhic Nobuil and Coire Dubh Mor round the imposing northern side of the mountain: this is the route described here.

It starts logically, if a trifle fiercely, up the blunt easternmost shoulder which leads to the quartzite-crowned balcony of Stuc a'Choire Dhuibh Bhig, 'Peak of the little Black Corrie', no longer a Munro though it well deserves to be. The succession of tops ahead looks high and steep but proves to be neither, and the route, rough going over the quartzite blocks, leads over twin-topped Bidean Toll a'Mhuic – 'Pinnacle of the Pig's Hollow' – and easily on to Spidean a'Choire Leith with its monstrous southern shoulder jutting over Glen Torridon. The shallow 'Grey Coire' – Choire Leith – hangs below this shoulder providing an ascent route, though from above the steep terraced hillside appears as a green slope, the grassy ledges masking the rock walls, and a descent – as anywhere on sandstone – requires careful route-finding. The easier regular route reaches the crest further east. Spidean is the highest summit with an extensive view over much of the north and west, from Ben Hope via the Cuillin to Ben Nevis.

Now comes the *pièce de résistance*, the crossing of the Fasarinen Pinnacles. Fasarinen are 'teeth' or 'talons', and these sharp and shattered sandstone fangs drop sheer into magnificent Coire na Caime on the north side. Ringed by steep rock and another chain of fearsome *aiguilles* to the west and cradling a tiny lochan, this 'Crooked Corrie' is Liathach's most impressive feature. In summer the pinnacles are not difficult but their exciting crossing is real scrambling and requires a steady head, while in winter the easier bypass, a spectacular path that snakes across the gullies and grassy buttresses falling south from the pinnacles, may prove formidable indeed. The second Munro is Mullach an Rathain – the 'Summit above the Horns'. Which horns? A rocky north-

east ridge curls round Coire na Caime to Meall Dearg (c 960 metres/3,150 feet) a chunky cone of red rock, crossing *en route* the five so-called Northern Pinnacles. Steep and loose, these towers demand real though easy rock-climbing. Meall Dearg is among the few 'technical' summits in Britain and in good winter conditions its ascent from the north followed by the round of Coire na Caime over both sets of pinnacles is one of the best mountaineering expeditions of its kind.

Though it is now possible to descend gradually to the westernmost end of the Liathach crest, our route now takes the scree-draped northern ridge, dropping down its left flank until gentle slopes lead to the remote lochan-studded strath where the path is joined and from where the sculpted northern flanks of the mountain can really be appreciated. It is now downhill, through wild country but on a good path, back to the start.

A Circular Traverse of Liathach

Length: 15 kms/9¼ miles
Total ascent: 1340 m/4,400 ft
Difficulty: a rugged and strenuous traverse, sometimes a little exposed, serious scrambling can be avoided: a high mountain, potentially serious and committing in bad conditions, rope might be useful
Note: area owned by NTS, interesting Visitor Centre at 905557. Ranger phone: Torridon 221

Start: large NTS car-park at 958569 beside A896 bridge below Coire Dubh Mor.

(1) From bridge, path ascends W of burn towards Coire Dubh Mor. After c 1.5 kms large sapling-topped boulder marks toe of shallow glacis spur falling across moorland from E face Liathach. Ascend spur, occasional cairns, towards prominent Y gully in centre grassy face. Narrow path zigzags steeply up heather strip R of gully, trends R through craglets to nose NE buttress below narrow upper cliffs. Round corner R mild scramble 30 m leads to quartzite scree, blocks, summit STUC A'CHOIRE DHUIBH BHIG (913 m/2,997 ft).
3 kms/2 miles

(2) Gradual ridge then steep rocky ascent lead over vague cairned top to blocky summit, cairn, BIDEAN TOLL A'MHUIC

(975 m/3,200 ft). Descend R of crest, rocky, traverse L to col, stony ridge ascends to boulders, sharp rocky summit SPIDEAN A'CHOIRE LEITH (1054 m/3,456 ft★). Bouldery descent, grassy ridge lead to 5 Fasarinen Pinnacles: either traverse direct, sustained exposed scrambling, or take narrow traverse path across steep slopes S flank to narrow col past difficulties. Final highest pinnacle AM FASARINEN (c 930 m/3,050 ft) accessible from path, easy scramble up gully. Long undulating grassy crest leads to minor top, avoid outcrops on LHS, stony slopes lead to OS cairn MULLACH AN RATHAIN (1023 m/3,358 ft★).
3.5 kms/2 miles

(3) Descend W 200 m to sandy shoulder whence follow N ridge until easy diagonal scree descent L leads to steep grassy slopes. Lose c 300 m (1,000 ft) height, take grassy spur NE towards W end Loch Grobaig. Cross outfall easily, at good path N bank go E. Path crosses vague boggy saddle, descends SE down Coire Dubh Mor to start.
8.5 kms/5¼ miles

Alternatives
(1.A) Regular ascent/descent path leaves road 936566 2 kms climbing to col just W Stuc a'Choire Duibh Bhig.

(3.A) Descend S from Mullach an Rathain by S ridge whence steep grass tongues drop to SE corrie, follow burn to road at 918555, or by Fasag stone shoot 800 m W.

Loch Torridon runs deep into the sandstone mountains of Wester Ross. The shapely pyramid of Liathach rises over the head of the loch in this view eastwards from near the crofting village of Ardheslaig.

The Slioch Horseshoe

Wester Ross, Northern Highlands

OS 1 : 50,000 Sheet 19

Slioch they call it – the 'Spearhead' – from the array of great pointed buttresses that support its broad crown. One of the most distinctive peaks of the Northern Highlands, its shapely sandstone shoulders rise from a plinth of grey gneiss to dominate the southern end of Loch Maree while its summit looks out across the so-called Great Wilderness. Easily accessible, Slioch is of the Great Wilderness but not part of it.

Loch Maree is the finest of the large Scottish lochs, 19 kilometres (12 miles) in length, it lies in wilder and more rugged country than its rivals. It was known long ago as Loch Ewe – as is the sea-loch into which it drains – and our walk commences at the little village of Kinlochewe at its head. Initially the path leads down the broad strath of the Kinlochewe River, gentle green farmland which seems strangely out of place beneath the grey pyramids of Beinn Eighe rising beyond the dark alders of the river bank. This is

an ancient path, a right of way down the entire northern shore of the loch along which, before the advent of the Kyle of Lochalsh railway, all mail for the Outer Isles was carried by runner to the little port of Poolewe. It is still a very beautiful journey through the waterside woods of the Letterewe Estate, which can be reached only on foot or by boat.

At the head of the loch the path traverses the shores of a pretty bay which mirrors Slioch rising above the birches, before crossing a footbridge over the torrent which issues from a dark and narrow defile that splits the hillside: this is Gleann Bianasdail, also known as the Fasagh Glen, the major outlet of the sizable Lochan Fada beyond Slioch, and with an excellent stalker's path leading through it, an important cross-country link. Our route now ascends to the lip of Slioch's shallow eastern corrie, more of a wide hollow than a corrie, before gaining the shoulder of Sgurr Dubh – the 'Black Peak' – by steep and unrelenting slopes.

This is the southern extremity of the Slioch horseshoe and here the wary may well encounter wild goats among the boulders. The ridge continues easily past two curious green lochans before a short rocky step leads to slopes of wiry grass and the desolate and undulating plateau. Patches of gravel and grey sandstone lend a moonscape atmosphere to the scene while an incongruous sandy pool of the kind unlikely to survive the summer hides beneath the final summit hump. It is worthwhile visiting the far western spur of the plateau which gives a fine view back across the craggy south-western flanks towards Kinlochewe and the Torridon peaks, but it is essential to continue to the twin northern summit, an eyrie looking steeply down on the bright ribbon of Loch Maree. The loch takes its modern name from Isle Maree, one of more than a score of islands clustered in the distance, where once the druids worshipped among the oaks and where pagan rites and bull sacrifices are said to have continued until the seventeenth century. Certainly St Maelrubha

Sgurr an Tuill Bhàin is the eastern peak of Slioch and this is the view towards it from below the north summit: the final ridge is unexpectedly narrow. The southern end of the Lochan Fada is glimpsed on the left.

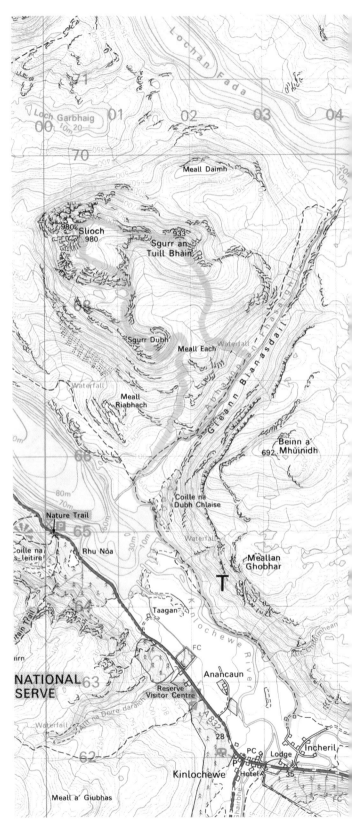

built a chapel there and the waters of his sacred well were believed, until quite recently, to cure mental disorders!

Be that as it may, the route onwards along the airy northern arm of the horseshoe provides a continuous prospect over the great trench of Lochan Fada and the serried ridges and summits of the alluring Great Wilderness beyond – some call it the Whitbread Wilderness after the redoubtable proprietor who while stalking the deer has eschewed the Land Rover and fought off variously the Hydro Board and mineral developers to continue the preservation of the finest area of unspoilt wild landscape in Britain. Long may it remain so. Beyond Lochan Fada rises A'Mhaighdean (pronounced Vyejun – 'The Maiden'), surprisingly similar to Slioch in outline and Scotland's most remote Munro, with the dark battlements of An Teallach (the 'Forge') easily identifiable in the distance.

A perfect narrow arete leads onto the final summit, pointed Sgurr an Tuill Bhàin ('Peak of the deep white corrie'), before easy slopes descend into the central corrie. The steep burn draining it gives the most interesting route down into the Fasagh Glen where the stalker's path is joined and followed back above the river with its delightful gorges, waterfalls, pools and bead-bonny rowans to the footbridge above the shore of Loch Maree.

A Circuit of Slioch

Length: 19 kms/12 miles
Total ascent: 1240 m/4,050 ft
Difficulty: excellent paths much of the way, otherwise good going though several very steep sections: the foot of this high mountain is a long way from habitation
Note: stalking information from Kinlochewe Estate, tel Kinlochewe 262.

Start: Incheril, limited parking at lane end 033624 before farm gate. (20 m/65 ft).

(1) Track passes R of farm, at junction go L to good path leading NW below hillside, by river, to shore Loch Maree and footbridge over river gorge.
4 kms/2½ miles

(2) Over bridge good path ascends NE towards narrow Gleann Bianasdail, levelling out after 500 m where rough trail forks L by twin cairns ascending hollow in hillside, steep, rocky in places, to Sgurr Dubh, after 200 m below rock buttress faint path contours L to very steep heathery slope, zigzag to summit Sgurr Dubh (c 730 m/2,400 ft). Follow broad ridge to saddle, round RH corrie edge to lochan, up steep narrow shoulder beyond to wide slopes leading to plateau and hump beyond, summit trig pt SLIOCH (980 m/3,217 ft★).
4.5 kms/3 miles

(3) Continue N 200 m to second hump, NORTH SUMMIT (980 m) whence strike E along plateau edge then narrowing ridge to thin saddle and summit SGURR AN TUILL BHÀIN (933 m/3,058 ft). Descend ridge SE to slight knoll where shallow spur falls R to corrie lip, small pond. Rough path descends steep ground L bank burn, cascades, waterfalls, to Gleann Bianasdail, take good path R to regain Loch Maree and retrace (1).
6.5 kms/4 miles to footbridge

Long-distance alternative
(3.A) In Gleann Bianasdail go L to outfall Lochan Fada, reach good path E side Gleann na Muice by stepping stones or crossing burn immediately N little Loch Gleann na Muice. Path becomes track to Heights of Kinlochewe and Incheril.
18.5 kms/11½ miles Slioch to Incheril

Dominating the southern end of Loch Maree, Slioch is seen here at dawn from the pine-scattered shore of Loch Maree near Grudie Bridge.

Ben More, the Roof of Mull Hebrides

OS 1 : 50,000 Sheet 48

'Mull . . . a hilly country, diversified
with heath and grass, and many rivulets.
Dr Johnson . . . said it was a dreary country,
much worse than Sky.' (sic)

James Boswell:
Journal of a Tour to the Hebrides 1773

'. . . in my journeys among the High Alps I
never found so much difficulty as here.'

Faujas de Saint Fond:
after attempting Ben More 1784

Perhaps the weather was terrible on both occasions and certainly Dr Johnson took little delight in mountains, but nevertheless both gentlemen were sadly mistaken for Mull is one of the most fascinating islands in the entire Hebrides while Ben More, its highest point and the only island Munro outside Skye, is a beautiful peak but in no sense a difficult one. The 'Big Hill', as its name translates, lords it over nine other summits rising above 2,000 feet (610 metres) besides a sizeable portion of the Inner Hebrides and is very much a

maritime mountain. Far gentler than the Cuillin of Skye yet still wild in a tempered way, these hills are geologically extremely complex and typically shapely: the conspicuous rocky cone of Ben Talaidh (761 m/2,496 ft) is surely one of Scotland's most imposing small peaks. Scots will need no prompting, but any southron mountain lover travelling the western Highlands should endeavour to climb Ben More and enjoy something of the intimate charm of Mull and its exceptional scenery: the road distance from Glencoe via the short ferries at Corran and Craignure is just 80 kilometres (50 miles).

Rising between two fine sea lochs and dominating them both, Ben More is a great pointed pile of basaltic lavas which radiates

Ben More is seen on a winter evening from the north-west across Loch Tuath. The traverse follows the skyline over A'Chioch on the left and then upwards to Ben More's summit before descending the left-trending ridge to the rounded shoulder of An Gearna.

several gracefully curving ridges and can be ascended easily from the roadside on either shore. However, the great grey scree slopes which the mountain throws down southwards are 'reminiscent of a slag heap' – to quote the SMC guide – and the discerning mountaineer will prefer to tackle the mountain from the lonely shores of the northern Loch na Keal – the 'Loch of the Cliffs'. The best route on the mountain, steep, spectacular but straightforward, traverses the worthy satellite of A'Chioch (the 'Breast') and leads directly to the summit.

The route starts almost on the beach where oyster-catchers dip and strut and seals watch quizzically from the lapping waves, at first ascending alongside the burn into Gleann na Beinne Fada. The torrent pours over a succession of waterfalls and several of its gorges must be 15 metres deep (50 feet) yet narrow enough to cross perhaps with an intrepid leap. Soon a steep ascent leads up to the crest of the Beinn Fhada ridge (the 'Long Mountain') where interesting going over grassy saddles and rocky outcrops leads towards the rugged wedge-shaped summit of Beinn Fhada rearing up like a miniature Gasherbrum IV.

From the broad saddle below Beinn Fhada the ridge up to A'Chioch appears deceptively easy but it soon steepens and narrows to become quite scrambly and the easiest route over the several little rock steps that bar the way is not always obvious. The bare domed summit of A'Chioch is surrounded by steep rocky slopes and from the small cairn the final arete rearing up to Ben More itself looks formidable – and in winter truly alpine. Taken direct in good conditions the ridge would be quite interesting for it is rocky and narrow and excitingly exposed on the northern side, but a series of grassy and mossy ledges on the steep enough southern flank turn all difficulties and the climbing ends suddenly on the plateau edge immediately below the summit cairn.

On a good day the astonishing view stretches from Ireland and the Outer Isles to the Cuillin and Ben Cruachan, but even in moody weather there is an inspiring panorama over the island-scattered western ocean. Awesome basalt cliffs close below frown down over Inch Kenneth and the mouth of Loch na Keal; Staffa rides the sea beyond like a viking galley while further still lies Bac Mor – the bizarre Dutchman's Cap – the Treshnich Isles and perhaps a white sail or two. The ancient Cathedral of Holy Iona is clearly visible a full 25 kilometres (16 miles) distant. If you have ever sailed this sea you will find this the most exciting view in the Hebrides.

The descent to the flat-topped shoulder of An Gearna is straightforward with interesting glimpses back across the craggy face of Ben More toward A'Chioch and its arete, but there is still a sting in the mountain's tail. The northern flanks of An Gearna are girdled by a low band of vertical and dripping black cliffs and these must be bypassed to left or right before a safe descent can be made into Gleann na Beinne Fada and the burn followed down to the shore.

The Ben More Horseshoe

Length: 13 kms/8 miles
Total ascent: 1300 m/4,275 ft
Difficulty: rough ground most of the way, some quite steep sections and several easy but exposed scrambly moves: good tactical route-finding required
Note: Magnetic rock renders compass unreliable here. Stalking information from Estate office, tel: Aros 410

Start: easy roadside parking at bridge 507367 on B8035 (5 m/15 ft).

(1) Rough path ascends W bank of burn 1.5 kms to waterfalls (in spate ascend pathless E bank) cross and climb steepening hillsides to gain N end Beinn Fhada ridge, cairn Pt 563. Continue SE along undulating ridge crest then steep semi-scramble above tiny lochan leads to flat summit and cairn BEINN FHADA (702 m/2,303 ft).
4.5 kms/2¾ miles

(2) Return to final tarn, descend S to wide saddle (c 525 m/1,720 ft), ascend narrowing ridge ahead, scrambling over short rock bands exposed on LHS to summit A'CHIOCH (c 850 m/2,790 ft). Rocky crest descends W then SW to narrow col, ascend steep arete above, exposed on RHS. Traces of path avoid difficulties by ledge systems on LHS, leading steeply to summit cairn, BEN MORE (966 m/3,169 ft★).
3.5 kms/2 miles

(3) Cross summit plateau NW along crag edge, descend stony slopes to gradual ridge fork, keep R above corrie to An Gearna plateau. Descend WNW from small cairn Pt 563 to avoid steep cliff band around nose of ridge, descending diagonally R below difficulties to rejoin ascent route near waterfall. Alternatively 500 m before reaching Pt 563 descend steeply N to pass E of cliffs.
5 kms/3¼ miles

Ben More and its satellites look impressive from the north over the sheltered waters of Loch na Keal: Beinn Fhada is the apparently small wedge-shaped summit at centre almost hidden by its own shoulder while A'Chioch and Ben More rise to the right.

Skye: the Storr and the Trotternish Scarp

Hebrides

OS 1 50,000 Sheet 23

'A walk upon ploughed fields in England
is a dance upon carpets compared to the
toilsome drugery of wandering in Skie'

Dr Johnson:
A Journey to the Western Isles of Scotland: 1775

Skuyö the Vikings called it – 'Cloud Island' – its high ground so often wearing a cloud cap as the dragon ships swept down the Minch. It is an apt title for this magical island, largest of the Inner Hebrides and famed for its Cuillin mountains; but Skye rises to another lesser range, no less unique in its way, liable to better weather and well meriting the attention of any mountain lover. Its 25-kilometre (15-mile) escarpment forms the spine of Trotternish, the long northern peninsula of the island, and while its summits rarely rise above 600 metres (2,000 feet) its crest falls eastward as a continuous line of frowning black precipices, often as high as 100 metres (300 feet), a landform as striking as any in Britain.

Apparently this incredible cliff is the largest landslip in these islands, dating to the retreat of the mainland ice-sheet in late Pleistocene times – the last ice-age – when the edges of a thick layer of basaltic lava, no longer supported by the ice, slipped away in a series of giant slivers like overlapping slices from a pre-cut bread loaf. Near the scarp's two extremities the rotting basalt has eroded into particularly spectacular architecture – the Storr and the Quiraing – both easily reached and well known. A long traverse

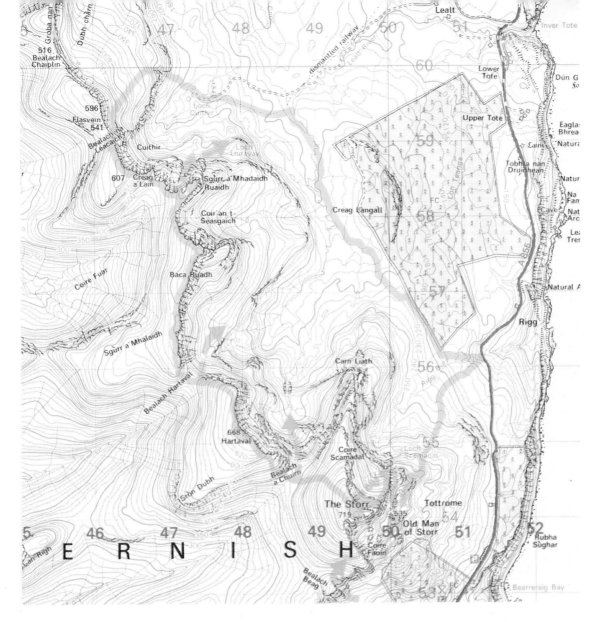

The Old Man of Storr and the weird basalt pinnacles surrounding it are seen to the south from the foot of the Storr cliffs: long island of Raasay lies in the sea beyond.

of the entire crest, a one-way trip of over 30 kilometres (20 miles) with no easy return, was first completed in 1901 but the route detailed traverses the best of the scarp in a reasonable day's circuit.

The extraordinary formations below the 180-metre (600-foot) cliffs of The Storr, the highest point in Trotternish, are usually reached from a Forestry Commission car-park at the northern end of Loch Leathan but for this route the Rigg Burn is followed, past banks of kingcups and through ferny dells to a delightful area of violet-sprinkled lawn just north of a dozen or so rickety pinnacles. Chief among them is the Old Man of Storr, a slightly leaning cigar-shaped pillar some 60 metres high (200 feet) and a conspicuous Skye landmark first climbed in 1955 by Don Whillans and his mates: Storr is said to mean 'decayed tooth', an appropriate enough title. Ravens glide around the corrie while awesome dark cliffs split by black gullies tower above and exploration is suggested before climbing to the Storr summit, the best route taking a narrow path that works north round the base of the cliffs into hanging Coire Scamadal. Here the decaying basalt at the corrie lip provides a rich environment for arctic/alpine plants including the Icelandic pur-slane (*Koenigia islandica*) found only here and in

Mull. Sensational views unfold as the cliff edge is followed upwards until a final buttress forces a traverse across into a wide grassy gully which emerges suddenly onto the greensward of the wide summit plateau.

A fine viewpoint, the Storr summit is a gentle place but with the vertical always close at hand one moves around it with care. Convex slopes sweep down to the first bealach and the route onwards over Hartaval to Baca Ruadh is easy with firm turf underfoot. This wide and lonely country belongs to the soaring eagles: the tiny white crofts scattered along the sea-fringe and the black specks of ships out in the Sound are a different world, a world inaccessible beyond the omnipresent cliffs. Beyond the 'Red Ridge' of Baca Ruadh the cliff edge becomes convoluted and the rock architecture exceptional once more. An impressive prow guarded by a narrow scrambly rock band juts from the main crest, but Sgurr a'Mhadaidh Ruadh – the 'Peak of the Red Fox' – can be easily bypassed. Creag a'Lain is the next summit and before climbing steeply up the edge of its great cliffs the face of the bealach beyond should be closely studied for it must soon be descended. Creag a'Lain would appear to mean 'Enclosed Crag' and its imposing face rears out of a strange cliff-girt hollow named Cuithir – the 'Narrow Glen' – the next objective.

Despite its formidable appearance the descent from the Bealach na Leacaich – the 'Pass of the Stony slopes' – is safe and easy albeit requiring careful route-finding: a direct line down these craggy slopes would be horrific though a possible ascent route can be picked out from below. Lilies float on the impressively situated Cuithir lochans at the head of a rough road and the remains of an ancient tramway: diatomite was once excavated here, a siliceous deposit formed from the remains of microscopic algae which infilled small post-glacial tarns and which has industrial uses. The tramway gives a fairly dry descent to the river which provides an interesting route through otherwise extremely rough country most of the way back to the Rigg Burn.

The Storr and the Trotternish Scarp

Length: 20.5 kms/12¾ miles
Total ascent: 1130 m/3,700 ft
Difficulty: easy walking, usually excellent going, careful route-finding essential in places: serious high ground attracting fierce weather, cliff edges always close
Note: easy descent E possible Bealach a'Chuirn, Bealach Hartaval, green gully 471584 before Creag a'Lain, escape always possible W

Start: limited parking on verge A855 at Rigg Burn culvert, 512562. (120 m/395 ft).

(1) Follow S fork Rigg Burn then ascend grassy corridor to ridge, fence, crest path climbs easily to grassy plateau overlooking Storr pinnacles and lochan. Path traverses N below main cliffs to little col, stile, continuing round L up short rock step into Coire Scamadal. Either head directly up to obvious wide green gully or ascend rocky L edge above cliffs traversing R to gully on faint cairned path below final crags. Steep grass leads to summit plateau THE STORR (719 m/2,358 ft).
5 kms/3 miles

(2) Descend grassy slopes NW to Bealach a'Chuirn, ascend L of broken crags to join cliff edge leading to summit HARTAVAL (668 m/2,191 ft), continue along edge crossing Bealach Hartaval and shoulder Sgurr a'Mhalaich to BACA RUADH (637 m/2,091 ft). Descend round corrie lip to col, avoiding SGURR A'MHADAIDH RUADH (587 m/1,926 ft) as desired, ascend steeply near cliff edge to summit CREAG A'LAIN (607 m/1,993 ft).
7 kms/4¼ miles

(3) Descend N to Bealach Leacaich. Immediately N of ancient wall drop R down soft scree c 100 m to horizontal sheep path traversing L above rocks to wide grass slopes. Descend steeply NE to twin ponds not on map. Follow stream descending from just N (469600) over lip to Loch Cuithir (180 m/590 ft).
2.5 kms/1¼ miles

(4) E of lake old tramway route descends ESE, after 1 km break R to River Lealt, follow river bank S, then E fork, to gain forestry edge, follow fence SE along to Rigg Burn, descend to start.
6 kms/3¾ miles

Eastward-facing basalt cliffs line the edge of the Trotternish escarpment as it stretches northward over Hartaval towards Baca Ruadh.

Blaven and the White Strand   Hebrides

OS 1 : 50,000 Sheet 32

'Oh Blaven! rocky Blaven!
How I long to be with thee again,
to see lashed gulf and gully
smoke white in the windy rain . . .'

probably Alexander Smith: 1865

Immortalized in song, celebrated by repute and beloved of climbers, the spectacular Cuillin mountains of Skye are unique in Britain. Despite the romantic claim of the Gaellic bards that this savage range was named from Cuchullin, the legendary 'Hound of Ulster' who ran a war-school on Skye, a more likely derivation is Norse and means 'Keel-like Ridges', a name applied also to similar mountains in Scandinavia.

There is the Black Cuillin and the Red, the former a serrated horseshoe ridge of thirty-one formidable gabbro summits surrounding remote Loch Coruisk, the Red an array of smaller more genteel conical peaks cloaked in granite screes and ranged to the north-east. There is but a single anomaly, one major peak, very definitely a Black Cuillin, which rises beyond the main range in what is really Red Cuillin territory at the head of the lovely Strathaird peninsula. To the Gaels it was Bla Bheinn, variously the 'Blue Mountain' or the 'Hill of Bloom', Sherrif Alexander Nicolson – he who first climbed Sgurr Alasdair, Skye's highest summit in 1873 – claimed it was the island's finest mountain, more recently Hamish Brown described it as the 'portentous postcript to the gabbro galaxy', but

to most mountain lovers it is just plain Blaven.

But Blaven is hardly plain, a superb peak, maritime and aloof, its great tousled head throws down rent and rugged walls east and west to form the spine of narrow Strathaird between the great sea lochs of Slapin and Scavaig. A long southern ridge sweeps down to the sea while four black satellites guard the summit from the encroaching Red Cuillin clustered to the north. Notwithstanding the explorations of Sherrif Nicolson and others, serious mountaineering started in Scotland with the discovery by members of the Alpine Club in the 1870s that there were still virgin peaks to climb in the Cuillin, though Blaven had been climbed in 1857 by a Professor Nicol and the young poet Charles Swinburne, which suggests that by its easiest

way Blaven is not a difficult mountain. Indeed of all the major Black Cuillin summits, Blaven is the most suitable objective for the experienced hill-walker with no rock-climbing pretensions.

The regular route takes the line of least resistance up the great steep and craggy shoulder that falls east from the summit into Coire Uaigneich (the 'Lonely Corrie'?) from where it is fairly unobtrusively marked and cairned: in poor conditions route-finding skills will be useful. Carefully avoiding precipitous ground, the ascent requires only a little mild scrambling, avoidable by diligent reconnaissance and never exposed. There are tantalizing glimpses northward over a narrow rocky bealach to Clach Glas, the jagged tower-like peak that appears as Blaven's smaller twin in most distant views: the traverse of the pair is a classic expedition first made in 1888 by the famous alpinist Charles Pilkington but it involves difficult and exposed scrambling.

As it zigzags up the eastern shoulder of Blaven, the route passes the head of this great gully which frames the summit of Clach Glas, the next peak to the north.

It has been claimed that Blaven is the best viewpoint in the Cuillin. Certainly the view includes a superb – and rare – panorama of the entire Main Ridge, all three Red Cuillin groups, the distant Storr, the Rough Bounds of Knoydart, the western seaboard and the Inner Isles. The summit ridge leads over the head of the great gully that splits the eastern flank to a second top before commencing a long descent to Camasunary where the white beach beckons towards the shimmering sea and pinnacled Rhum.

Continuously interesting, the ridge is sustained at harder-than-walking standard until grassy slopes – crossed by a good traverse path which can be used to avoid Camasunary itself – lead to the deserted lodge in the green meadows behind a lonely and beautiful bay. The name of this place appears to mean 'Bay of the White Strand' and it would be worth the climb just to walk the shore and swim maybe in the deep river channel at its western extremity. Unfortunately this tranquillity was interrupted in 1968 by an ill-

conceived military attempt to blast an unwanted jeep-road over the Strathaird peninsula and through to Coruisk, luckily it was prevented but not before the old track linking Camasunary to Kilmarie on the Elgol road had been ruined. This is the final section of the route: stalwart walkers will cut the corner through the 'corrie of St Mary's kirk' – Cille Mhaire – which is rough terrain though shorter than the road which is easy going and unfrequented.

Over Blaven to Camasunary

Length: 15 kms/9½ miles
Total ascent: 1300 m/4,250 ft
Difficulty: rugged strenuous itinerary involving tactical route-finding, a little mild scrambling on a large craggy mountain deserving respect: a committing route once started on S ridge descent

Start: good roadside parking at 561215, old bridge beside A881 Elgol road. (10 m/30 ft).

(1) From bridge 200 m N, path ascends N bank Dunaiche burn to lower corrie thence climbing steeply L into Coire Uaigneich beneath craggy E face Blaven to fade by stream fan below dark cleft. Turn N, ascend grassy rake diagonally up great shoulder, traces of path, cairns, take easiest line through rocky outcrops to crest of shoulder. Path zigzags up steep stony slope past tops two big gullies, across scree, boulders, to gap in summit rock band, short scramble to OS cairn and summit BLA BHEINN (928 m/3,044 ft★).
4 kms/2½ miles

(2) Descend S 20 m to little col, easy airy rock ramp leads L across broken crag to shallow gully and cairn SOUTH SUMMIT (924 m/3,033 ft) continue S avoiding blind ridge on R, best route cairned. Descend stony crest, dropping L round each difficulty, occasional mild scrambly moves, to steep grass slopes, flat green spur crossed by traverse path, and Camasunary shore.
3.5 kms/2¼ miles

(3) Rough track climbs E to wide saddle Am Mam (185 m/610 ft). Descend c 400 m, strike L across hillsides following c 150 m contour into Cille Mhaire corrie. Short ascent leads to wide boggy saddle (210 m/690 ft), descend steep grassy slopes N to Dunaiche burn near waterfall, rejoin ascent path far bank.
7.5 kms/4¾ miles

Alternatives
(2.A) From c 200 m S of S summit descend steep stony slopes SE, hints of path, avoiding cliffs on L, to narrow col above head Coire Uaigneich, broken slopes drop into corrie, rejoin ascent route.
4.5 kms/2¾ miles

(3.A) From Camasunary cross Am Mam but continue track to Kilmarie (4 kms/2½ miles), follow road N to start.
9.5 kms/6 miles

The south ridge of Blaven rises from the lonely meadows of Camasunary where a deserted cottage stands behind the white strand.

South Uist, the Mountains and the Sea

Hebrides

OS 1 : 50,000 Sheet 22

> 'Of these islands it must be confessed
> that they have not many allurements, but
> to the lover of naked nature.'
>
> Dr Johnson:
A Journey to the Western Isles of Scotland, 1775.

Tir nan Og, the Isles beyond the Sunset, the Islands of the Blessed. The mysterious islands of the far west have ever beckoned, even if the Long Island – the chain of the Outer Hebrides that stretches from Barra and the Uists to Harris and Lewis – is not quite as remote as that mythical archipelago of Gaellic legend. Few folk associate South Uist with mountains, nevertheless the mountaineer on Skye or the yachtsman beating across the Little Minch will be well aware of two prominent peaks rising high above the horizon-hugging shape of the island. Actually three worthy summits spring from a rugged mass of gneiss which rears steeply from the indented eastern shore to drop more gently westward towards the loch-scattered moorland, green machair and white sands of the Atlantic coast.

This walk traverses all three of these summits and must be one of the finest expeditions of its kind in Britain, long but always interesting and atmospheric with that heady mixture of mountains and sea. A strong party could obviously complete the circuit in a long day, but would be unable to linger to enjoy the stupendous views of ocean and islands or to explore the intricacies

of summit and glen. Starting along the attractive serpentine shores of Loch Eynort, the route climbs through the heather towards the obvious low point in the long southern ridge of Beinn Mhor and the hidden ravine which crosses it. At first the ridge is wide and peaty but soon becomes scabbed with patches of glacis and sprinkled with erratic blocks. Beyond a second strange defile the mountain asserts itself and the

narrowing ridge sweeps up towards Beinn Mhor: a glance back down this elegant grassy crest reveals sea on three sides, a spectacular situation. From the summit however the view is truly unique, to the north-west the great stacks of St Kilda rise from the wide ocean a full 100 kilometres (62 miles) distant, while the jagged crest of Rhum floats south-eastward on the Hebridean Sea.

A narrow arete leads onwards from the summit, a row of small spiky tops and miniature gendarmes liberally hung with moss and grass from which a succession of bold buttresses and deep gullies fall some 250 metres (850 feet) into Glen Hellisdale: several climbs have been made

Though only of modest height, Beinn Mhor and its surrounding peaks are visible throughout the Uists. Here Hecla (left) and Beinn Mhor are seen to the south from Benbecula across the shallow Bagh nam Faoilean – the South Channel.

here. A short way past the northern summit the regular route takes the north-west ridge but our traverse descends round the head of Glen Hellisdale to a wide saddle at the base of a craggy wall guarding the route upwards onto Ben Corodale. This barrier can be turned on the left by a steep uncompromising slog but a more entertaining route follows the obvious grass rake, more spectacular but quite straightforward, which ascends rightwards across the cliff to gain the pleasant seaward ridge of the mountain. Best described as a rocky turret, the top of Ben Corodale is reached easily or by a good scramble, but the way ahead is not obvious for sizable crags almost encircle the summit. However a grassy rake descends to easy slopes below and a wide shoulder littered with rock outcrops and little ponds. Ben Corodale is also known as Feaveallach, probably a corruption of Feith Bealach – the Boggy Pass – which succinctly describes the next saddle, a waste of peat hags below the slopes rising to Hecla. Obviously once a Viking sailing mark – for there is a prominent Icelandic volcano of the same name – Hecla is another fine mountain, and the west ridge leads first to a craggy top which provides a satisfying – but avoidable – scramble, whence a short rocky arete leads to the bouldery main summit. Now the view northwards opens up, over a myriad lochs, lochans, islands and islets towards the distant blue line of the Harris peaks, while Skye looms across the Little Minch behind the massive bulwark of Waterstein head. From the northern summit, Point 564, the grassy ridge falling seawards gives an excellent descent to Usinish Bay.

Set into the grassy hillside, the stone-walled Usinish bothy is not difficult to find. Kept shipshape by shepherds and military parties from the Benbecula rocket range, thus snug refuge is pretty basic but storm-proof and furnished with rough bunks and a few old pots and pans: visitors should bring sleeping bags and a light stove. In good weather the return route south-ward down the coast is delightful with steep hillsides above the sea linking a series of narrow and secluded glens. Particularly evocative is Glen Corodale where now ruined cottages gave sanctuary to the Young Pretender for three weeks in 1746 while the authorities combed the island for him. In rain and mist however the return route can be hard going and the navig-ation tricky, especially through the complex terrain leading to the Bealach na Hoe.

A Traverse of Beinn Mhor and Hecla

Length: 28 kms/17 miles, plus
Total ascent: outward – 1250 m/4,100 ft; return – 650 m/2,150 ft
Difficulty: virtually trackless, rocky in places but usually excellent going on high ground, several slightly exposed sections but direct route avoids any scrambling. Return route more rugged, some bog and deep heather: tactical navigational skills useful. This is wild, remote and unfrequented country and should be respected accordingly
Notes: compass unreliable on Hecla. For NW ridge regular route leave road at 768341. B&B at Arinambane roadhead, phone Bornish 379. Hut-type accommodation nearby at Gatcliff Trust's Howmore hostel, warden at cottage 759564

Start: roadhead beyond North Locheynort, ask permission to park at Arinambane croft 789283.

(1) Good path leads E above shore but disappears at 805287 Sloc Dubh inlet E side, ascend by burn E into shallow corrie, more steeply into defile Bealach na Hoe (c 200 m/660 ft). Follow broad ridge N over Beinn nan Caorach, cross deep gash Bealach Crosgard, climb narrowing ridge N to flat shoulder, continue NW along cliff edge to trig point BEINN MHOR (620 m/2,034 ft).
7 kms/4¼ miles

(2) Continue NW along narrow arete, almost scrambly, exposed on R, to minor top, then wider ridge leads to shelter circle NORTH SUMMIT (608 m/1,994 ft). Descend N to flat shoulder then E down broad slabby ridge – best route is wide grassy gully R of crest – to broken ground of wide Bealach Hellisdale (c 290 m/955 ft). Grassy rake, wide, easy, ascends diagonally R across cliffs above Bealach to join broad ridge above leading NW to rocky turret BEN CORODALE (527 m/1,729 ft).
3.5 kms/2¼ miles

(3) Grassy rake immediately below summit drops W through cliffs to easy slopes, then broad broken ridge descends to wide peaty saddle Bealach Corodale (c 300 m/985 ft). Ascend steep slope above to wide ridge leading E to rocky summit HECLA (606 m/1,988 ft).
3 kms/2 miles

(4) Descend NE to col, contour R to gain grassy ridge dropping SE towards Usinish Bay. Bothy at 850333 below grassy hillside (c 10 m/30 ft).
3.5 kms/2¼ miles

(5) Return route follows rugged coast S, steep slopes above sea link glens, rough going. From boggy Glen Liadale strike SW, pass lochan Glen Cormascot whence broken rocky hillsides lead to Bealach na Hoe. Retrace route to start.
10.5 kms/6½ miles, plus

The pride of Beinn Mhor is its narrow summit crest, this is the view south-eastward from the north summit towards the main top: Loch Eynort is seen below on the right and the Cuillin of Rhum in the far distance, left.

Safety and Access

'The recollections of past pleasures cannot be effaced ... There have been joys too great to be described in words ... Climb if you will, but remember that courage and strength are nought without prudence, and that a momentary negligence may destroy the happiness of a lifetime. Do nothing in haste; look well to each step; and from the beginning think what may be the end.'

With those memorable lines Edward Whymper closed his book *Scrambles Amongst The Alps* which despite being first published in 1871, is still probably the greatest mountain narrative in the English language. He had good cause to voice such sentiments for after reaching the coveted summit of the Matterhorn for the very first time, he was involved in a tragedy which clouded his entire life thereafter; an avoidable accident which killed four of his companions and which today we would blame on negligence. Admittedly he was writing of the Alps and we have no Matterhorns here in Britain, not quite, but the same strictures apply, for although the hazards among our subtle British hills are far less apparent, they are no less real.

Our hills are all things to all men – there is a challenge somewhere among our wonderful uplands for everyone and the routes described in this book cover a fantastic variety of terrain. Certainly first-time ramblers ambling along the Malvern crest on a balmy summer's day may be forgiven for wondering how they could possibly be courting danger. As a teenager my own introduction to the Malverns was a double traverse with the hills plastered in hard frozen snow, and we made the return leg after nightfall by moonlight. It was an unforgettable experience that Whymper would surely have understood, but in such conditions even a sprained ankle could have resulted in an exposure case and an epic midnight rescue by gum-booted policemen, themselves at risk slithering around steep and icy slopes. However, we were aware of the hazards – such as they were – and we were suitably equipped for traversing the small mountain chain that the Malverns had temporarily become.

How much fiercer the Cairngorms, where I have skied on the very route described on page 160, in April, stripped to the waist. Yet in the same place, in the same month but another year, I have fought for survival, hardly able even to crawl, in a blizzard of Antarctic ferocity. Such are the British hills. The lesson to be learnt from these experiences is that even our most apparently benign terrain can swiftly become hostile in the extremes of weather and conditions which can afflict our hills at all seasons. Every walker should be aware of this fact and it must temper his activities and his equipment.

But this is a where-to-do-it rather than a how-to-do-it book, and safety – indeed sanity – on the hills are subjects well covered elsewhere: Whymper so succinctly summed up the ethos. Suffice to stress three obvious yet salutary points. First is that the selection of equipment and clothing is 'horses for courses': if spare clothing and emergency gear is not in your rucksack you can't use it, but too much of it –

unneeded – will ensure a miserable overloaded trip at the best, and at the worst engender a situation where it eventually becomes necessary. Second is that skill with map and compass is a prerequisite for virtually all upland walks, indeed useful on any country outing. In poor visibility or confusing country such skills are obviously essential, but even following a right of way across the fields in perfect visibility they can save time, effort and frustration. Thirdly, and perhaps most important of all, we must each know our personal limitations. We can know them only by experience, to which there is no short cut. Thus never be afraid to retreat: it is better to have tried and turned back than never to have started. Nothing ventured, nothing gained. But pushing beyond one's limits is a foolish game.

In modern Britain, with continual and growing pressure on our countryside and wild places, access is often a contentious issue. All land belongs to someone or somebody, and in England and Wales, even in our ten National Parks, the only access, as of right, is along properly registered Rights of Way or to certain, but by no means all, classes of common land. However, many landowners, such as the National Trust or Forestry Commission, will allow virtually unrestricted access to their wild country holdings, other private landowners kindly permit access to certain areas of open country while the National Parks or local authorities have negotiated access agreements to yet others. Sometimes it is just a matter of habitual use and 'nobody minds' but often somebody does mind, and with good reason, for instance when lambing is taking place, or grouse shooting, or – like it or not – the military are exercising.

In short, if you enter land you do not own, against the wishes of the landowner, you are committing the civil offence of Trespass.

In Scotland the situation is slightly different. The act of 'trespass' is not defined in statute and, unlike south of the Border, is not in itself an offence and although a landowner has the right to insist that 'trespassers' leave his land, he must prove nuisance or damage in court before an individual can be excluded or sued. Over the years responsible behaviour and mutual respect between landowner and hill-walker have resulted in a situation whereby, in practice, there is reasonable freedom to roam open country at will.

Having said that, in Scotland's upland regions – besides the sheep and grouse that (as in England and Wales) provide employment and income for local people, there is also deer stalking on which the local economy may well depend. Typically from mid-August to mid-October indiscriminate hill-walkers in many parts of the Highlands may do damage by disrupting stalking and at this season the walker should contact the local gillie or estate office before venturing onto the hills to ensure that the legitimate interests of both parties do not clash. Thankfully in Scotland there is still a tradition of courtesy, consideration and amicable co-operation between landowner and walker.★

Unfortunately this is not always true in the different

★An extremely useful Access booklet is published by the Scottish Landowners Federation in conjunction with the Mountaineering Council of Scotland and may be obtained from the Federation at:
18 Abercromby Place, Edinburgh EH3 6TY

situation that exists south of the Border. Thoughtless behaviour and vandalism by a minority have sometimes soured the goodwill of many landowners towards the majority. But – certainly in my own experience – if approached politely most landowners will be pleased to allow him or her reasonable access across their open land. In one notable instance we were threatened by an irate gentleman, complete with shotgun, who – it transpired – had been rudely abused by trespassing yobbos on his own land the previous weekend and wanted no more with walkers. But we were all country lovers and man-to-man diplomacy resulted in an invitation to a tea at the castle!

'I know there is no right of way, but do you mind if we go up the hillside here onto the ridge?' I once asked a farmer in a remote Welsh valley. 'Oh naw, go up wheneffer you like, as long as it's only you and your mate – but I don't want big partiss up there, see.' Was the very reasonable reply.

To sum up, always be courteous in the countryside, if in doubt ask permission, scrupulously observe the Country Code, leaving the hills as you would wish to find them, with no sign of your passing.

The Country Code

- Guard against all risks of fire
- Fasten all gates after you
- Keep dogs under proper control
- Keep to footpaths across farm land
- Use gates and stiles – avoiding damage to walls, fences and hedges
- Leave no litter – take it with you
- Be careful not to pollute water supplies
- Protect all flora and fauna – do not pick flowers
- Respect the countryside and the way of life of the folk who live there

Bibliography, Useful Addresses, Acknowledgements

Interesting Background Reading for Hill-Walkers

A Cambrian Way – Richard Sale (Constable 1983)

The Country Life Guide to Weather Forecasting – S Dunlop and F Wilson (*Country Life* 1982)

Fitness on Foot – Peter Gillman (World's Work/*Sunday Times* 1978)

Geology and Scenery in England and Wales – A E Trueman (Penguin 1971)

Geology and Scenery in Scotland – J B Whittow (Penguin 1977)

Guide to Britain's Nature Reserves – Jeremy Hywel-Davies and Valerie Thom (Macmillan 1984)

Hamish's Mountain Walk – Hamish Brown (Gollancz 1978, Paladin 1984)

The High Mountains of Britain & Ireland – Irvine Butterfield (Diadem 1986)

The Hill Walker's Manual – Bill Birkett (Oxford Illustrated Press 1988)

Mountain Navigation – Peter Cliff (published by Peter Cliff 1987, distributed by Cordee, Leicester)

Mountaincraft and Leadership – Eric Langmuir (Scottish Sports Council/MLTB 1984)

The Mountains of England & Wales (so called 'Bridge's Tables') – George Bridge (Gastons/Westcol 1973)

Mountaineering – John Cleare (Blandford 1980)

Munro's Tables – (Scottish Mountaineering Trust)

Countryside Commission Official Guides to the National Parks (ten volumes) – various authors (Webb & Bower 1987)

Ordnance Survey Outdoor Handbook – Michael Allaby (Macmillan 1987)

Speak to the Hills, an anthology of twentieth-century British and Irish mountain poetry – ed Hamish Brown and Martyn Berry (Aberdeen University Press 1985)

Walking, Hiking & Backpacking – Tony Greenbank (Constable 1985)

Relevant Magazines

Climber – Holmes McDougall Ltd, 7th floor, Plaza Tower, East Kilbride, Glasgow G74 1LW

Great Outdoors – also Holmes McDougall Ltd

High – Springfield House, The Parade, Oadby, Leicester LE2 5BF

Country Walking – Emap Pursuit Publications Ltd, Bretton Court, Bretton, Peterborough PE3 8DZ

Odyssey – Chatsworth Publicity Services, High Bridge House, High Bridge Street, Newcastle upon Tyne NE1 1EW

Some Useful Addresses

British Mountaineering Council – Crawford House, Precinct Centre, Booth Street East, Manchester M13 9RZ

Long Distance Walker's Association – 29 Appledown Road, Alresford, Hants SO24 9ND

Mountaineering Council of Scotland – Hon Sec, Rahoy Lodge, Gallanach Road, Oban PA34 4PD

National Trust – 36 Queen Anne's Gate, London SW1H 9AS

National Trust for Scotland – Suntrap, 43 Gogarbank, Edinburgh EH12 9BY

Nature Conservancy Council – Northminster House, Peterborough PE1 1UA

Rambler's Association – 1/5 Wandsworth Road, London SW8 2LJ

Youth Hostel's Association – Trevelyan House, 8 St Stephen's Hill, St Albans, Herts AL1 2DY

Useful Weather Forecast Telephone Numbers

Special Mountain Forecasts:

Peak District	– 0742–8091
Lake District National Park	– 099–662–5151
North Yorkshire	– 0632–8091
Snowdonia National Park	– 0286–870–120
Scottish Highlands	– 041–248–5757

Weathercall Regional Forecasts:

Devon and Cornwall	– 0898–500–404
Malverns and Shropshire	– ,, ,,–410
Central Wales	– ,, ,,–414
Yorkshire Dales	– ,, ,,–417
Southern Uplands	– ,, ,,–422
Galloway	– ,, ,,–420
NW Highlands/Hebrides	– ,, ,,–425

Acknowledgements

It would be impossible to research, write and photograph a book like this without the assistance, co-operation and hospitality of many people all over the country: I wish I could list them all. I am especially grateful for the crucial assistance of: David Archer (Snowdonia National Park), Mike Couling (Welsh Water Authority), Brian Griffiths (Clwyd County Council), Andrew Jenkinson (Scenesetter Publications), Mr Lane (Dyfed County Council), Graham Little (Mountaineering Council of Scotland), Rae Lonsdale (Yorkshire Dales National Park), Beverley Penney (Ramblers Association), Mrs Richards (Powys County Council), Roland Smith (Peak National Park), Lesley Smithson (British Mountaineering Council), Roger Stevens (Brecon Beacons National Park), Tom Wall (NCC Stiperstones Ranger), and indeed that of many other officers and officials of National Parks, County Councils, the Nature Conservancy Council, and the National Trust besides so many private individuals. Thank you all.

My thanks are due also to the contemporary poets from whose work I've received inspiration and from which I've taken the liberty of quoting a few apposite words: Ivor Brown, Huw Jones and Roger Redfern.

Index

Page numbers in *italics* refer to illustrations. Where appropriate summits and tops ascended during walks have been indicated in **bold** type.